SEATED IN HEAVENLY PLACES

The Authority Of The Believer

by Denis Audet

Published by New Jerusalem Ministries
International Publications. P.O. Box 1557,
St. Cloud, MN 56302.

Acknowledgements

This book has been written as an act of obedience to the Holy Spirit. Whether or not I have been faithful is up to you, dear reader, to judge, according to God's word and His Spirit. By nature, I am not a writer of the word, but rather a doer of it. And so if there is a kernel of truth in this book, let the glory rest with the One who is the Truth, who brings light to His Word.

I have learned that when a person is obedient, the Lord leads witnesses to encourage and help him get the job done. I praise the Lord for the witness of my wife, Grace, who resolutely reminded me of my need to be obedient, and her words of encouragement to seek the Lord and finish the task. I thank my former colleagues of Okontoe Fellowship, some of whom took over my work load in order that I might write this book. I also want to express my appreciation for all the people who literally prayed this book into existence and the faithfulness of Irene Leingang, Leatrice Teigen, Mary Calva and John Nelson who helped me type and edit the manuscript. Finally, a special appreciation goes to Gene Jurek for illustrations, layout and cover.

TABLE OF CONTENTS

v

Introduction

In all your ways acknowledge me, and I shall direct your paths. This is my promise to you, my people. Give each day to me and I shall fill it to overflowing with myself and my work which is massive this new year . . . the things that I have promised you five years back will begin to happen in this year. You shall see things — signs and wonders — far beyond your wildest expectations. You can expect me to move in ways that people have never seen before, at least in this generation, and believed. You shall feel my presence for I am now able to communicate with you in new ways; for you are learning the truth; you are becoming my body and my body is becoming larger and larger. And I rejoice as I see people coming — from every line, from every color, from every nation, from every tribe, from every little hamlet, from every big city, from all around this great universe. I am drawing my people together in a way they have never been drawn before. You are my body, my body is growing, and I want it to grow and grow and grow so that Heaven will be filled with the songs of praise of the people of God; and earth will be forgotten in its tragedies as I deal with it with my justice. Your hands shall be touched by mine and all you touch will be healed. You shall lift your hands in praise as you are now, and I shall touch your hands. You shall feel me endue you with power. You shall feel the strength pouring down through your arms and you shall go forth, and whatever you touch I shall make whole . . . as you speak my words, you will see my power, and those who hear will understand . . . Remember, my children, to stand on my word — *My Word,* my children, *My Power —*

not yours, My people are crying, and I have heard their cry, and I am bringing the Good News to them. Be ready, be ready. I am preparing you — I have prepared many of you, and I shall send many of you. There will be opportunities to proclaim my truth as never before. And let the signs follow — so people will believe.

There shall be great movements of My Spirit across this world, and in the midst of the wars and strife and fears and all that seems to be collapsing there is a'building My Church. My Church is a'building, and it is growing and is becoming my body, and I am calling people from every nation and where you go you will find people ready to believe. I am sending out thousands, tens of thousands. I am sending millions. I want this world to be saturated with the truth. Behold, as you go forth in My strength, you shall be fully satisfied, and I shall be satisfied for the harvest will be reaped and brought to Me in abundance beyond what you have dreamed before. Be prepared, My loved ones. This night I am speaking to people in community after community all across the world — I am telling the same message — those who have failed to believe before will believe by the power of My Spirit. Those who have sought healing will receive it. Those who have given up hope will find hope; for I bring it to them by the power of My Spirit. And those of you who walk in My Spirit will be swept into this mighty, mighty army of God. And we shall go together into victory in spite of what the world sees in us. For I am gathering My people. So rejoice My children, rejoice for in this year the movement of My Spirit will significantly draw men unto me — everywhere ... Do not miss a single opportunity that I set before you, for the warfare will be great, but I claim the victory.

Does God speak to you like that? More importantly, are you a part of this great victorious army that God is building? If not, would you like to be? Armies are equipped and authorized to do battle. Are you equipped? Do you know your authority as a believer in Christ? Can you fight the good fight of faith for the King of Kings, Lord of Lords? It doesn't matter how old or young you are, or how weak or strong you are. God is enlisting His people to be His army.

Several years ago there was a filler story in a newspaper. The story was about a town constable some 70-odd years old who flagged down a trucker speeding through a little town. The constable was directing traffic for children at a school crossing. As he held out his hand to let the children cross, he saw a truck coming too fast to stop. So he blew his whistle which was around his neck and the truck shuddered to a stop half-way into the crosswalk. The little old man drew himself up to his five-foot-five height, walked up to the semi and commanded the trucker to come out. With all the authority of a general he started dressing down this man who was all of six-foot-four, two hundred pounds and one third his age. Then he whipped out a pencil and a pad and ticketed him for speeding and warned him to slow down. The trucker meekly took the ticket and got into his cab and crawled out of town.

What made that big man in the enormous truck stop, take the scolding and accept the ticket? Was it the constable's impressive appearance? His tin whistle? No, of course not. The trucker stopped because of the badge and uniform the constable was wearing. He stopped because of the authority the constable had. That authority represented someone and something that was bigger and more powerful than this little five-foot-five-inch, 70-odd years old man. That authority was delegated to him either by the state or the local municipality. And if that weren't enough, he stopped because that officer represented the law of the land and to go against him would be to go against the United States government.

As God's people, we have been delegated authority from the Lord of the universe. In fact He is the One who has ordained all authorities (Romans 13). This authority that we have as believers is not natural, but supernatural and that is why all human comparison and illustrations of authority fall short. We not only have the delegated authority, but also the delegated power to do the works of the God of the universe. That divine authority not only resides in heaven, but in every child of God who has Jesus Christ as his Savior and Lord. By faith, we ourselves are seated in heavenly places. So when I talk about the authority of God, I also include the power to do it. Neither one is something we possess, because both come from God. By faith, this authority and power are ours to express that the kingdom of God is within us. Now, there is a distinction between authority and power. While a man in a car may have the power to go across an intersection, he certainly does not have the authority to go against a red light. But Jesus is giving all his responsible and obedient children the green light to move by His authority and power.

It is one thing, however, to have this power and authority residing in you and another to know that you have it. That is the thrust of the first part of this book: to acquaint you with your authority as a believer.

I remember reading an historical account of some Scottish immigrants in Australia in the mid 1800's. Most of them were farmers. The tracts of land they bought were poor. The soil was sandy and the rain came infrequently. For three to four generations, these families eked out a miserable existence, not knowing that underneath that land was one of the world's richest deposits of gold. They had it, but they did not know about it.

I submit to you that there are many of God's children that have the riches of the kingdom of God in Christ Jesus within them, and they do not know it. In their ignorance, they are bound, struggling, wounded, and hurt.

They cannot fulfill the divine destiny that God has planned for them in the church and in the world. They cannot be proclaimers of the Good News, healing, and deliverance until they first experience it for themselves.

A middle-aged woman came for ministry several years ago. She was a Christian, but a defeated one. She was bound by a spirit of fear that had paralyzed her throughout her life. When we proceeded to show her her authority in Jesus Christ, she immediately took authority over this spirit and renounced it from her life. As soon as she had received deliverance, she started laughing so loudly and hard that tears came streaming down her cheeks. One of the members of our team asked her if she were seeing the demon of fear. Between peals of laughter, she chortled, "Yes." She went on to describe the demon. It was less than 6 inches tall, green, with a sad do—I-have-to-leave look on its face. Growing more serious, she said, "To think for all these years, I let this spirit immobilize me." She then went over to the demon and stomped on it and it disappeared. She immediately had a vision of Jesus and was overcome with His presence. He seemed to fill the whole room and even go beyond the room. She repeated over and over again, "He is so big! He is so big!" In a rather dramatic way, God was showing that woman her authority as a believer. It is based on Jesus who has been given all authority in heaven and on earth.

When Jesus was on this earth in the flesh, he attended the local synagogue. As the word was to be read, He got up and read the prophecy of Isaiah 61.

The Spirit of God is upon Me.
Because he anointed Me to preach the gospel to the poor.
He has sent me to proclaim release to the captives
And recovery of sight to the blind,
To set free those who are downtrodden,
To proclaim the favorable year of the Lord.

5

He closed the book and said, "Today this scripture is being fulfilled in your midst". (Luke 4:16-20) He was saying to His hearers that He was the fulfillment of that prophecy. What was described in this prophecy was the ministry of the coming Messiah. Now focus on this, brothers and sisters: Jesus, who is the same, yesterday, today and forever, is still fulfilling His ministry and that prophecy; only He is fulfilling it through you and me. He has given us the authority to do and receive His ministry for ourselves, the body of believers, and the world.

Once we know whose authority we have, it follows that we need to see how His authority and power can be released in our life. This basically is the subject of the second part of the book. God's power and authority becomes available to us only when we meet His conditions as Christians. Just as electrical power can be used only when the appropriate wires and outlets are installed, God's authority and power can become effective in the world and the church only when we let ourselves be used as outlets for that power. If God's power is not evident today in the church and the world, it is because we have failed to be channels. The failure is in us, not in God.

Sometimes we are like my son when he was about two or three years old. When I tried to put his coat on him, he might get a hand or his arm in it and then something or someone would distract his attention. He would leave me with the coat or drop it onto the floor. Now God, for the sake of the world and His church, wants to lay His mantle, His cloak of authority and power upon His people. He wants His will to be done on earth as it is in heaven. Yet, sometimes, knowingly or unknowingly, we walk away from His divine intention and authority. Some of the problem stems from bad theology, rather than an unwillingness to do God's will. Satan has also misled God's children to live beneath their privilege. Others simply do not know which step to take. They need to grow and stand fast in their walk with God and act on the promises of His word. His word not only reveals the authority we have, but also shows how we can receive and release it in our lives.

Bill Barr, Jr., director of Okontoe Ministries, recounts a conversation that he had with a young woman. She had been spectacularly saved and delivered from the drug and occult scene. As an art student in college, she not only dedicated herself but her art to Jesus. In fact, in order to make a clean break with her past, she was led by the Lord to destroy some of her artwork which had been influenced by the demonic world in which she lived. So she enjoyed new beginnings. Yet, in her new-found faith, she struggled more than she needed to. Like Lazarus she was raised from the dead. She had the resurrected life of Jesus in her. All she needed was help in removing the bindings from her hands and her eyes.

She wondered what was the matter. Why wasn't she getting the victory? One day as she was showing Bill some new paintings she had finished, the Lord graphically revealed to Bill precisely what the problem was. One of her pictures was a temptation scene. Satan was portrayed larger than life in brilliant colors looking grotesque and evil. In contrast, Jesus was drawn about half as big as Satan in pale pastel colors. That was the problem! Bill was able to share with her the reason she wasn't getting the victory in her life. She was still not assured of her authority as a believer. Satan loomed large in her life, just as he did in that picture. She needed to see with the inner eyes of faith that Jesus was the greater one. He needed to be more vivid in her life. God's Word assures us "Greater is He that is within us (Jesus) than he that is in the world (Satan)." Satan is a defeated foe. By His death and resurrection, Jesus earned the right to take the keys of the kingdom of darkness and set the captives free. With His armor, God has given us the ability to fend off Satan's attack and even cause him to flee. That girl needed to know her authority under Jesus and to be able to release His authority in her life.

This book is not only a teaching about knowing our authority and how to release God's authority, it is a testimony of God's faithfulness to His word and His people. The book has evolved out of a ministry to thousands of people. It is a testimony of limited people (living beneath their privilege) suddenly becoming unlimited people, discovering their authority and becoming a part of God's great army. Throughout these pages you will see that this book is also a testimony of my personal pilgrimage to find the authority and power of God for myself. Although I did not originally intend it to be that way, I believe the Lord wanted it that way. He undoubtedly wants you to see and perhaps identify with my struggle and human frailties and know that beyond a shadow of doubt, it is His authority and power not mine (or yours).

Dwight L. Moody said "I am sick of hearing people asking for crumbs from God's table. Crumbs are good enough for cats and dogs, not for sons and daughters." While I did not bark or meow, I must confess I certainly did a lot of grumbling and whining until I learned how to get up to God's table. In the following pages, I invite you to come and sit beside me. There is plenty of room. Let's feed on the promises of His word. While you are at it, feast and meditate on Paul's prayer to the Ephesians. Make it your prayer.

I thank God continually for you and I never give up praying for you, and this is my prayer; That the God of our Lord Jesus Christ, the all glorious Father, will give you spiritual wisdom and the insight to know more of Him; that you may receive that inner illumination of the Spirit which will make you realize how great is the hope to which He is calling you, the significance and splendor of the inheritance promised to Christians and how tremendous the power available to us who believe in God. That power is the same divine energy which was demonstrated in Christ when He raised Him from the dead and gave Him the place of the highest honor in heaven, a place that is infinitely superior to any command, authority, power or control which carries with it a name far beyond any name that could be used in the world or the world to come. (Ephesians 1:15-21 Phillips)

Chapter I

Authority for The World

Part I — To Witness to the Power of the Gospel

As a child in Sunday School, the first scripture verse I memorized was John 3:16.

> For God so loved the world that He gave His only begotten Son that whosoever believeth in Him should not perish but have everlasting life. (KJV)

Later when I was saved at age 17, I was encouraged to personalize this verse and say God so loved me that He gave His only begotten Son . . . It was a good idea, but I tended to forget the world. Somehow, unconsciously, I limited God's ministry and authority to the church and His people. Those who witnessed to the world were specialists like Billy Graham, other evangelists, and missionaries. It was not until many years later that I realized that God has given every child of God the authority to fulfill the great commission. It was not an option, but a mandate, a command. Jesus assured His disciples that as they proclaimed the Gospel, He would be with them always — those that received them would receive Him. As freely as they received from Him, they were to freely give. It is because Christ died for the world that we are responsible to God for the world. On numerous occasions, the Lord has shared His love for the lost and how He wants us to reach out to them on His behalf. Consider the following prophecy, for example:

> I've called you to be my people, and to be my people means to stand with me . . . to speak as I speak . . . to act as I act, to share with others the news that I have given to you. To lead the flock. To proclaim the news to the nations. To reach out to those who are hungry and thirsty for Me. Who are hurting, who are lonely. So far lost. To reach out to those who are weak and broken. Who are destitute. Who are so desperate for My love. Be My love — express My love to the destitute of the world. Those in high places. Those in low places. Those in far away places. Those in jungles. Those in cities. Those in government. Those in the churches. No matter what social standing. No matter what color. No matter what race. No matter what denomination. I weep for My children. The orphans that are spread over the world — who do not know that I am their Father. That I have come to save them and to set them free . . . the lonely, destitute people of the world overcome by fear and anxiety. People with no hope. People who cannot understand how to live in the face of destruction. No joy. People who have no love. My people, My sheep that are spread out on a thousand mountains. That do not know where the Shepherd is. Go to My sheep. Lead My sheep. Be My sheep. I am your Shepherd. I called My sheep to the mountain of my kingdom. The green pastures of My universe. To the rivers of sweet water. Rivers of Living Water that flows from My Throne.

In the third chapter of Ezekiel, God commissioned the prophet to speak on His behalf to the house of Israel. God warned Ezekiel that if he did not proclaim His words of warning, those who rebelled would die in their sin, but their blood would be on the prophet's hands. In other words, God was holding Ezekiel responsible for the message. We as Christians are also responsible for God's message.

In Acts 10, the centurion Cornelius, a devout and godly man, receives a visit from an angel. The angel commands Cornelius to send his servants to Joppa and bring Peter to his house. While they are on their journey, Peter has a vision of a sheet coming from the sky with all kinds of food forbidden by Jewish law to eat. A voice from heaven declared all things kosher (edible). God, through all this, was preparing Peter to eat and be in a Gentile house. Peter received the messengers of Cornelius and immediately went to preach the Gospel. Much to Peter's surprise, Cornelius and his whole household were saved.

You might wonder in this whole episode, "Why did God go through all the trouble of sending an angel to Cornelius and then prepare the heart of Peter to preach the Gospel to the Gentiles? Why didn't He let the angel proclaim the message?" The answer, of course, is that the angels of God have no authority to preach the Gospel. Only God's children have that right.

Don Basham, author, teacher and editor of *New Wine,* a magazine of Christian Growth Ministries, shared a letter written by a child. To me it was a testimony of how desperately God wants to use us regardless of age. The authority to witness to the Gospel of Jesus is for all believers. Here is her letter:

Dear Reverend Basham:

Hello! This is my testimony. My name is Wendy Ann Kerr and I am 10½ years old. I suppose I never would have gotten hold of your book, "Face Up With a Miracle", except for well, I was able to read when I was 2½ (8 years ago), and spell pretty good at 6. So I read lots of grown up books. Well, one day I began to glance through the book and thought that might be a good book to read.

I started reading. It was good! When you told about the baptism in the Holy Spirit, I wanted that very much. At the end when you told how to receive it, I was thrilled. Next day, I went into the woods in the back of our house and received it. I was happy.

One day my sister got a very bad cut. It just wouldn't heal. It ached and ached. I prayed for her. After she said, "Your hands felt funny . . . just like Jesus." She is four years old. My first convert was a girl named Deidra. She was born again and later received the Holy Spirit. She has told all her friends about Jesus since. (She is five years old.) My second convert was a 4 year old named Christopher Beers. He has not received the Holy Spirit.

I have been very happy since I received. Praise the Lord!

Wendy Kerr[1]

The high calling of every Christian, regardless of age, is to reproduce Christ in as many lives as possible.

A number of years ago I was a house guest of a Spirit-filled couple in Austin, Minnesota. The ministry team, of which I was a part, was offering teaching seminars at their church. Since our meetings were in the evening, I had a good deal of time on my hands during the day. But as it turned out, the time wasn't really in my hands, it was in God's hands. I started playing on the guitar and singing some gospel tunes with my hosts' two children who were about 7 and 9 years old. We were having a rousing good time, so much so that some of the neighborhood kids, about 4 of them, wanted to come and join in. It was about this time that I began to get an inkling that the Lord wanted something more than a sing-along. That afternoon He impressed me to sing one particular song — "The Gospel Riders," written by some anonymous author.

[1]"Evangelism," *New Wine,* Ed. Don Basham, Christian Growth Ministries, July/August, 1976, Vol. 8, page 2.

Matthew, Mark, Luke, and John
Keep on singing' that old gospel song
Matthew, Mark, Luke, and John
Keep on singin' that old gospel song.

We are the gospel riders
Gypsies of the Lord
We are the mountain climbers
All you children of the Lord.

At the end of the chorus the song leader was to insert the name of a person.

is a ridin'
is a ridin'
is a ridin'
He's (she's) a ridin' for the Lord. Repeat. Chorus.

I could see where the Lord was leading me. I asked the kids if they wanted to be gospel riders. I explained that a gospel rider is someone who shares the good news of Jesus Christ. Then I explained in very simple terms the gospel message and asked them if they would like to receive Christ and His Holy Spirit. To my surprise, they all eagerly nodded and asked Christ to come into their life. Luke 18:15 became very real to me, especially where Jesus said:

Suffer little children to come unto me
forbid them not for of such is the Kingdom of God.*

Like the Pied Piper I started leading the children through

---

*Most people shy away from sharing the gospel with young children because they reason that a child won't understand it. But a child is able to understand the spiritual reality of Jesus long before he can understand the doctrine. It is the Holy Spirit that convicts us anyway, and not our minds. The ability to articulate it can come later. Just as our Christian walk is a continuous walk of deeper commitments and understanding, so it is with a child.

the house and out the back door singing the Gospel Riders; this time adding my name and the children's names to the chorus. Denis is a ridin', James is a ridin', Joyce is a ridin', etc. Pretty soon we were wending our way through the backyards of the houses and vacant lots, gradually picking up more and more young people. Everyone was asked if he wanted to be a gospel rider and if he wanted to receive Christ. At one point we spotted two girls looking at our long chain of children singing the "Gospel Riders" song. The Lord impressed me to ask some of the children to witness. I asked one boy, Tommy, who couldn't have been more than 8 years old to share the gospel message with the two girls. They seemed hesitant at first and I tried to help Tommy by trying to quote a tract from a Jesus People Church in Minneapolis; but somehow I drew a blank. God did that intentionally because out of this little 8 year old boy came the exact words from that tract. "How much do I love you? Jesus says, 'This much.' and he opened His arms wide and died." Well, that incident and the witnessing that followed blew me away. Many of those children that day not only became children of God, but also spiritual fathers and mothers to other children.

I'll never forget that afternoon because it was God's opportunity to show me again that the Gospel is still powerful and He uses anyone that is willing to exercise His authority to witness to His presence. Our authority is based not only on Christ's commandment to go into the world, but on the supernatural power of the gospel itself. Paul had to remind the Thessalonian, Corinthian and Roman churches of this fact even in his own day.

> Our gospel did not come to you in word only but in power and in the Holy Spirit and with full conviction (I Thess. 1:5).

15

For the Kingdom of God does not consist in words, but in power (I Cor. 4:20).

For I am not ashamed of the gospel, for it is the power of God for salvation to everyone who believes, to the Jews first and also to the Greek (Rom. 1:16).

The problem is that many people don't believe that it is power. Is it any wonder when, under the guise of scholarship, the Word of God is demythologized, spiritualized, and even humanized and reduced to a dead work of ethics?

A student at one of our midwest seminaries asked his New Testament professor what was the gospel of Jesus Christ. The professor's response was, "Well, you are asking a very hard question; books and books have been written on this subject and are still being written. We need to look at the historical Jesus in the context of the traditions of the early church and the theologies of the individual writers of the gospel. But, someday we'll get it sorted out." Can you imagine the Philippian jailer, about to run himself through with his sword, asking, "What must I do to be saved?" And Paul's response is "Well, you see, you're asking a hard question; books and books will be written about this . . . someday . . . ". No, Paul knew the power of the gospel. And while it may sound like foolishness to the world, it has the power to redeem the world and change people's lives. In the face of all the cynicism and criticism about God's Word, we need to reaffirm the power and simplicity of the gospel.

This is what happened to our ministry. As soon as we started believing God's word was true, we suddenly saw miracles happen, people being changed and set free. We were doing the works of Jesus, with little or no effort on our part. When people would ask us, "What's happening? What's going on?", the only valid answer was, "Jesus is

16

happening and we're going with Him." As soon as we believed God's Word was power, we no longer tried to program God any more. He programmed us.

For years I attended church organizations and clergy meetings where we would discuss the problems and issues of the day within and outside the church. We would form ad hoc committies to discuss and influence people, the mass media, men and women of good will. We'd organize, form more committees, and try new programs and nothing much would happen. People wouldn't be changed. Sometimes we would debate issues and get angry with so-and-so for not seeing it our way. Most of the time, we would spend very little time in the Word unless we could use it as a proof text for our view. We ended up judging the Word instead of letting it judge us. But the most liberating thing was to discover or rediscover the power of the Gospel. This allowed me to lay aside all the frustrations and the burdens of being issue-oriented. All I needed to be was Jesus-oriented.

One day as I came out of a frustrating clergy meeting where the issue concerned battered wives, the Lord spoke to me and said, "You have seen the pitfalls of being issue-oriented. When you chose issues instead of Me and My Word, the end result is justifying a position or people – in this case battered wives – at the expense of judging and condemning other people – in this case husbands. My Word convicts, My Word reconciles, My Word renews, My Word recreates, and you need never apologize for that or be ashamed of it." At this particular meeting, two feminists were presenting their case for battered wives. They were accusing the ministers of not helping their cause because, as one put it, "You clergymen are always trying to get these people reconciled." By implication, the husband was judged a lost cause and he needed to be kicked out, rather than reconciled. They didn't believe

17

it was possible for God to change the man and make him a new creature in Jesus Christ. But, that's the Good News and we need not apologize for it. God does not want us to dissolve the marriage relationship, to free one person and leave another person in bondage so that he can beat up some other woman. He wants to heal and reconcile all parties. You and I have been called to bear witness to the power of this life-changing Good News.

So, we have the authority to witness to the Word, because God's Word is power. But that power needs to come through people who themselves are empowered by the Holy Spirit. The necessary ingredient for witness is the infilling or baptism of the Holy Spirit.

In the first chapter of Acts, the disciples were told by Jesus to stay in Jerusalem until they were endued with power from on high. Then Jesus went on to tell them the reason for needing that power.

> Be My witness both in Jerusalem and all Judea and Samaria and even the remotest parts of the earth. (Acts 1:8)

The primary purpose of Pentecost and the baptism of the Holy Spirit was and still is to bestow power for witnessing to the Gospel. It's not for speaking in tongues, although that is part of the package if you want it. It's not for exercising the gifts of the Holy Spirit, although this is a necessary blessing that follows. It is for witnessing the presence and power of the Living Word. Through the baptism of the Holy Spirit, we ourselves become the medium for the message, a letter read by all men (II Cor. 3:2-3).

The testimony of scripture reveals two acts (free acts of grace) or stages in the unfolding drama of salvation. In the first act, the spiritually dead person becomes spiritually alive through the act of conversion. In the second act, the

18

spiritually alive person becomes spiritually filled through the act of Pentecost.

In the act of conversion, people confess Jesus to be their Lord and Savior. They experience the new birth. They are "born again." What is born again is the human spirit which has been touched and regenerated by the Holy Spirit (John 3). Because they are cleansed by Jesus' blood, they become sons and daughters of God the Father and the Holy Spirit bears witness to it (Rom. 8). As a result, their names are written in the Book of Life. In the second act of Pentecost, we confess and ask Jesus to be the baptizer in the Holy Spirit. By faith we invite the third person of the Trinity to not only make us fit for heaven, but also for earth. We invite Him to sanctify us, purify us, and empower us to be God's disciples, to substitute Christ's life for our lives. Through the power of the Holy Spirit, we are inviting Jesus not as a house guest or a guest of honor in our lives, but rather we are asking Him to take up residence; to occupy the living room of our social lives; the bedroom of our private lives; the library of our intellectual lives; the recreational room of feelings and the kitchen of our appetites. Now, this doesn't happen all at once. But the baptism of the Holy Spirit opens the door for that step by step walk of faith.

The common misconception of the baptism of the Holy Spirit is that the Holy Spirit is given to us to make us spiritual giants. But in reality, the baptism is given to reduce us so that more of God's Spirit can dwell and flow through us. In the process, by faith, Jesus exchanges our life for His so we can say with Paul —

I have been crucified with Christ; and it is no longer I who live, but Christ who lives in me; and the life which I now live in the flesh I live by faith in the Son of God, who loved me and delivered Himself up for me. (Gal. 2:20)

John the Baptist prophesied that the one who would come after him would baptize not with water for repentance, but by the power of the Holy Spirit. Now Jesus not only became the Baptiser in the Holy Spirit, but also set Himself as an example for us to follow. In the Gospel accounts, we read that Jesus who was born of the Spirit went to the river Jordan, submitted to John's baptism by water and was baptized with the Holy Spirit. Three Gospels portray the Holy Spirit coming down as a dove and the Heavenly Father speaking:

This is my beloved Son, in whom I am well pleased.
(Matt. 3:17; Mark 1:11; Luke 3:22)

While Jesus lived 30 years in perfect obedience to the Father, the baptism by the Spirit marked the beginning of His ministry to the world. As obedient followers of Christ, pleasing to the Father, we need to claim that second blessing of Pentecost for our lives, if we haven't already done so.

Many people have theological hang-ups with the term baptism with or in the Holy Spirit. But the apostle Peter in describing the Pentecostal experience of Cornelius and his family to the council at Jerusalem uses the following terms. 1) The Holy Spirit fell upon them; 2) This came as a promise of Jesus to baptize with the Holy Spirit; and 3) It was a gift — the same gift that they received at Pentecost (Acts 11:15-17). The baptism with the Holy Spirit is a promise for us today. Like salvation, it is a free gift from God. We need to claim it by faith and have the Holy Spirit fall upon us.

Some people identify the baptism of the Holy Spirit with water baptism, a baptism of repentance for salvation. And yet, according to the scripture we see that, while they can go together, they are uniquely different. In the eighth chapter of Acts, Philip the evangelist comes to Samaria and proclaims the message of Christ to the people there with signs following (which, incidentally, should be the norm rather than the exception). The biblical account goes on to say that they believed Philip's message (in other words, they were converted) and they were baptized. The baptism here refers to the baptism of repentance in water in the name of Jesus (v. 12). In verse 14 it says that Peter and John heard that the Samaritans had received the Word of God and they subsequently went down and prayed for them in order that they might receive the Holy Spirit (v. 15). Why? Because He had not yet fallen on any of them (v. 16). And so they laid hands on them that they may receive the Holy Spirit. Here we have the distinct account of believers being baptized into salvation and afterwards receiving the Holy Spirit through the laying on of hands by the apostles.

The apostle Paul has his conversion experience on the Damascus road and later with the laying on of hands by Ananias, he receives the baptism of the Holy Spirit (Acts 9:17). Cornelius, on the other hand, in listening to the gospel message preached by Peter is converted and receives the baptism of the Holy Spirit. And this incident forces Peter and his friends to rethink their theology.

21

And all the circumcised believers who had come with Peter were amazed because the gift of the Holy Spirit had been poured out upon the Gentiles also. (Acts 10:45)

How did Peter and his friends know that they were baptized in the Holy Spirit? Answer: they heard them speak in tongues — which is a consequence of the baptism of the Holy Spirit. They also knew that Cornelius and his household had to be saved before they could receive the gift of the Holy Spirit. And this knowledge prompted Peter to say:

Surely no one can refuse water for those to be baptized, who have received the Holy Spirit just as we did, can he? (Acts 10:47)

And so he ordered them to be baptized, in the name of Jesus.

In chapter 19 of Acts, Paul meets some disciples of John the Baptist. He asked them into what baptism have they been baptized and they replied, "John's baptism". Paul explains and reminds them that John the Baptist, who baptized with a baptism of repentance, told the people to believe in Jesus who was coming after him. Now notice in the next verse, they receive a believer's baptism in the name of Jesus.

And when they heard this, they were baptized in the name of Jesus. (Acts 19:5)

Following their water baptism, which is an expression of faith and conversion to Christ, Paul lays hands on them and the Holy Spirit comes on them.

And when Paul laid his hands upon them, the Holy Spirit came on them and they began speaking with tongues and prophesying. (Acts 19:6)

In all of the above accounts, we find the distinction

between the baptism of the Holy Spirit and water baptism. This undoubtedly accounts for the use of the plural word baptisms in Hebrews:

> Therefore, let us leave the elementary teachings about Christ and go on to maturity. Let us not lay again the foundation of repentance from acts that lead to death, and of faith in God, instruction about baptisms, the laying on of hands, the resurrection of the dead, and eternal judgment. (Heb. 6:1-2, New International)

Notice, this is considered elementary. We need to get beyond the discussion and debates of the baptism of the Holy Spirit and water baptism. This is basic, bedrock stuff. The baptism with the Holy Spirit isn't an option that we have. It isn't a fringe movement. It's at the dead center of God's will and necessary for us to fulfill the great commission. (This is why I didn't include this discussion in the second part of this book.)

A person has only to read the biographies and auto-biographies of great men and women of God — such as John Wesley, Dwight L. Moody, Charles Finney, Madam Guyon, General Booth and others — to discover that they experienced the baptism of the Holy Spirit. This is what made them mighty witnesses for Christ. Today God is fulfilling His promise that came through the prophet Joel, that He would pour out His Spirit on all flesh (Joel 2:28-32). Millions of people are discovering first hand that when God says He "is pouring out His Spirit on all flesh," He means all flesh — not on evangelists only or ministers or missionaries, but on all flesh. He is no respecter of persons or denominations. The tremendous movement of His Spirit which involves the baptism of the Holy Spirit is cutting across all doctrinal lines, and all denominations. This is not a sectarian movement. All the theological picket fences that the denominations have erected to hinder us from becoming Christ's universal body are being quickly inundated by God's living waters – the Holy Spirit. You can become part of that if you aren't already.

The baptism of the Holy Spirit, whether it is received through the laying on of hands or alone in prayer, comes by faith. By faith, we simply ask Jesus to be our baptizer in the Holy Spirit. Jesus says you receive not because you ask not. Even though Jesus sees our need for this gift, He will never force Himself upon us. I received Jesus as my Lord and Savior when I attended a Youth for Christ meeting at 17 years of age. As I put up my hand and asked Him to come into my life, I found, as John Wesley put it, "my heart strangely warmed." From that time on I had, for better or for worse commitments to Him, and I know I was hooked up to God. Yet it wasn't until 15 years later that I realized that there was something more.

The Lord led me to pastor two churches, an Indian mission church and another church 18 miles away. While I busied myself with my pastoral duties, I found myself constantly drained trying to meet the needs of everyone. I preached Christ-centered messages. A few people were changed. More people came into the church. But when I looked at scripture, I saw a great deal of disparity between what the disciples were doing and what I was doing. I saw Peter preaching one sermon and three thousand coming to know the Lord. In contrast, I saw myself, along with other pastors, preaching three thousand sermons and maybe getting one convert. In Acts I saw men endued with the power of the Spirit preaching a powerful gospel. In contrast, I saw myself straining and struggling to get people interested in God.

Finally one day I closeted myself in my cold, drafty study and feebly gave God an ultimatum. I told Him that if something didn't happen soon I was going to quit.

Many of my classmates in the seminary had done just that. I had no doubt that God called me into the ministry, but God put into my heart the need for something more. And that something more was the baptism of the Holy Spirit. While I was at the seminary, some of my classmates had come into this new dimension of the Spirit. I was fearful of it because 1) it seemed totally un-Presbyterian*; 2) I was scripturally ignorant in spite of my major in New Testament studies; 3) my liberal theological studies based on so-called modern scholarship de-emphasized, and all but eliminated, the supernatural. While I didn't buy the whole package, I certainly was affected by it.

But God always leaves a witness to the truth of His Word. And that witness came in the form of a rotund, cherubic grocer who helped me start an Alcoholics Anonymous meeting in our community. This man was on fire for the Lord. Everything was Jesus this and Jesus that. His simple unwavering, uncritical reverence for the Word of God amazed me. Even more amazing was his testimony of how Jesus freed him from 15 years of alcoholism. He no longer was one step away from being an alcoholic, because Jesus had given him the victory. It wasn't a matter of his strong will. He simply let Jesus take over this area of his life and God changed him. When this man spoke, his words didn't fall to the ground. They didn't tickle the ears of the people either. They hit home and God was given the glory. What astounded me was how this unlearned man could witness with so much authority. But then I was reminded of the Pharisees who said the same thing of the unlearned fishermen. What I saw

*Little did I know that such Presbyterian giants as Charles Finney, John Hyde and A. B. Simpson (Founder of Missionary Alliance) were Spirit-filled.

I wanted and needed. This man was a Full Gospel Business-men's Fellowship* International and Regional Director and an elder in the Foursquare Gospel Church. That authority to witness was not only based on his belief in the power of God's Word, but he himself through the Holy Spirit, was the vessel for that authority to move unimpeded through him.

One night, after an AA meeting, instead of huddling around a coffee pot in the church basement, we invited this grocer to come into our house next door. Kneeling on the hardwood floor of our living room, we asked him to lay hands on us and pray with us for the baptism of the Holy Spirit.

My wife and I received it by faith, not by how we felt at that moment. In our case the feeling came later and so did the devotional language. About a week later as I was awakening out of a deep sleep, I felt a power flow through me that I had never experienced before. That power was so strong that I could not move or speak. I knew it was God's love pouring through me like rivers of living water. But with that love, I was fearful because I knew that this love was a holy, purifying love that could destroy me. Mentally I asked the Lord to stay His hand. Years later I read that this same experience happened to men like Charles Finney and Smith Wigglesworth. Since then, I have also met other people who have had this same experience.

That same week, after this strange and exciting encounter with God, the Lord brought to mind that I had wrongly answered a question in a communicant class. One child in my confirmation class asked, "If God is love,

*The Full Gospel Businessmen's Fellowship International, founded by Demos Shakarian, is an interdenominational lay witness to the movement of the Holy Spirit.

why must we fear Him?" In several places, the Bible tells us that the fear of God is the beginning of all wisdom. We are told to fear God, to keep His commandments. My answer was simply to use the term reverence. But after that experience, I had to go back and amend that and say, "when it says fear, it really means fear." Yes, even in God's love there is a special kind of fear. A fear because of His holiness.

At this point, let me interject that we need to be careful in sharing experiences because our faith does not rise or fall with experiences. It depends solely on God's Word and His faithfulness to His Word. We, therefore, shouldn't look for experiences, because we live by faith and God in His sovereignty works in different ways with His people.

With the baptism, I not only had this experience with God, but more importantly, scripture became alive to me. People came up to me and said, "Preacher, you preach differently. What happened to you?" The town gossip, with tears in her eyes, asked, "Would you forgive me for all the mean things I said about you?" An unbeliever called me and said, "That prayer you had for my little daughter who was sick was answered immediately." People began asking me to pray for people for healing, because they saw something happening. What was happening was the beginning of the release of the Spirit in my life. That is the new anointing we need to witness to the power of the Gospel of Jesus Christ.

Once we recognize that the Gospel is power and we become vessels for that power through the baptism of the Holy Spirit, what then? We are called to fulfill the great commission and make disciples. The world's and our neighbor's blood is upon us if we do not witness to the presence and reality of Christ. Now it is easy in this day and age to anticipate the coming of Christ and the rapture of the church. But the second coming doesn't mean that the church is to batten down the hatches 'til He returns. In fact, the apostle Peter reveals that the coming of the Lord is being delayed until the whole world receives the proclamation of the Gospel (II Pet. 3). His coming, therefore, hinges on our witness.

Chapter 2

Authority for The World
Part II — To Make Disciples

And Jesus came up and spoke to them, saying, "All authority has been given to Me in heaven and on earth, Go, therefore, and make disciples of all the nations, baptizing them in the name of the Father and the Son and the Holy Spirit, teaching them to observe all that I commanded you; and lo, I am with you always, even to the end of the age." (Matt. 28:18-20)

When the resurrected Jesus commissioned His disciples (with the promise that He would be with them empowering them and directing them), He did not say, "Go and make converts," or "Go and make church members." He said, "Go and make disciples." Much of what has taken place in the past two thousand years has been the former — converts, or worse still, unregenerated members — and both the church and the world have suffered for it. The bottom line for all evangelism, for all witnessing is to make disciples. Those that are evangelized must become evangelists.

When we look at the mathematical progression that enters in making disciples, we can begin to have some idea how the message of Jesus was spread so rapidly during New Testament times. They had no satellite TV communications systems, phones, or mass media to use and yet they turned their world upside-down. They were able to do that because they were obedient to the Word which says that we are to make disciples. If, for example, you were to win one person to Christ in one year and train that person to win people to Christ and they in turn would win and train one person per year and so on, in the space of 32 years, less than a generation, over four billion people would be won to the Lord. This is equal to the population of the world. But this is not happening. In fact, we are losing the battle in terms of the population growth. Fewer people are receiving the Gospel of Jesus Christ than are being born. Discipleship is a sign of maturity and the lack of it, a sign of immaturity.

The writer of Hebrews chides the Christians who have never progressed beyond the stage of babyhood.

> For though by this time you ought to be teachers, you have need again for someone to teach you the elementary principles of the oracles of God, and you have come to need milk and not solid food; for everyone who partakes only of the milk is not accustomed to the word of righteousness, for he is a babe. But solid food is for the mature who because of practice have their senses trained to discern good and evil. (Heb. 5:12-14)

Babies in the natural world cannot reproduce. Generally they cry a lot, need a lot of attention, and are irresponsible. This is understandable, but can you imagine seeing a grown man helpless, irresponsible, fussing, sucking on a bottle of milk? It would be rather ludicrous, yet in the spiritual realm, these comparisons are not far from the truth. Many of God's people are helpless. Either by intent or in ignorance, they have not become doers of the Word. While they should be teachers of the Word and spiritual fathers and mothers training, nurturing their spiritual offspring, they themselves are in constant need of nurture.

When we look at the average church, we find five categories of commitment with certain gradations in between:

1. Those people who sometimes live morally exemplary lives, but are not committed to Jesus. They have the form of religion, but not the Spirit simply because they have not confessed Him as their personal Savior.

2. Those who have committed their lives to Jesus as Savior but not as Lord. They have sonship with Him but no fellowship with Him. They are the undisciplined backsliders, the carnal Christians who ride the fence between the world and the things of God.

3. Those who have committed their lives to Christ as both Lord and Savior but lack authority. They either attempt to do the works of God in the flesh or look to the leadership, the so-called professionals, to do the work of Christ. Many times they have the problem of legalism and feelings of condemnation.

4. Those who have seen the need to have the power of God flowing through their lives. They have been baptized in the Holy Spirit but like the Corinthian church, their motives are wrong. They are not walking in the Spirit. They are the "bless me" type who want God to bless them, but they have no real desire to bless Him and the world. They desire the inheritances and promises of God, but they have no desire to be God's inheritance.

5. Finally, we have God's Spirit-filled disciples, knowing where they fit in the body of Christ, reproducing themselves, exercising God's authority and expressing the fruits of the Holy Spirit, especially love.

This last category should be the ultimate goal of all training in discipleship. Paul encourages Timothy, his disciple, to make other disciples.

> The things which you have heard from me in the presence of many witnesses, these entrust to faithful men who will be able to teach others also. (II Tim. 2:2)

Much of the problem in witnessing to the point of discipleship lies at the feet of religious leaders who have perpetuated this immaturity. While much of it is due to sheer ignorance of scripture, many take great pride in having people look up to them and be dependent upon them.

As a student pastor in Leavenworth, Kansas, I had the good fortune of being used to bring a man to Christ. It was like picking a ripe plum. Some one had planted and watered, and I was around for the harvest. The man was a young farmer, hungry to know more about God. He sought me out whenever he could. And I was just as excited about sharing with him. Sometimes we would talk until two in the morning. I encouraged him to begin witnessing to his new found faith in the church and in his home. His zeal and ardor for the Lord was infectious and fun. But then there came a day when the calls stopped. He didn't need me. At first my pride was pricked. I felt abandoned and useless, but then the Lord spoke to me in my innermost being.

> My son, do you want him to be dependent upon you or Me?

I was stunned for a moment but then for the first time I understood what it meant to be a spiritual parent as well as an earthly parent. Psalm 127:3-4 offers us a beautiful word picture of what children are in the eyes of God. It has both a spiritual and natural application.

Behold children are a gift of the Lord, the fruit of the womb is a reward. Like arrows in the hand of a warrior, so are the children of one's youth.

Whether we are raising biological, earthly children or spiritual children, we need to treat them like arrows in a warrior's bow. We need to hold them tight, aim them right, and then give them flight. My problem was that I wanted to hold on to my new found convert and make him dependent upon me instead of God. As spiritual fathers and mothers, we need to hold on to them and let them grow in love; and aim them right by nurturing, training, and teaching them to be doers of the Word; and finally, give them flight by letting them become mature disciples. In Ephesians 4:11-13, Paul lays out the various offices of the church and reveals what their common purpose is; namely, to build and equip God's people into mature, unified Christians for the work of service:

And He gave some apostles and some as prophets, and some as evangelists and some as teachers, for the equipping of the saints for the work of service to the building up of the body of Christ until we all attain to the unity of the faith, and of the knowledge of the Son of God, to a mature man to the measure of stature which belongs to the fulness of Christ.

You will notice this maturity doesn't take place in a vacuum. Maturity and discipleship involve relationship. If we are to be spiritual parents, this means that discipleship involves commitment to one another in the family of God. The unity of faith that Paul is talking about is not simply agreeing about doctrine or our faith in Jesus Christ. Rather it is a lived-out response to it among the brethren. Jesus spent three years establishing a real relationship with His disciples. He taught them, corrected them, ministered to them, and showed by example how they were to minister. He gave them on-the-job training, sent them out two-by-two on trial runs, and then commissioned them.* In this whole process, He stretched their faith. Above all else, He showed them His love and His Father's compassionate heart and how to care for each other.

I have observed people belonging to Spirit-filled groups. I have listened to anointed teachers who conveyed the message of Jesus and how to minister by His power and yet nothing much happened. One day I asked the Lord what was the matter. And the Lord spoke to me very clearly. He said, "My son, discipleship begins and ends with loving relationships." Of course, while this should be happening in the family, it needs to carry over into the spiritual family of God. Jesus said, "By this all men will know that you are my disciples, if you have love for one another." Loving, caring relationships are both the vehicle of discipleship and the medium for the message of Jesus Christ. We are the living epistles that are to be read by all men. The Pauline epistles use the term "body of Christ, bride of Christ." All these terms are used to describe a relationship between Christ and His disciples. One Hindu commented to a missionary friend, "I love the Christ you preach, but I can't stand the Christians." And yet the message is Christ in us, the hope of glory. We are called by Jesus to be the salt of the earth, a light to the world, but the salt will never get out of the shaker or the light will always be under a bushel if we never establish a loving relationship towards others as well as to the world.

---

*Jesus sent out His disciples by twos (Luke 10) for there is extra power and authority when we represent the church — two or three gathered in His name (Matt. 18:19-20).

The apostle Peter illustrates the relationship of the family of God by comparing it to living stones, being built up as a spiritual house of a holy priesthood, a place to offer up spiritual sacrifices acceptable to God through Jesus Christ (I Pet. 2:5). The Holy Spirit wants to bind us together with the super glue of Christ's love.

A young lady shared with me a vision of her church that the Lord had given to her. As she was interceding for the people in her church standing against the broken relationships within that church, the Lord showed her that the people represented a pile of bricks. They were not joined together in love, and they could not bless the Lord, each other or the world.

In recent years, many leaders are seeing that Sunday and midweek services and family night get togethers have not met the need for discipleship. As a result, small nurture groups have sprung up in churches where the people are not only taught principles of discipleship, but experience loving relationships. My wife and I have proved the importance of this to ourselves. When the Lord has brought people our way we have been impressed to establish Paul-Timothy relationships with them and encourage them to do the works of God. If they aren't Christians, we lead them to Christ and have them baptized in the Holy Spirit. In the atmosphere of loving relationships, we minister to them and have them minister to us. We show them how to pray and witness and minister to other people. Then there comes a day when the Lord will say to us "let them do it." I can't begin to tell you the joy there is in this. In these last days, the Lord is compressing the time that needs to be spent in demonstrating the power of God, establishing relationships, and having people reproduce themselves.

One summer I found myself short on staff. Since we always minister in twos, the Lord impressed me to call a friend of mine, Eli, and teach him to minister by His power and share His ministry. Now I had already established a relationship with Eli and his family. Both Eli and his family had had ministry for inner healing. He was a born-again, Spirit-filled elder and treasurer of a local Presbyterian church. This particular time both he and his family were having their faith stretched because he was unemployed. When I called him up, he leaped at the chance and said it would take his mind off of his unemployment.

I began to share with him all that Jesus taught us. Part of the sharing involved the very practical areas of clothes, food, money, emotional encouragement, and prayer. Years before when my wife and I started our ministry without salaries, he was one of the many saints who pressed money into our hands and encouraged us to keep going. Now it was our turn, only this time God wanted to give us a deeper relationship, leading to mature discipleship. I encouraged Eli to attend several of our seminars on counseling in the Spirit and help minister with me. He sat in on some of our counseling ministry. We prayed together, shared together, and ministered together. He watched me lead people to Christ, introduce them to the baptism of the Holy Spirit, and minister healing of soul, body, and spirit and deliverance. Pretty soon, he started moving in the power of the Spirit, getting words of knowledge, visions, prophecy. Finally, there came the time when the Lord prompted me to let him lead in ministry. The same Holy Spirit that used me used him to heal and deliver God's people.

But that wasn't and still isn't the end of this story. Around about this time, there was a flyer that came to Eli's church about a conference on healing and church administration in Canton, Ohio. Since the church had no pastor at this time, some of the other Spirit-filled elders felt impressed to send Eli to this conference. They even offered to pay his way, which was a miracle in itself. It also happened that another pastor in a nearby town was planning to go, so they both went to the conference. While they were at the conference, the speaker gave his introductory speech and then said, "The Lord has impressed me to have Eli B. speak." My friend Eli at this point got a bit shaky and queasy and looked around hoping that there would be another man by the same name. No such luck! Reluctantly, he arose and headed toward the podium with no idea of what he would say. But as he came forward to the lectern, the Lord immediately gave him a message. The essence of the message was that God wanted clean vessels for His healing ministry.

After he had spoken, people began to mill around drinking coffee. One man motioned Eli to come over to a corner where they could talk with a measure of privacy. The man was a minister, and asked Eli, "Don't you think God can use anyone for His ministry?" Eli knew by the word "anyone" the man was referring to himself. Immediately the Lord gave Eli a word of knowledge (supernatural information) about him. Eli responded, "No, you need to be His child first. The Lord also wants you to deal with this sin of homosexuality in your life." The man, who gave no outward appearance of his homosexual life style was stunned and said, "How did you know about this?" Eli simply said, "The Lord told me." This opened the door for Eli to share with this minister in a loving way. He led him to Christ and the baptism of the Holy Spirit. By the power and authority of Jesus, Eli showed him how to exercise his authority as a believer and be delivered from his homosexuality and many other problems that he had in his life.

The man later went to see his former lovers and witnessed to them about what God did in his life; how Jesus freed him from the hypocritical and sinful life. He shared the good news with them and one of them received the message of Christ. That Sunday, he preached to his congregation of 450 members. With the special anointing of the Holy Spirit, he shared how for the first time he knew what it meant to be a new creature in Christ, to be forgiven and delivered from the sins of the past. He then asked his congregation to forgive him for preaching a watered down gospel, one that had no power to change lives. He had an altar call and went forward himself to make his confession public. Over eighty percent of that minister's congregation came forward, many with tears in their eyes.

The pastor shared all this with my friend and disciple Eli. Needless to say, that one incident made my whole summer. We need to catch hold of this for ourselves, because this is bedrock New Testament living. When I look at my life and many others that God has used to make disciples, I know that discipleship or discipling has nothing to do with abilities, only availability.

One woman on our staff, for example, came to us deeply hurt by her past, so hurt that she wondered whether God loved her, let alone could use her. As we shared, ministered and expressed God's love toward her, we could see the Holy Spirit building faith in her. As she sat in ministry sessions with others, the day came when the Lord spoke and said, "Let Betty do it." With an incredulous look on her face, she said "Who me?" "Yes, you", I firmly replied. Hesitantly at first, she led a woman through a prayer of faith and deliverance. Because Betty was new to this, the demons in the woman receiving counseling spoke out and questioned both Betty's and the woman's authority. Together we stood against the demons and told them to keep quiet in the name of Jesus. I asked the woman to confess aloud, "Greater is He that is within me, than he that is in the world." (I John 4:4) After that, Betty continued to lead her in renouncing these spiritual forces that were binding her and prayed for her inner healing. The woman's contorted expression changed before our eyes to a radiant victorious smile. God changed her face as if she had had plastic surgery. But Jesus wasn't through. He told me to let Betty give that woman a power blessing. As I shared this with Betty, once again she gave me that "Who me?" look. She stood six feet in front of the woman and asked God to bless her. The power of God came through that woman and she fell limply backwards in my arms. As I laid her down on the floor, the Lord continued the cleansing and healing process in her. First she wept, then the joy of the Lord fell on her as she laughed and giggled with holy hilarity. Attempting to get on her feet, she fell back on the couch drunk in the Spirit, just like the disciples were at the time of Pentecost.

While we have seen the power of God countless times, this was a special time. God was not only healing and delivering one of His saints, but He was making a full-fledged disciple out of Betty. I saw her flex her spiritual muscles for the first time that day. Today, her life is not the same. Several years ago, God gave her a vision for a special ministry to the "hard core" people who need to live in Christian community for a while — people who have never experienced the love of God's people and healing power of Jesus. Today, this ministry is slowly becoming a reality for Betty, but it couldn't have happened until she herself experienced the Gospel as power for her own life. It couldn't have happened until she was endued with power from on high. It didn't happen until she established a relationship with a loving, caring, healing body of believers. This is what Jesus did when He was with His disciples and we can do no less as we are called and given authority to witness to the world and make disciples.

Chapter 3

The Authority to Reign
and Live in the Kingdom of God

I've often heard the expression, "He's so heavenly minded that he's no earthly good." The truth is if we are really to be of any earthly good, we need to be heavenly minded. The Bible even goes further and reminds us that we are citizens of heaven; we are seated in heavenly places and, what's more, the kingdom of God is within us. God desires His will (and therefore His rule) to be done in us as it is in heaven. Our authority to witness to the world and make disciples is based on our authority to live and reign in the kingdom of God while we are still here on earth. In His priestly prayer Jesus prayed to the Father that He not take His disciples out of the world, but keep them from the evil one (John 17:15). The dimension of the Spirit is what keeps us from the evil one and enables us to be in the world and not of the world. Paul reminds the Corinthian church of this truth when he says:

Now we have received not the spirit of this world, but the
Spirit who is from God that we might know the things
freely given to us by God, which things we also speak, not in
words taught by human wisdom, but in those taught by
the Spirit, combining spiritual thoughts with spiritual
words.

But a natural man does not accept the things of the Spirit
of God, for they are foolishness to him, and he cannot
understand them, because they are spiritually appraised,
but he who is spiritual, appraises all things yet he is
appraised by no man. For who has known the mind of the
Lord that should instruct him? But we have the mind of
Christ. (I Cor. 2:12-16)

Notice the last line. We *have* the mind of Christ. It is
because we have the mind of Christ that we can reign and
live in God's kingdom. Salvation, God's righteousness, and
His way of looking at things are utter foolishness to the
natural man. To argue and debate spiritual truths with
someone who is unspiritual is folly.

One member of our ministry team was a missionary in
India. In addition to preaching the Word, he studied the
religion of the Sikhs and used to get in great debates with
them. Then one day the Lord in His still small voice said,
"You win all the arguments, but you still lose the people."
Why? Because the natural man does not understand the
Spirit of God, God's way of thinking and living until he is
convicted and spiritually hooked up to Jesus.

The truth of this was never made more real to me than
when we were counseling a particular couple. They were
panic stricken over their delinquent, adopted 10 year old
son. In our first encounter with them and their son, there
was no doubt that the boy ruled the home. The couple
adopted him when he was 8 months old and raised him
in an extremely permissive atmosphere. The child would
even curse them in public, when things did not go his

own way. He was constantly truant at school which made his rebellion a legal problem. Social workers were counseling the family and some were frustrated to the point of suggesting the child be placed in a school for the incorrigible.

Despite all this, we shared the Bible's spiritual truths about rearing children. We discussed with them how God gave them authority over their child, and how, contrary to the world, we love our children by discipling them. We also mentioned that the reason why their son was unhappy was simply because he had not honored them. Things were not well with him, even though they gave him everything he wanted. The promise of well-being to those who follow the fifth commandment − a long life and blessing to those who honor their parents − was not available to him. As we continued to share with them, we felt they were attentive to what we were saying, but somehow the words were not getting through to them. It seemed that our words were falling to the ground. When they left, we asked the Lord why and the Lord revealed to us it was because the couple did not know Him. Jesus said, "I am the Way, the Truth, and the Life." We can only know the truth when we have the personified Truth of Jesus Himself and He alone can help us implement this Truth for our life by the power of His Spirit. This does not mean that the Gospel and its truths are not rational. On the contrary the truth of Jesus needs to be rationally understood with the mind. Without the Spirit convicting the unbeliever or illuminating the believer's heart, these truths have no effect. It is like switching on an unplugged lamp. Unless we are plugged into the Holy Spirit it does not shed light to the inner man or motivate him. Without the Spirit bearing witness to our regenerated spirit, we are put in the position, as Paul says, of "always learning but never coming to the knowledge of the truth" (II Tim. 3:7).

The following week, we had a second conference with them. Before we progressed any further, we led them to Jesus and salvation and hooked them up to the Truth. Then we proceeded to tell them essentially the same thing that we said the week before, only this time they received it not only in their heads, but in their hearts and spirits. Through the power of the Holy Spirit, they were able to implement it in their lives and in the life of their son. The first week we spoke only to their minds, the second week we were able to speak through their minds to their spirits.

Now this will be a lot easier to comprehend when we understand the biblical concept of man. The Bible reveals that a person is made up of a soul and a body. The soul (rendered psyche in the Greek, from which we get the words psychology and psychiatry) is the place of self-awareness, the personality of the person (Matt. 11:29, 26:37f). It is made up of the mind, the will and the emotions. The mind is the vehicle of thought (comp. Lamentations 3:20-21). The will enables us to make decisions. The emotions express how we feel in our soul. The body is composed of the flesh and the five senses — sight, touch, smell, taste and hearing. The soul and the body are the basic area where the natural man functions. There is a third dimension to man according to the Bible — the dimension of the spirit. Just as a radio or television set has a receiver to pick up certain frequencies so the human spirit has the capacity to receive spiritual things and sense things beyond the reason of the mind. The human spirit seems to function in three areas: 1) intuition, 2) conscience, and 3) fellowship with God. With respect to intuition, the human spirit allows us to be aware of God and as believers communicate with Him, to know and understand His Will and live accordingly (e.g. Rom. 1:20; I Cor. 2:6-16). The conscience enables us to tell right from wrong by which we feel guilt or have a clear conscience (e.g. Heb. 9:14; 10:22; I Tim. 3:9). The conscience, however, can be seared by persistent sin and deceitful spirits (I Tim. 4:1-2). Finally, the human spirit affords fellowship with God. It allows us to commune with Him and worship Him in spirit and in truth (Jn. 4:24). The spirit of the natural man, while it is aware of God, is for all intents and purposes dormant (Eph. 5:13-14). It can only be awakened or resurrected by the Holy Spirit that convicts and regenerates it.

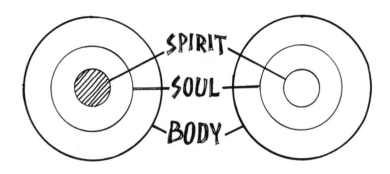

You might wonder how it got that way in the first place. Scripture tells us that Adam and Eve were originally created as spiritual beings who had a soul and lived in a body. They were created to have communion with God forever. But when they sinned against God by eating the fruit of the tree of knowledge, they lost that communion. They not only experienced physical death, but spiritual death as well. They became natural beings. And we who are Adam's offspring are two dimensional people, too. We live primarily in the area of the soul life and the flesh. But Jesus, the second Adam, revives and restores the third dimension in our lives – the spirit. This is what happens when we are born again. The rebirth that comes to us as a matter of confession with the mouth and belief in the heart (Romans 10:10) awakens our spirit to the reality of God as Spirit. That is why Jesus told the Samaritan woman, "God is Spirit and those that worship Him must worship Him in Spirit and Truth." (John 4:24)

Another way to illustrate this phenomenon is to picture the natural man looking at himself and the world in a mirror. Before we are saved, everything is centered on ourselves and our world. Sin only allows us to reflect upon ourselves. Behind that mirror which represents the ego, centered on itself (which is to say sin), is the dormant spirit. When the Spirit of God comes upon a person and he is saved, the Holy Spirit strips away the self centeredness, the equivalent of the silver of the mirror and allows the mind to be transparent like a window to the regenerated spirit. This process gradually accelerates as the person renews his mind through study of the Word of God and becomes obedient to the promptings of the Holy Spirit. Jesus says, "My sheep hear My voice." We need to hear His voice and put our mind into captivity to Jesus.

But what about the many Christians who are saved, yet who live as if they were only two-dimensional people? The human will can prevent the mind from being transparent to the human spirit and the promptings of the Holy Spirit. To use our illustration again, you have seen people stroll down a sidewalk and look into a store window, but they are not looking at the displays in front of them. They are primping and using the background light as it shines on the window. They are using the window as a mirror again. Likewise many Christians let themselves be caught in the background light of circumstances, selfishness, pride, etc., so that their minds are no longer transparent to the things of the spirit. Paul, in addressing the Galatian church, speaks precisely to this problem.

> Having begun in the Spirit, are you going back to the
> flesh? (Gal. 3:3)

In other words, are you going back to living in the soul
and the body and thus closing yourself to the leading of
the Holy Spirit? To the Colossian church he prayed that
they would see things from God's viewpoint, and be filled
with His wisdom, and have understanding and discernment
of spiritual things. (See Colossians 1:9-15 – Phillips.)
God's purpose is for us to be three-dimensional people, led
by our human spirits inspired by the Holy Spirit.

The Lord reinforced the truth of His word when He
spoke a word of prophecy one New Year's Eve. He had
already revealed His intention of building His army and
how He wanted to use us as a part of His army to draw all
men to Himself. He went on to say the following:

> You shall be aware of My Presence as never before. You
> shall be aware that it is I that moves. It is I who wins, it
> is I who woos people to Me. It is I who loves them enough
> to die for them, enough to let you die for them. That is
> My purpose for mankind in the coming year. I am talking
> to you about it now because you have given Me your
> minds. You have been willing to accept the new dimension
> of what I am calling you to live. *I have made you three-*
> *dimensional people now.* And I call you into it. And I
> would purpose for my world newness of life, and awareness
> of hope, the rare, wonderful, beautiful feeling of knowing
> that I am totally in control. When you see soaring prices
> and when you begin to take the counsel of your fears, stop
> and remember that I am in control. Remember that I will
> prepare everything – that I will give you all you need. I
> shall open doors. I shall proclaim the truth through you,
> if you will only be My people . . .

So we are called to live as three-dimensional people ruled
by the Spirit of God.

Returning to the couple with the rebellious ten year

old son; when they received Christ they not only received insight to the biblical truth of kingdom living, but also received the power to live it through Him. The apostle Paul understood this even for his own life, when he said:

> For we know that the law is spiritual, but I am of the flesh sold into bondage to sin.
>
> For that which I am doing, I do not understand; for I am not practicing what I would like to do, but I am doing the very thing I hate.
>
> But if I do the very thing I don't wish to do, I agree with the law, confessing that it is good.
>
> So, no longer am I the one doing it, but sin which indwells me.
>
> For I know that nothing good dwells in me, that is, in my flesh; for the wishing is present in me, but the doing of the good is not.
>
> For the good that I wish, I do not do; but I practice the very evil that I do not wish.
>
> But if I am doing the very thing I do not wish, I am no longer doing it, but sin which dwells in me.
>
> I find then the principle that evil is present in me, the one who wishes to do good.
>
> For I joyfully concur with the law of God in the inner man, but I see a different law in the members of my body waging war against the law of the mind, and making me a prisoner of the law of sin which is in my members. (Rom. 7:14-23).

Paul, in this chapter, sees the dilemma of all mankind, wanting to do good, but not able to do it because there is a civil war going on inside them. Paul seeing the problem, cries out: "Wretched man that I am, who will deliver me from this body of death?" He answers his own question: "Thanks be to God through Jesus Christ our Lord" (vv. 24,

25). In preaching and counseling to people (like that couple with the ten-year-old child) about making certain moral and spiritual choices for their lives and families, we used to constantly be frustrated by people who somehow didn't know better, who seemed to be powerless even when they wanted to make the right choices. Some would explain, "If only we had a better upbringing, or more faith, or your faith, or better circumstances, or . . . I'd be able to do what I am supposed to do." But the answer wasn't in any of these things. We assumed that if these people could intellectually comprehend and affirm certain truths, even biblical truths, they would be able to resolve it. But this is not necessarily true. The problem didn't need to be resolved so much as it and they needed to be redeemed. While we will touch on this in a later chapter on inner healing, we need to see the sin factor in relation to reigning and living in the kingdom of God. The Word of God says the heart is deceitful above all things (Jeremiah 17:9). Sin puts blinders on our spiritual eyes and cuts us off from the power of God working through us to do His will. Forgiveness, on the other hand, removes the blinders and allows God to work through us.

While this may seem obvious, I find that there are far too many Christians that are struggling in Romans 7. They are striving to do things for God. That striving is in the flesh which Paul says is a body of death. By faith they need to move on to Romans 8 and let the Spirit of God bear witness with their spirit that they are sons and daughters of God. As sons and daughters, our relationship isn't based on what we can do for God, but on what God has already done for us in Jesus Christ. A life of faith which is a gift of God, frees us from bondage to legalism and condemnation and striving to measure up to God. Faith sees with the eyes of God the perfection of Jesus in us.

There is a story about a farmer who was driving a horsedrawn wagon with a load of produce. Along the road, he met a man with a huge sack of potatoes slung over his back. Being neighborly, he invited the man to hop on. The man accepted the invitation, but still kept the load of potatoes on his back. When the farmer asked why he left his load on his back instead of resting it on the wagon, the man said that he didn't want to burden him or his horse. Now a person would be foolish to do a thing like that, but no more foolish than when Christ offers to carry our sins on the cross and remove the burden of guilt and condemnation under the law, and we still carry the burden of the law by striving to please Him with our righteous efforts. Paul says that all our righteousness is as filthy rags. All our striving as two-dimensional people is useless because of the sin factor in our members. Paul further adds, "If righteousness comes through the law, then Christ died needlessly." (Gal. 2:21) That is why we are called to live by faith and are justified by faith (just as if we had never sinned). Faith lives in the third dimension — the spirit — and draws on Christ's death and resurrected life to do the work, the will and righteousness of God.

Drawing on the righteousness of God also includes drawing on His forgiveness and judging sin as sin. Now the people of the world cannot and will not recognize sin unless they are convicted by the Holy Spirit and receive forgiveness unto salvation. Take the problem of alcoholism, for example: according to the world, it is not seen as a sin but rather a sickness. Homosexuality is not even considered a sickness, but an alternative life style. Abortion is not murder, but a human right. The world has even gone so far as to modify words to remove the recognition of sin. Words, such as making love, or having an affair are so much easier on the ears, as well as on the conscience, than the words fornication and adultery.

God has given all His children the authority and right to judge righteously within ourselves — to see with His eyes and deal with sin. This is important for kingdom living because in order to live and reign in the kingdom of God as three-dimensional men, we need to simply agree with God when we sin. We are called to confess our sins before God. Confession simply means agreeing with God that we have sinned. If we refuse to agree with Him, the Word says we make God a liar and cut ourselves off from His Word and what He has to say to us. (See I John 1:10, Phillips). The apostle John reveals how God judges sin in our lives and how we must judge it too — with His righteousness.

> Here, then is the message which we heard from Him, and now proclaim to you: God is light and no shadow of darkness can exist in Him. Consequently, if we were to say that we enjoy fellowship with Him and still went on living in darkness, we should be both telling and living a lie. But if we are really living in the same light in which He eternally exists, then we have true fellowship with each other and the blood which His Son Jesus shed for us keeps us clean from all sin. (I John 1:5-7)

As God's people, we need to see that no matter what the offense, or how far we have walked away from God, we are still His children. Sin means missing the mark. It involves losing our fellowship with God — and that is serious enough — but, we don't lose our relationship.

I have three children. My relationship to them as their father remains the same regardless of how they act. There are times when they are disobedient and grieve me, but that does not change my love for them. My relationship as the father remains the same even though my children may be out of fellowship with me. The same thing is true in our relationship with God the Father. Even in our sins, we can have the perfect assurance that God doesn't abandon us (no more than I would abandon my children). It is within His divine nature to always call us back and seek to reconcile us through His Son Jesus. This is true for us as believers as well as for the world. Jesus is our high priest and intercessor and His blood shed on the cross covers the sins of the past, present, and future. He restores our fellowship with the Father. In Hebrews 4:14-16, we read:

> Since we have a great high priest who has passed through the heavens, Jesus the Son of God, let us hold fast to our confession. For we do not have a high priest who cannot sympathize with our weakness, but one who has been tempted in all things as we are, yet without sin. Let us, therefore, draw near with confidence to the throne of Grace, that we may receive mercy and may find grace in the time of need.

When we sin and ask forgiveness we have the promise:

> If we freely admit that we have sinned, we find Him reliable and just — He forgives our sins and makes us thoroughly clean from all that is evil. (I John 1:9)

By faith, we need to receive that forgiveness. This truth needs to be emphasized because there are many of God's children that are caught up in the judgment of the world. There is subtle, sometimes not so subtle, judgment on our jobs and in our social life. Satan, the prince of this world, is the accuser of the brethren. He always tries to condemn God's children, especially those who have unresolved sin. But the good news is that there is no judgment in Christ Jesus. There is no condemnation. There is simply unconditional love and mercy from Him.

The Lord reminded me of this one time when a brother in Christ and I were both struggling and looking for

51

direction for our respective ministries. Certain people questioned our integrity and our ministry. We felt the death of a dream and a hope. Fear, doubt, discouragement, resentment, impatience with God and ourselves and even with each other all added up to the final equation of condemnation. But as we wept and confessed our sins to God and to each other, the Lord spoke these comforting words:

. . . I know it's so hard for you, I want to say it again to you. I never sit in judgment of you. I never say, "Oh, you foolish children." I never say that. I stand before the Father day and night and say, "No, they are not foolish children. They are my people. They are made righteous by my righteousness." I plead your cases before the Father day and night. I am your Advocate. I have pled your case and I have won! And the Father has granted me the right to speak to you in this way tonight. He has told me to do this to assure you, that even though He is judge of all – and He will judge each one of you clearly – and I'll be there because I am the Judge, too. But He has said, "Tell them that what I have said is true! I bring to you peace, my children. I bring to you forgiveness, I bring to you non-judgment! I bring to you life that doesn't deal with death at all . . . not even death of a hope, death of a desire, or death of a dream, or death of anything that would keep you from being my people. I bring to you life, for I am Life. Can your spirits comprehend what I am saying? This is spiritual truth from God Himself. Do you understand? All thoughts of Me are Life. All thoughts of me are hope. There is no death in me, there is no condemnation in me. There is only radiant hope. There is only life . . .

God's people need to comprehend that Jesus, the Way, the Truth, and the Life brings life, not judgment. In fact, Jesus is never going to judge us for the sins we asked forgiveness for. When He forgives, He forgets. He pardons our sins into eternal forgetfulness. He can do that because

His blood not only covers our sins but remits, removes our sins. He erases our sins just like an eraser removes chalk on a chalk board.

One Christian brother, under deep condemnation by Satan questioned that. As he shared his past sins and the problems that he reaped from them, he blurted out, "How can God forgive me for all those things I've done?" He persisted in this questioning even when he told us that he had asked God's forgiveness for them. At that point, the Lord helped us out with a vision. In the vision there was Jesus and a man weeping at the foot of Jesus. Just like this man that we were counseling, the man asked to be forgiven for his sins and Jesus said, "I forgive you." But then the man persisted and said, "How can you forgive me for all my sins?" And Jesus, matter of factly, said, "What sins?" You see, He had already forgotten them. We need to forget them, too. We have no right to bring them up again. This includes the sins we have asked forgiveness for and other people's sins against us for which they have asked forgiveness. The Word of God commands and promises the following:

> Do not call to mind the former things, or ponder things of the past. Behold, I will do something new, now it will spring forth; will you not be aware of it?
>
> I will even make a roadway in the wilderness, rivers in the desert.
>
> I even I, am the one who wipes out your transgressions for my own sake; and I will not remember your sins (Isaiah 43:18, 19, 25) (Hebrews 8:12).

When Jesus was left alone with the woman caught in adultery, He asked if any were there to condemn her. And the woman looking around for her accusers, saw no one. They could not remain and justify their condemnation of

53

her because of their own sins. Jesus responded, "Neither do I condemn you, go your way; from now on sin no more." (John 8:11) After we receive forgiveness for our sins, we need to forget the past and press on to our high calling.

In ministering to the couple with their ten-year old son, we were privileged to minister righteousness to them. As we exhorted, encouraged, corrected, reproved them, just as we do thousands of others, we were fulfilling the role of every Christian with the body of Christ. We are not only called to judge and minister righteousness for ourselves, but also to judge and minister righteousness to the body of Christ. This is our priestly function. Our living and reigning with God is a corporate venture. We are fellow saints of God's household. (Eph. 2:19) Collectively, we are a chosen race, a royal priesthood, a holy nation, a people for God's possession (I Peter 2:9). Paul graphically illustrates that fellowship by comparing us to a holy temple made for the Lord. We are being fitted together by the Holy Spirit as a dwelling place for God with Christ as chief cornerstone. (Eph. 2:20-21) He further compares us to a body fitted together, properly working with each individual part, growing together, building each other up in love (Eph. 4:16). All of these illustrations are indicative of the fact that we need to build each other up and minister the righteousness of God.

A young man on our summer staff, when he first came up to our wilderness camp on the Gunflint Trail, expressed his enjoyment of the wilderness. Later, the Lord spoke to him in a prophecy:

My son you rightly love My creation, but you will not really enjoy the wilderness until I remove the wilderness from within your life through the help of My body.

54

God wants to do the same thing with us all. He wants to remove the wilderness of sin and selfishness in our lives. While He uses His Spirit to convict us of our sin and need for righteousness, He uses the body of believers to minister His righteousness.

Paul confronted the Corinthian church with the sin of immorality of one of its members (I Cor. 5:1-13).

> Do you not know that a little leaven leavens the whole lump of dough? (v. 6)

> Clean out the old leaven, that you may be a new lump, just as you are in fact unleavened. For Christ our passover has been sacrificed. (v. 7)

> Let us therefore celebrate the feast, not with old leaven, nor with the leaven of malice and wickedness, but with the unleavened bread of sincerity and truth. (v. 8)

Paul here draws on the Jewish practice and celebration of the Passover with unleavened bread, a memorial to the time when God delivered them from Egypt (See Exodus 12). He makes an analogy between the leaven (yeast) which permeates and affects the whole body of Christ. What he is saying by this is that the body of Christ needs to be treated as an organic unit. Just as our whole body is affected by a cut or disease, so Christ's body is affected in the same way in the spiritual realm. That is why Paul speaks to them later and says if someone in the body is hurting, all are hurting (I Cor. 12:26). This is a spiritual truth. When pastors and leaders within the body of Christ comprehend this truth and minister to it, they will inevitably experience revival in their midst. When they don't, they can expect division, suspicion, lukewarmness, even death.

Now Paul goes on to focus on where the ministry of God's righteousness begins.

> I wrote you in my letter not to associate with immoral people. (v. 9)

> I did not at all mean with the immoral people of the world or with the covetous and swindlers or with idolaters; for then you would have to go out of the world . . . (v. 10)

God doesn't want us to have a siege mentality. That is, He doesn't want us, like so many sectarian groups, to run away from the world and build our little fortress blocking out our witness to the world until Jesus comes. No, Jesus died for the world and the church is a gift of God to the world. In fact, the church is in the world to fulfill the will of God for the world. As a chosen race, a royal priesthood, a holy nation (which God is building within us), we are a witness of how God can change darkness (evil) into light (righteousness). It is precisely because we are the salt of the earth and the light of the world that our major concern is not with the attack of Satan from outside the church, but within the church. Someone has said, "When a person is lost, Satan is glad. When he becomes a newborn Christian, Satan is sad. But when he sells out to Jesus and desires to please God by being His disciple, Satan gets mad." He not only gets mad, he gets scared because his kingdom is threatened. And so he tries to destroy the fellowship of the believers and the testimony of the Holy Spirit. There is a battle going on. If the church is God's army, the army needs to be committed to each other and unified by His Spirit and His righteousness. Where there is no unity and commitment to each other, then defeat is predictable. That is why Paul comes down hard on the people within the church.

> But actually, I wrote to you not to associate with any so called brother if he should be an immoral person or covetous, or an idolater, or a reviler or a drunkard, or a swindler, not even to eat with such a one. (v. 11)

For what have I to do with judging outsiders. Do you not judge those who are within the church? (v. 12)

But those who are outside, God judges. Remove the wicked man from among yourselves. (v. 13)

Evidently, the man was unrepentant in his immorality. In fact, he was probably flaunting his incestuous relationship with his father's wife. As a result, Paul had decided to deliver him up to Satan for the destruction of his flesh that his spirit may be saved. (v. 5) But to reiterate, when Paul uses the term 'judge' he doesn't mean condemnation. Jesus Himself said, "Judge not lest ye be judged . . . " but also told the Pharisees that they wrongly judged according to appearance and needed to judge righteously. (John 7:24) They judged Jesus according to appearance, for example, as a law breaker of their tradition when He healed the man with the withered hand on the Sabbath. They should have judged Jesus righteously and seen by this healing the mercy and goodness of God. Judging righteously means that we see with the eyes and heart of God what is evil and what is good. Judging righteously also means, we judge the sin and not the sinner. This is what Paul means by judging in this passage. Peter means the same thing when he says judgment begins in the household of God. (See I Pet. 4:17) Notice that Paul makes the distinction between those outside the church and those in the church. In Chapter Six, he reproves the Corinthians for having lawsuits against the brethren and having things settled by unrighteous unbelievers. He reminds them that some day all God's people will be judging the world and angels. They, therefore, needed to judge righteously among themselves. Because we have the authority to judge righteously in ourselves, we have the authority to judge and minister righteousness in the community of believers.

Paul, in fact, encourages his disciples to exercise that authority:

> These things speak and exhort and reprove with all authority. Let no one disregard you. (Titus 2:15)

> I solemnly charge you in the presence of God and of Jesus Christ, who is to judge the living and the dead and by His appearing and His kingdom: preach the word, be ready in season and out of season, reprove, rebuke, and exhort with great patience and instruction. (II Tim. 4:1-2)

Jesus, Himself, in Matthew 18 shows how we are to minister to the brethren in the body. He tells us that if a brother sins, we are to reprove in private. Many sins and problems brought on by sin would be resolved at this point if we cared enough to confront the offender. Jesus further instructs that if the offender doesn't listen one needs to call others in as witnesses to confirm the facts. Many times Satan can magnify the problem in our minds, and we need disinterested parties. Besides, in the counsel of many, there is wisdom. This is certainly true when two people have been hurt by each other. But then Jesus says if the person refuses to be reconciled or listen to them they are to tell it to the church. Why? Because the sin affects the whole body. Finally, if the offender refuses to listen to the church, Jesus says, "Let him be to you as a Gentile and a tax collector." In other words, if the offender refuses to submit to the righteousness of God, he is to be considered as a part of the world. This may seem hard, but God always leaves the door open for reconciliation. Many times, people sin and hearts harden precisely because there is no righteous example. There is no positive encouragement and loving commitment to each other. As a royal priesthood, we need to minister the righteousness of God one to another and build up the body of Christ.

But what is the standard of judging righteously and

ministering righteousness? The answer is the Word of God:

> All scripture is inspired by God and profitable for teaching, for reproof, for correction, for training in righteousness; that the man of God may be adequate, equipped for every good work (II Tim. 3:16-17).

> Let the Word of Christ rule in your hearts, with all wisdom, teaching and admonishing one another with psalms and hymns and spiritual songs, with thanksgiving in your hearts to God (Col. 3:16).

In the world, where everyone is doing what seems right in his own eyes, there is no gauge, no standards. Everything is relative. There is simply a consensus morality and spirituality. The kind that says, "If everyone is doing it, it must be right," or "Everything is permissable if we do it in love." The tragedy is that this kind of mentality is creeping into the body of Christ. The reason why, of course, is that the Word of God is no longer considered the infallible rule of faith. When this happens, we tend to reduce and water down the gospel and make it more palatable to the world. In the name of making the gospel relevant to the world, we become irrelevant to the gospel. When the authority of the Word of God is questioned, there is always the tendency to come up with a progressive kind of revelation. This leads us to make arrogant assumptions. The assumption, for example, that says, "That may have been the early Christian church's understanding of things, but today, with our scientific disciplines (e.g., medicine, psychology, etc.) and world view, we have a clearer insight to these things. The end result is that we judge the Word of God instead of letting it judge us.

But the truth of the matter is that the Word of God is unchanging because God is unchanging. Jesus, the Living Word, is the same yesterday, today and forever, and the written Word is the same yesterday, today and forever.

59

Why? Because the Holy Spirit, who is inextricably tied into the Word of God, bears witness to the fact. The phrase in II Tim. 3:16 usually translated "inspired by God" in the Greek literally means "God breathed". Scripture is the training ground for righteousness, and therefore for kingdom living, because the Holy Spirit uses it to implement God's will and judge us righteously (individually and collectively). Both Scripture and the Holy Spirit enable us (as three-dimensional people) to see if we are being led by God's Spirit or the spirit of this world.

In this respect, while Scripture is unchanging, it is not static, but vital and dynamic. The Bible uses two Greek words to explain this phenomenon. One word refers to the universal word – Logos. The other word refers to the specific word of God to you as a believer — Rhema.* For example, if I were to say, "Jesus saves", that is the truth. It is the universal word – Logos, regardless of whether you believe it or not. But if you were an unbeliever and I were to proclaim this word to you and you were convicted by the Holy Spirit and given the faith to receive Jesus as your personal Savior, that universal word Logos (Jesus saves) would turn into Rhema, a personal word for you. The gift of faith given by the Holy Spirit is the dynamic element in the Word of God. That is why the writer of Hebrews can say the following:

> The Word that God speaks is alive and vital, it cuts more keenly than any two-edged sword; it strikes through to the place where the soul and spirit meet, to the innermost intimacies of a man's being; it examines the very thoughts and motives of a man's heart. No creature has any cover from the sight of God; everything lies naked and exposed before the eyes of Him with whom we have to deal (Hebrews 4:12-13, Phillips).

*There are a few exceptions when they seem to be used interchangeably.

On one occasion, I was counseling a man in his late 20's (whom we will call George) who had recently come to know the reality of Christ in his life. When Christ came into his life George was convicted to marry the girl with whom he had been living. She claimed to already have been a Christian. I led George to Christ, counseled them and married them. But they were no sooner married, than Satan started getting his licks in. Because of their pre-marital relationship, distrust and jealousy came into the picture. Accusations cropped up. Tempers flared. Satan convinced George to divorce his wife. He was convinced that it wasn't worth the struggle, and maybe he shouldn't have married her in the first place. I received a tearful call from his wife. I went over to their apartment and tried to convince George that this was wrong. I told him it wasn't his love or lack of love for his wife that was going to sustain their marriage, it was God's love for both of them that would keep them together. I read him part of the marriage vows they had taken, "What God has put together, let no man put asunder." But the more I talked to George the more hardened and determined he was to divorce her. In fact, he had already gone to a lawyer and filed for divorce. When I left their apartment, I felt utterly helpless and useless. I shared the way I felt with my wife Grace and the Lord gave her a scripture passage from Malachi 2:13-17. She felt that I was to share this with George and I should use the Living Bible paraphrase.

> Yet, you cover the altar with your tears because the Lord doesn't pay attention to your offerings anymore, and you receive no blessing from Him. "Why has God abandoned us?" you say. I'll tell you why; it is because the Lord has seen your treachery in divorcing your wives who have been faithful to you through the years.

> You are united to your wife by the Lord. In God's wise

plan, when you married, the two of you became one person in His sight. And what does He want? Godly children from your union. Therefore, guard your passions! Keep faith with the wife of your youth.

For the Lord, the God of Israel, says He hates divorce and cruel men. Therefore, control your passions, let there be no divorcing of your wives.

You have wearied the Lord with your words.

"Wearied Him?" you ask in fake surprise. "How have we wearied Him?"

By saying that evil is good, that is pleases the Lord! Or by saying that God won't punish us — He doesn't care.

I looked at that passage and I related to my wife that this was a pretty hard saying. I thought it would cut off what little communication was left. With some doubts and a lot of fear, I dutifully went to see George, and assured him that I wasn't going to argue with him. I affirmed that I loved him as a brother in Christ and that I had a word from Scripture for him. Leaving the Bible open on the couch, I said my good-byes and left. About two in the morning, George called and said, "I can't sleep. I looked at that passage and it seemed that it was written in caps a foot high. I can't go through with the divorce; I'm calling it off."

What convinced him? Certainly not my words. But God's Word accompanied by the Holy Spirit did. And the (Rhema) Word would give him no peace until he agreed with God that it was wrong to file for divorce. That Word became the standard of righteousness for him. The Holy Spirit used that Word to get beyond his mind, set on divorce, to his spirit and convicted him of God's righteousness. While my wife and I were instrumental in ministering the righteousness of God, it was actually God's Word accompanied by the Holy Spirit that restored him to righteousness.

If God's Word is the standard for all righteousness and we are to minister this righteousness through the power of the Holy Spirit, in what manner do we do it? The answer of course, is in Love. God's Word says, "Let all that you do be done in love (I Cor. 16:14). Faith works through love (Gal. 5:6). It does no good to whip people with the truth even when it is God's Word. Very early in the pastorate, I thought of myself as a budding Billy Graham, but people didn't always receive me that way. God showed me that the truth is not enough. The Holy Spirit is the one who convicts. Many times, I found myself trying to convict people in the most unloving way. But the gospel is the good news of how God loves us and died for us and redeems us.

In the light of this truth, I remember hearing a story about Dwight L. Moody. He met an evangelist from England and invited him to come to America and preach. Soon afterwards, the evangelist took Moody up on this invitation. Since the evangelist was relatively unknown in the United States, Moody hired a small hall for him in Chicago, then went off on another crusade. But it wasn't long before the evangelist was packing them in and they were forced to hire bigger halls. Upon hearing this, Moody cut his itinerary short and went home to find out the reasons for the man's success. As he listened to the evangelist and saw the people responding, he was convicted by the Holy Spirit to change his whole manner of preaching. This young evangelist, instead of scaring people into the kingdom with God's judgments, was merely preaching the love of God.

Jesus loves us where we are. This is central to the Gospel message. But He doesn't leave us where we are. His love bids us to grow. With Jesus' love in us, we need to bid people to grow by loving them into the Kingdom of God. Consider the following passages:

> Even if a man is caught in any trespass, you who are spiritual, restore such a one in a spirit of gentleness, looking to yourself, lest you, too, be tempted. Bear one another's burdens and thus fulfill the law of Christ. (Gal. 6:1, 2)

> And so, as those who have been chosen of God, holy and
> And so, as those who have been chosen of God, holy and gentleness and patience; bearing with one another, and forgiving each other, whoever has a complaint against anyone; just as the Lord forgave you, so also should you. And beyond all these things, put on love which is the perfect bond of unity. (Col. 3:12-14)

Time and again I have witnessed what love, which is the perfect bond of unity, can do in a congregation. In one of the nearby towns, for example, there is a man whom we'll call Tom. Tom came from a non-Christian home. He was unloved, neglected and even abused as a child. He grew up a bitter and cynical person. Nice people called him a wet blanket and others something worse. To say that Tom had an abrasive character would be like calling the Grand Canyon a crack in a wall. He fit in socially like feet fit in gloves. As you can imagine, Tom was not easy to get along with. He met a family who invited him to their church. Miracle of miracles, he heard the message of the love of Jesus Christ at that small church, received Christ as his Lord and Savior, and Baptizer in the Holy Spirit. But because of his past, he didn't change overnight. The people at that church not only preached a message of love, but they lived it. It didn't matter that his conversation was crude. It didn't matter that sometimes he was sharp and angry. They simply loved him into the kingdom. In their love for him, they ministered encouragement and correction. As Tom gradually opened up to them, he was also able to receive inner healing from the hurts of the past. Many times, some of the more mature Christians in all humility

64

and sincerity would ask him advice and even ask him to pray and minister to them. This blew him away. It broke down his defenses; it tore down the psychological walls that Tom had built up out of fear of being hurt. He discovered that he was needed. They needed him to complete the body of Christ. Today, you would have trouble recognizing Tom, because his whole countenance is changed. The joy of the Lord is his strength. Tom is too busy building up and ministering to the rest of the body to dwell on his past hurts. Today, when I preach in that church, I always feel the special presence of God. And why shouldn't I feel that way? Those people are ministering the righteousness of God. They have such a love for one another that the kingdom of God is not only in their hearts but in their midst.

Chapter 4

The Authority to Build up the Body of Christ Through the Gifts of the Holy Spirit

We have established that we have authority for the world to witness to the world and make disciples. We also have the authority to stand against the world and the Evil One and live and reign in God's kingdom while we are here on earth. There is a realm of authority, however, that we should consider which enables us to build the body of Christ. In the remaining chapters of Part I, we need to recognize our authority 1) to exercise the gifts of the Holy Spirit, 2) to forgive sins, 3) to heal the inner man, 4) to heal the outer man, and 5) to deliver from spiritual bondage and curses. These areas of authority help us to collectively render the church (the bride of Christ) spotless and wrinkle free. Individually, they help us to render our spirit, soul and body complete and blameless before the coming of Christ.

In addressing the Corinthian Church, Paul says that he does not want them to be unaware of spiritual gifts (I Corinthians 12:1). We should not be either. God wants to use each individual Christian for the building up of His body. Paul goes on to enumerate the gifts of the Holy Spirit which help us to build the body.

Now there are varieties of gifts, but the same Spirit. (v. 4)

And there are varieties of ministries and the same Lord. (v. 5)

And there are varieties of effects, but the same God Who works all things in all persons. (v. 6)

But to each one is given the manifestation of the Spirit for the common good. (v. 7)

For to one is given the word of wisdom through the Spirit, and to another the word of knowledge according to the same Spirit. (v. 8)

To another faith by the same Spirit, and another gifts of healing by the one Spirit. (v. 9)

And to another, the effecting of miracles, and to another prophecy, and to another the distinguishing of spirits, to another various kinds of tongues, to another the interpretation of tongues. (v. 10)

But one and the same Spirit works all these things, distributing to each one individually just as He wills. (v. 11)

The above gifts of the Holy Spirit are ministry tools which are the out-workings of the Holy Spirit.* We, in our

*While I will confine myself to the manifestational gifts in this book, there seems to be some Biblical and experiential evidence for holding three distinct categories of spiritual gifts. There is, for example, the functional or motivational gifts in Romans 12, i.e., prophecy, teaching, mercy, exhortation, etc. Secondly, the office or ministry gifts as described in Ephesians 4:11 and in I Corinthians 12:28f, i.e., apostles, prophet, evangelist, pastor, teacher, etc. Finally, the above manifestational gifts as described above in I Corinthians 12: 2-11. While all these are charisms, it is my belief that the nine manifestational gifts are universal gifts given by the Holy Spirit to meet the needs of every and any member of the Body of Christ, regardless of their functional gift or office.

ministries, look at these as a nine-prong plug which we daily plug into to minister to God's people and build them up. One day as we were sharing a teaching on the authority of a believer, the Lord exhorted us with these words:

> O My people, many of you are hurting and wounded. Many of you are longing for the day to claim your inheritance when you shall be healed and totally free to be my people. But I tell you, my dear ones, if you are to receive your inheritance, you are to receive it now; not someday, not tomorrow, not next week. Not next month or next year, but now. You are in my kingdom now if you are in My kingdom at all.

The Lord has demonstrated to us time after time that the reason why so many people are not functioning and exercising their authority to witness to the world and live and reign in God's kingdom is precisely because they themselves are hurting, wounded and bound. They need to be built up individually so that they can bear the fruit of the Holy Spirit and be three-dimensional people. They also need to be renewed collectively so that they can minister healing to each other and truly fit into the Body of Christ. The gifts of the Holy Spirit are vehicles for ministering God's healing power and building up God's people collectively and individually.

If I can use the analogy of a car to describe the individual Christian's spiritual walk; the car is the salvation wagon in which we receive Christ. The Baptism in the Holy Spirit is the gas, the fuel to move us to do the work of God and the gifts of the Holy Spirit are the oil in the crankcase to lubricate us and allow us to function properly. The best aspect of the gifts of the Holy Spirit is that they can function regardless of the spiritual temperature, like 10W40 oil. God can use the most or the least mature Christian as His vessel for these gifts. The Corinthians, for example, were immature Christians. Paul calls them baby Christians. He encouraged them to exercise the gifts for the common good. They were not given for an ego trip or to cause division among the brethren. On the contrary, they were to be exercised in love and in a loving manner. That is why Paul sandwiches his talk on the gifts with the need for self-sacrificing love in I Corinthians 13. Love is one of the fruits of the Spirit and Jesus said that it is by their fruits (or lack of them) that you will know them (Matthew 7:32). The fruit, especially love, is the measure of maturity in the Christian. The gifts, on the other hand, are tools like hammer and saw. Tools are not to be admired for themselves. They are there for constructive building. Now, tools in the hands of immature children can be destructive, but that doesn't mean that they should be avoided as some traditional churches have done. On the contrary, Scripture tells us the gifts of the Holy Spirit should be used in obedience to the moving of the Holy Spirit (See I Corinthians 12:7-11) and in love (I Corinthians 13:1, 14:1). In fact, everyone is to use them (I Corinthians 12:7, 14:26) and no one is to come behind in any gift (I Corinthians 1:7). Paul further instructs: 1) to not be ignorant concerning spiritual gifts, (I Corinthians 12:1), 2) to not neglect them (I Timothy 4:14), 3) to stir them up (II Timothy 1:6), 4) to seek to excel in them (I Corinthians 14:12). Nowhere does he say ignore them or that they are for a particular generation or particular class of people. God wants us to exercise the gifts of the Spirit in a mature and loving way to build up the Body of Christ.

Because the gifts are given for the building up of the Body of Christ, and because Jesus sent His disciples out two by two, we always minister at least in twos, as representatives of the Body of Christ. Jesus said whenever two or three are gathered in His Name there He is in their midst. There is power in the Body of Christ. It says in Scripture, "One can put to flight one thousand, two, ten thousand" (Deut. 32:30). In functioning as the Body of Christ, we invite Jesus to be the wonderful counselor in our midst. As we submit to Him body, soul, and spirit, we ask that the gifts of the Holy Spirit would be manifested through us. While one person leads in the Spirit, the other prays in the Spirit and each changes off according to the leading of the Spirit. The Lord has used me, and many others, in the same way to function in all nine of the gifts to meet the needs of His people.

In order to see the way these gifts function, let's take them one at a time and see how they work in the Bible, and how we use the gifts to build the Body of Christ.

WORD OF WISDOM

Paul says, " . . . to one is given the word of wisdom through the same Spirit" (I Corinthians 12:8). The word of wisdom that Paul is talking about is not natural wisdom or advice, but supernatural wisdom, the wisdom of God. Many times it comes as an answer to some problem or to silence an opponent. In the Old Testament, King Solomon asked God for wisdom to rule and God gave it to him (I Kings 3:5-28). This gift was manifested when two women came before him with two babies — one dead and the other alive. Both claimed the live one was her own. One of the women had accidentally suffocated her own child during the night, and according to the other woman she exchanged it for hers while she was asleep. Because there were no witnesses present, there seemed to be no solution to the problem. It was one woman's word against the other. But then the word of wisdom was given to Solomon. Solomon commanded a sword be brought to him and he ordered the living child to be divided in two, half to one woman and half to the other woman. The result was that the natural mother loved her child so much she was willing for her child to be given to the other woman rather than have it slain. The other woman, on the other hand, was willing to have it slain and divided. The response of these two women made it clear who was the real mother of the living child. Those that heard and witnessed Solomon's answer to the problem also recognized it was the wisdom of God.

> When all Israel heard the judgment which the king had handed down, they feared the king; for they saw that the wisdom of God was in him to administer justice. (I Kings 3:28)

Jesus as the Messiah, fulfilled the prophecy of Isaiah 11:2, which promised that the Spirit of the Lord would rest on him with the spirit of wisdom and understanding:

> The Spirit of the Lord will rest on him, (the Spirit of wisdom and understanding, the Spirit of counsel and strength, the Spirit of knowledge and the fear of the Lord. (Isaiah 11:2)

The classic example of His exercising the wisdom of God was occasioned when the scribes asked Him a loaded question to trap Him, "Is it lawful for us to pay taxes to Caesar or not?" It was a trick question. If Jesus answered yes, He would be considered a friend of the Romans and at the same time unpatriotic towards the subjugated Jews. The Jews in turn could justify their hatred for Him. On the other hand, if He answered no, His enemies would report Him to the Roman authorities as seditious. That was the problem. The gift of wisdom was manifested through Jesus when He said, "Show me a denarius. Whose head and inscription does it have?" They said, "Caesar's," and He said, "Then render to Caesar the things that are Caesar's and to God the things that are God's (Luke 20:24-25)." You can imagine how nonplussed they were. The result was that they could not trap Him. The account continues, " And they were unable to catch Him in a saying in the presence of the people; and marvelling at His answer, they became silent (Luke 20:26)."

Now this same Jesus promised His disciples that they would be given wisdom (Luke 21:14-15):

> So make up your minds not to prepare beforehand to defend yourselves, for I will give you utterance and wisdom which none of your opponents will be able to resist or refute.

God is still manifesting His wisdom for and through His people today. Many people come to us with some seemingly insurmountable problems and difficulties. God has the answers. A typical occasion, for example, was when a man came to us with his sister. They wanted prayer for his wife who had gotten involved in one of the cults. While she would let her children go to the parochial school, many times she would take them to her cult meeting. Upon hearing this, our first inclination was to take a position of alarm and have the husband confront his wife with the sin of her cult involvement. After all, he was the head of the house, even if he did appear to be a mouse. But that was not God's plan or His wisdom. God had a better plan. Later, He revealed that there was a spirit of rebellion in the man's wife, and a confrontation over the cult activity would only have further alienated her. God is in the business of reconciling people. In His wisdom, He showed us that we needed to speak with the husband about his relationship with Jesus. The reason his wife was involved in

72

the cult in the first place was that she was starved for something spiritual and in her rebellion, she was willing to take Satan's counterfeit. Both of them had the forms of religion, but lacked the spirit. Christ needed to be real in their lives. When confronted with God's wisdom, the man had to admit that he was a Sunday-only Christian, and that he needed to have Christ in his heart throughout the week.

This opened the door for us to lead him to Christ and take authority over some of the problems in his life. He was introduced to the Baptism of the Holy Spirit and encouraged to attend the Life in the Spirit Seminars held by his church. We led him through Scripture and taught him briefly how he needed to be the spiritual head of his family by loving his wife as his own body, praying for her and doing spiritual warfare for his wife and children. Together with his spirit-filled sister, we bound the spirits of rebellion and rejection and fear of rejection in his wife and we loosed the spirit of salvation on her. The end result of this ministry was that in less than six months, the man's children received Christ and were baptised in the Holy Spirit. The change in the lives of her family so shocked the wife that she eventually abandoned her cult meetings and was led to Christ by her sister. This could not have happened without God's wisdom entering into the picture. He knew that once the whole family let their light shine, this wife, in spite of her rebellion, would be won to that light.

God's wisdom is never contrary to His Word. In fact, it always supports it. On another occasion, we had to minister to a woman who had four children. She wielded her authority as a believer and got total victory for the hurts in her life. This included the hurts caused by her husband who had abandoned her and her family. But that wasn't the end of it. She wrote us a letter and asked how she could win her husband back. I must say at first I had no answer. But as I prayed and asked for God's wisdom, the answer came. Scripture says, "But if any of you lack wisdom, let him ask of God, Who gives to all men generously and without reproach, and it will be given to him (James 1:5)."

Suddenly, my thoughts were flooded with a four-point plan of action. The Lord led me to have the woman ask her children to forgive their father. She had already done that for herself while she was with us for ministry. The Lord did not want anyone in her family binding the husband by any unforgiveness. Secondly, Jesus inspired me to encourage the children and mother to let their light shine so that their dad and husband would see their good works and glorify Him. Since he had left them, they could do that only in their letters to him. They were to express their love for him and share what God had done to change their lives. This was to be done in a non-judgmental, non-preaching way. Thirdly, I encouraged the woman, as a matter of confession before God in the spiritual realm, to be in submission to her husband and claim the promise of I Peter 3, "Namely, wives, be subject to your husband, so that he might be won without a word." In a very practical way, she expressed that submission by letting her husband know in her letters how she would value his judgment and wisdom on certain decisions that had to be made for the family. In other words, let him feel needed. It was very easy for the wife to take an independent stance precisely because her husband had left her. But in the spiritual realm, this did not allow God to enter the picture and put pressure on him to be responsible to his wife and children. If God can even use Satan for His purpose (as he told us), He certainly can use a wayward, unbelieving husband to do His Will if we trust Him (not the husband) to work through the husband. For the fourth step, Jesus showed me something entirely new.

He revealed that because a husband and wife are one flesh and under a covenantial relationship with Him, they have a God-given right to do spiritual battle for each other. I asked her to get together with her spirit-filled prayer group and ask God to reveal to them (through a word of knowledge) the spiritual forces that were affecting her husband, and then bind them up in the name of Jesus. I sent the letter to her and four weeks later I got an answer. She and her family had done exactly what I had written. Her husband was coming home permanently for Easter. God in His wisdom knew what would bring that man home and He was faithful to the promises of His Word.

WORD OF KNOWLEDGE

Hand in hand with the word of wisdom, God gives us His word of knowledge to minister and to build up His people. The word of knowledge comes when the Holy Spirit reveals information about a person that you had no previous knowledge about. A word of knowledge also comes as the Holy Spirit reveals a particular scripture which specifically applies to a given problem or situation. Many times, it will provide not only the answer, but offers hope and even convicts a person to change his or her ways.

The word of knowledge was manifested through Jesus when He confronted the Samaritan woman about her marital status at Jacob's well. When Jesus commanded her to go and call her husband, the woman answered and said that she had no husband. And Jesus responded, "You have answered well, 'I have no husband;' for you have had five husbands, and the one whom you now have is not your husband; this you have said truly (John 4:17-18)." How did He know about her marital status? The Holy Spirit revealed it to Him as a word of knowledge.

Many times, the Lord will also give us a word about a person's past that they either have blocked out of their minds or have difficulty in acknowledging. One day, for example, we were ministering to a young college gym teacher. Her husband had left her and she was deeply wounded; so much so that she was unable to share and open up to receive God's inner healing. She confessed that there were things in her past that she was ashamed of and for which God couldn't possibly forgive her. At this point, we seemed to be at an impasse. Then the Lord revealed to me He wanted her to receive forgiveness for her homosexual relationship that she had with another woman. There was nothing that she had done that He would not forgive. When I shared this word of knowledge with her, it was like opening a dam. God loved her so much that He revealed her sin not to condemn her for it, but rather to let her receive His forgiveness and deal with it. Once she understood that, she poured out all her problems and received ministry for them. The word of knowledge was the key to her receiving God's forgiveness and inner healing.

Many times, a word of knowledge will be expressed as a vision. One day as I was praying with a woman, the Lord gave me a vision of a baby in a womb. When I shared this with her, she broke down and she said that she did not want this last baby. The vision enabled her to resolve her guilt feelings and ask God's forgiveness.

What about the word of knowledge that gives a scripture to convict or to offer hope? Jesus promised us that the Spirit would bring to remembrance all that He said (John 16:13). In a previous chapter, I shared that my wife had a word of knowledge using scripture for a parishioner who was filing for divorce. The scripture from Malachi 2: 13-16 expressed God's hatred for divorce. The Word so convicted him that he stopped the divorce proceedings.

On another occasion, a nurse who was a former missionary worked in a private psychiatric clinic. After receiving some ministry, she shared with us that she was under severe persecution from her superior, a psychiatrist and avowed atheist. The point of conflict was when she quietly prayed with some of the clients as the Lord led and with some of the Christian staff. There was no problem until one of the patients gratefully shared with the doctor how much better she felt since she had prayed with the nurse. Instead of being elated, he was enraged. From that point on, she was a marked woman. He not only told her to stop praying with people, he constantly criticized and found fault with her work. Sometimes, he would go out of his way to put her down before her coworkers. As we prayed with her, one member of our staff received a word of knowledge through scripture which offered hope, encouragement and vindication. The word was a strong word, however, from Psalm 7:8-17:

> The Lord judges His people; vindicate me, O Lord according to my righteousness and my integrity that is in me. (v. 8)
>
> O let the evil of the wicked come to an end, but establish the righteous; for the righteous God tries the heart and minds. (v. 9)
>
> My shield is with God Who saves the upright in heart. (v. 10)
>
> God is a righteous Judge, and a God Who has indignation every day. (v. 11)
>
> If a man does not repent, He will sharpen His sword; He has bent His bow and made is ready. (v. 12)
>
> He has also prepared for Himself deadly weapons; He makes His arrows fiery shafts. (v. 13)

Behold he travels with wickedness and he conceives mischief, and brings forth falsehood. (v. 14)

He has dug a pit and hollowed it out, and has fallen into the hole which he made. (v. 15)

His mischief will return upon his own head, his violence will descend upon his own. (v. 16)

I will give thanks to the Lord according to His righteousness, and will sing praise to the name of the Lord Most High. (v. 17)

This word of knowledge not only promised God's vindication of her and offered her peace, but also proved prophetically true. The verbal abuse she received lessened considerably. In less than a year, the doctor was felled by terminal cancer. But before he died, God gave this nurse an opportunity to get reconciled with him and let God's love be expressed. Whether he received Christ through that witness, only God knows.

GIFT OF FAITH

There is another gift that we pray for to minister and build up God's people and that is the gift of faith. When we talk about the word "faith" we need to see three elements of faith:

1. The gift of faith
2. The saving faith
3. The fruit of faith

Saving faith is the assurance of our salvation and our standing with God. It is the life lived in fellowship and obedience to His Word and Will (Hebrews 11:38-39; Romans 1:17; Galatians 3:11).[2] It is the motivational

[2]Derek Prince, *Faith to Live By,* Christian Growth Ministries Pub., Ft. Lauderdale, Florida, 1977, page 15.

power for the gift of faith to be exercised. It is the faith that believes that God is the rewarder of those who seek Him (Hebrews 11:5). It is the faith that we walk and live by.

The gift of faith is the dynamic expression of God's love and mercy based on that saving faith. It is faith in action when the promises of God (be it healing, miracles, deliverance, etc.) become the promise for now. The gift of faith turns the universal promises (the Logos) into the present (Rhema) for us now. Jesus promises this gift explicitly when He said, "If you have faith as a grain of mustard seed, you will say to this mountain move here to there and it shall move and nothing shall be impossible to you (Matthew 17:20)." The gift of faith can make seemingly impossible situations possible. In every case this gift must correspond to God's Will and Word. The gift of faith expressed God's ability to do His supernatural work.

The fruit of faith, the third element of faith, expresses God's character as revealed in Jesus Christ — His trust-worthiness, His faithfulness, His commitment to us; and our commitment to Him. While the fruit and the gifts are not mutually exclusive, the fruit is the result of our mature walk with Him. The gift of faith on the other hand does not necessarily relate to maturity in the faith. It is there simply to meet the need to build up the body of Christ.

In a sense, the three phases of faith are expressive of the persons in the Trinity and their ultimate intention that we be God's inheritance; that He be all in all in our lives. God the Father desired to receive a family of sons like his first born (Romans 8:17). Faith for salvation opens the door for our participation in His very life and purpose; as well as appropriating all that God desires to share. It qualifies us to live and reign with Him in His righteousness. Jesus, the second person of the Trinity, desires to receive a glorious body for his expression (Eph. 1:23). Faith as a fruit allows us to express His character and our life hid in Him. The Holy Spirit desires a temple of living stones for His eternal abode (Eph. 2:20-22). The gift of faith enables Him to build and heal that body individually and collectively so that it may be complete before the coming of our Lord. All three members of the Trinity through these three phases of faith can receive honor, glory and satisfaction.

Jesus expressed all three of these phases of faith when He was faced with the decaying body of Lazarus. He prayed, "Father, I thank thee that Thou hast heard me, and I know that Thou hearest me always." In this confession He expressed faith in His righteous standing with the Lord and His trust that God always hears Him and is faithful. With this relationship established and His trust in God, He boldly and confidently expresses the gift of faith by commanding Lazarus to come forth (John 11:43).

Jesus found the gift of faith in God in many people. To the woman with the issue of blood he said, "Thy faith has made thee well" (Luke 8:48). To the Canaanite woman who sought deliverance for her daughter who was demon possessed, Jesus declared, "O woman, your faith is great; be it done for you as you wish" (Matthew 15:28). Jesus marveled at the faith of the centurion who believed that all He had to do was say the word and his servant would be healed (Luke 7:9). Hebrews 11 shows that this gift of faith was given to people in the Old Testament. The prophet Elijah, for example, expressed the faith of God when he was instrumental in bringing the widow's child back from the dead (I Kings 17:20-24).

But what about Biblical faith for today, particularly the gift of faith? We have seen the gift of faith exercised as we prayed for the healing of memories, wounded spirits, healing of broken relationships, deliverance and physical healings.

A 25-year-old woman was brought to our ministry center by her spirit-filled mother. I say 'brought by her mother' because she was emotionally devastated by her broken marriage and so heavily sedated that she was not mentally capable of making any decisions on her own. As we started to pray she sat sucking her thumb as if wanting to go back in her mother's womb. We prayed for the gifts of the Spirit to be manifest through us and wondered at the same time how we were going to get through to her. But God's gift of faith came to her as well as us. As we received words of knowledge and wisdom, she became aware enough to offer and receive forgiveness, deliverance, and inner healing for herself. We did not see the full results of that ministry until weeks later. God transformed that young woman's life from one of bondage and hopelessness to one of radiant promise; from zombie-like state to a vibrant joyful personality. Sometimes the gift of faith comes as part of a healing process as in the above case, and sometimes as an instantaneous miracle. But in either case the gift of faith is there to make it happen.

GIFT OF HEALING

The gifts of healing and miracles work hand in hand with the gift of faith. While we sometimes use the word healing and miracles interchangeably, I believe that healing usually follows a natural process whereas miracles defy or go beyond the natural process or laws as we understand them. While we talk more about healing and our authority to heal the outer man in another chapter, we need to see that the gifts of healing are plural. This would lead us to conclude that there are various types of healing which can include the healing of spirit, soul and body.

Jesus not only healed the sickness but blessed the whole person.[3] Like all other gifts of the Spirit, the gift of healing is a gift that we do not hold onto or even possess; in other words we are not the healers. Rather the gift of healing is a direct gift of God's grace to the person with the need.

In the Old Testament, one of God's redemptive names is Jehovah Rapha, usually translated, "I am the Lord, your healer" (Exodus 15:26). Jesus was also the fulfillment of the prophecies that expected the Messiah to heal the sick (Isaiah 35:5-6; 61:1). He healed the sick out of His compassionate heart and sent His disciples to do the same (Mt. 10:8). The Word of God further promises that one of the signs that will accompany those that believe is that they will lay hands on the sick and they will recover (Mark 16:18).[4] I find that the more we believe that God desires to heal his people, the more readily available is His gift of healing.

A former co-worker discovered this for himself when his ministry was short-circuited by major coronary attacks. Between taking dilators to expand his blood vessels and pills to calm his system so he could sleep, his life style was limited to say the least. Under orders from his physician, he was to avoid climbing stairs or carrying anything more than a briefcase. And yet the Lord gave him a vision for a church without walls, a family camping ministry located in the boundary waters of Minnesota. But the vision could only be carried out by a healthy man; a man who would be able to lift things like canoes and do general maintenance,

[3] Seigfried Grossman, *Charisma,* "The Gifts of the Spirit", Trans. by Susan Weisman, Key Publishers, Inc., Wheaton, Illinois, 1971, p. 42.

[4] Arnold Bittlinger, *Gifts and Graces,* Trans. by Herbert Lassen, William E. Erdmans Pub. Co., Grand Rapids, Michigan, 1968, p. 34-35.

besides traveling and teaching across the country. As he was lying in his bed with a second coronary, he lamented, "Lord, I am only half a man, how can I accomplish the task you gave me unless I'm healed. Won't you heal me?" The Lord instructed him to put his hand over his heart and immediately a sensation like an electric current went through his body. He was healed. A check with his internist confirmed it.

GIFT OF MIRACLES

In addition to the gift of healing, the work of miracles touches not only on healing but covers a wide range of supernatural works. This gift, as we have said before, is a God-given ability to perform acts which seem to override or contradict natural laws. In the Old Testament, for example, we have the incident where Joshua prays for the sun and moon to stand still until the enemies of the Israelites were defeated (Joshua 10:12). The parting of the Red Sea (Exodus 14:21) and the widow's inexhaustible supply of oil and flour (I Kings 17:8-16) are just a few examples of God's miracle working power in the Old Testament.

In the New Testament there is the account of Jesus' first miracle of changing water into wine (John 2:1-11). Then there is the account of His walking on water (Mt. 14:25-53); feeding the multitude (Mk. 6:45-53) and the raising of the dead (John 11:38-44). Another miracle, of course, which seems to be overlooked by many people is the miracle of being born again — from being spiritually dead to being spiritually alive. When the disciples came back after performing great works of deliverance and healing, Jesus said, "Nevertheless, do not rejoice in this, rejoice that your names are recorded in heaven (Luke 10:20)."

In recent years there have been reports of God's people witnessing resurrections, people having been officially declared dead and coming back to life.[5] In the recent Indonesian revival there have been several accounts of bodies being in partial stages of decay that have been revived. There have been incidences of walking on water and water changing into wine.[6] All miracles that were performed by Jesus. And why not? Jesus promises that "Greater things will you do in my name" (John 14:12). We have witnessed the daily miracles of people being reborn into a new life in Christ. We have seen the miracle of people instantly being delivered from demonic bondage. Jesus said, "If I cast out demons by the finger of God, then the kingdom of God has come upon you" (Luke 11:20). People with one short leg and built-up shoes have had their legs grow out before our very eyes.

My wife has personally witnessed not only God multiplying food but changing the taste of food as she prayed over it. Several years ago she was temporarily working as a cook in a restaurant. As things sometimes happen, everything went wrong. The special was macaroni and cheese. She had not only scorched the cheese sauce, but put too much salt in it. It tasted terrible. There was neither time nor cheese enough to make another batch. The waitresses asked, "What will we do?" She said, "Serve it I guess. I'll pray." They were skeptical but had no better suggestions. My wife simply prayed, "Lord, I know we

[5] Betty Malz, *My Glimpse of Eternity*, Spire Books, Fleming H. Revell Co., Old Tappan, N. J., 1977. Betty Malz's story of her death, glimpse of eternity and return to life is just one of many accounts that corroborate the truth of the Scriptures.

[6] Mel Tari, *Like A Mighty Wind*, Creation House, Carol Stream, Ill., 1971.

don't deserve it, but we surely would appreciate it if you could make this stuff taste good, and so would the customers. Amen." With great hesitation the waitresses served the first orders and waited. Soon they were back in the kitchen asking excitedly, "What did you do, Grace? They say it's the best they've ever tasted!" When my wife assured them that all she had done was pray, they were still doubtful even though they knew she had no time for anything else. Besides the telltale brown flecks were still in the cheese sauce. A little later they witnessed an extension of the same miracle. There was possibly one half cup of macaroni and cheese remaining when two more orders came in. Neither customer would accept a substitute, so again my wife prayed, "Please, help Lord," and she emptied the pan and served two full portions. Everyone was a little surprised and each one was glad that the other had seen what they had seen, a miracle from God.

God has promised us through prophecy and His word that in the days ahead as we walk in His strength and believe as His children, He will demonstrate more of His miracle working power.

GIFT OF PROPHECY

The gift of prophecy is another gift that we constantly need for the building up of the body of Christ. Prophecy is an inspired Word from God given through a yielded vessel. Paul places a high value on this gift when he exhorts, "Ernestly desire the spiritual gifts, especially that you may prophesy" (I Cor. 14:1), and again, "I want you to speak in tongues, but even more to prophesy" (I Cor. 14:5). The purpose of prophecy is primarily to comfort, encourage, and build up the body of believers (I Cor. 14:31).

85

> One who prophesies speaks to men for edification and
> exhortation and consolation. One who prophesies edifies
> the church.

Prophecy is not first and foremost foretelling as commonly understood, but rather forth-telling. It may involve a glance back in the past or a look into the future but nearly always with the purpose of giving light, correction, or encouragement to the present.[7]

The gift of prophecy as well as the office or ministry of prophet was common in the Old Testament. Sometimes God spoke audibly as He did to the prophet Samuel concerning judgment to Eli and his sons. Visions are also a part of God revealing Himself as was the case of Isaiah, who was confronted with God's holiness in the temple (Isaiah 6:1ff).

Using a proverb, Jesus characterized Himself as a prophet without honor in his own country and in His own house. (Mt. 13:53-58). People in His day recognized Him as such (Mt. 16:14; Lk. 7:16, 24:19; Jn. 4:19) and His enemies argued against this claim (Jn. 7:52; Lk. 7:39). Like the Old Testament prophets, Jesus had visions. As He was being tempted, He saw all the kingdoms of the world in a moment's time (Lk. 4:5). At His transfiguration, He, along with some of His disciples, was able to see and speak with Moses and Elijah about His suffering and crucifixion (Mt. 17:1-8).

In the book of Joel (2:28) we have the promise that this prophetic spirit would be poured out on all the people of God. Peter acknowledges the fulfillment of this prophecy on the day of Pentecost, when he says,

> But this is what was spoken through the prophet Joel:

---

[7]Arnold Bittlinger, *op cit*, p. 42.

> And it shall be in the last days, God says, That I will pour forth of My spirit upon all mankind; And your sons and your daughters shall prophesy, and your young men shall see visions, and your old men shall dream dreams;

> Even upon my bondslaves, both men and women, I will in those days pour forth of My Spirit and they shall prophesy . . . Acts 2:16-18

God is still using prophecy to build up His people today. Someone has quipped, "God's power and gifts didn't peter out when Peter petered out." This is true for our day, too. I can remember when I received my first prophecy. There were over 500 people gathered at a praise and prayer meeting. All sorts of doubts and questions came in my mind. Is this from me or is this from God? What happened was after a long pause the Lord gave the same words to someone else who had the courage of conviction to offer it. Many times God will accommodate His budding prophets by allowing them to feel something. He used to accommodate me by letting me feel the anointing in the back of my head. By contrast, the first prophecy given to one member of our staff appeared as a ticker tape across his mind. Still another would feel his hands raise up like balloons. But God doesn't want us to rely on these helps. He simply wants us to trust Him and hear His voice.

There have been various accounts of God speaking audibly to His people. While I have personally heard the Lord call my name when I was 7 years old, and I have heard some people testify of God speaking audibly, these occurrences are the exception rather than the rule. God usually speaks in the still small voice. When He speaks, He not only edifies you and the body of Christ, but also confirms His Word.

Many people who are used for the first few times in prophecy are fearful of saying something out of their flesh. But they need to put their fears, as well as their pride, aside and realize that what they say will be tested not only by time, but also by the congregation and the prophets. In other words, let his word be weighed by the prophets. This is done in the spirit of humility. There should be no stigma with making a mistake. The question to ask ourselves is, "Are we more concerned with making a mistake or with having the people of God edified?"

Usually the more we speak, trusting the Lord to speak through us, the more purified the message will be. The old saying, "Practice makes perfect" applies here too. It's like learning to walk. We don't learn to walk as children without falling down a few times. Eventually we try and try again and become more confident as we listen to the voice of God and speak forth in obedience.

More often than not, as we minister to God's people, God has a word of encouragement for that person. A typical example of that was when a psychologist friend brought his wife for inner healing. He was gloriously healed the week before. Like him, she had suffered rejection from her father. Her father had urged her mother to abort the child. At that point the parents did not realize that twin daughters would be born to them. The mother refused to abort and the father persisted in his rejection of his children after they were born. As we ministered to her for the healing of memories and a wounded spirit, the Lord spoke a word of comfort and encouragement through her husband:

> My daughter, I have known you from the beginning of time. I knew you while you were being formed in your mother's womb. I knew you when you were still an un-fertilized egg coming down the left fallopian tube of your mother. I saw you and your sister fertilized with your father's sperm. Your sister was born before you and you

were not expected by your parents. But I claimed you
both and have a divine purpose for both of you and your
families . . .

As the prophecy went on, the Lord affirmed his Father love
for her and assured her that her life was not without
purpose.

Sometimes the Lord will give guidance through
prophecy that will confirm what is already in the heart of
the person. A young man for example came for ministry.
He had tried many jobs and business ventures and was unsuccessful in all of them. After the ministry time the Lord
kept on giving me the message, "Christ for the Nations,
Christ for the Nations." I asked the young man, "Does
that mean anything to you?" I had known that this was a
charismatic Bible School founded by Gordon Lindsay. But
I had no idea where it was located. The young man then
shared with me that he felt the Lord was calling him
into the ministry, and over and over in his mind the Lord
was telling him to go to Dallas, Texas. "Well," I said,
"Let's check and see where Christ for the Nations is." I
remembered seeing a Gordon Lindsay booklet on our book
rack . . . Checking the flyleaf I saw to my surprise that it
was located in Dallas, Texas. The young man applied, was
accepted and is gloriously happy with God's direction for
his life. In our everyday ministry we continually ask for
guidance and the Lord is faithful to give it.

Many times we say "a picture is worth a thousand
words." The Lord knows that, too. That is why along with
the gift of prophecy He often uses visions to instantly
reveal a truth. In a previous chapter I shared that there was
a man who questioned whether God could forgive him for
the evil things that he had done in the past. At this point
the Lord gave a brother in Christ a vision of a man kneeling
before Jesus confessing his sins and crying out, "How can

you forgive me for all my sins?" And Jesus, matter of factly said, "What sins?" You see Jesus had already forgiven them. In this vision, He was only affirming His Word that promises that when we ask forgiveness, He wipes out our transgressions and remembers them no more (Isaiah 43: 25; Hebrews 8:12; Jer. 31:34). When He forgives, He forgets and pardons our sins to eternal forgetfulness. That man needed to know that. As my co-worker shared this vision with him, he was able to be at peace with himself and with God and receive that total forgiveness himself.

DISCERNING OF SPIRITS

The seventh gift that Paul mentions is the gift of discerning of spirits. The gift of discerning of spirits is different from the general discernment that every Christian believer possesses. While every believer as a three dimensional person has a certain understanding of God's ways and His Will, the gift of discerning of spirits is the supernatural ability to differentiate between divine, demonic, and human powers in others.

In the Old Testament, this was needed to distinguish the true prophets from the false ones. Micaiah (I Kings 22), for example, was able to discern that the court prophets were inspired by a lying spirit.

Jesus discerned Satan speaking through Peter when He rebuked Peter for saying that he did not have to go to Jerusalem and suffer and be killed (Mt. 16:22-23). Minutes before Jesus had asked the disciples who they thought He was and Peter confessed He was the Son of the Living God, Jesus discerned that this statement was not the product of Peter's mind but it was revealed to him by His Father in heaven (Mt. 16:17). Paul discerned that a slave girl's correct observations about him and his ministry sprang from an evil spirit and not from the Holy Spirit (Acts 16:16-18).

This gift of discerning of spirits is necessary to ministry to God's people. We are always called to test the spirits, and see if they are from God. Why? Because Satan and his cohorts are liars and deceivers and we need to know what is of God and what isn't.

For example, this gift came into play when we were ministering to a man who had given his life to Christ a few months before. He wanted to receive the baptism in the Holy Spirit. As we laid hands on him and agreed with him to receive it, he started to speak in tongues. Immediately the Lord gave us discernment that this tongue was not inspired of the Holy Spirit. It was Satanic in nature. When we addressed the spirit to stop in the Name of Jesus, a demonic leer came on the man's face. The Lord revealed through a word of knowledge that it was a spirit of deception. This opened the door for further ministry and deliverance from past occult activities.

Sometimes the Lord will let you see the demon itself in the spiritual realm. On one occasion, for example, we were at a retreat house and one of the members on our team saw a spirit floating down the hallway. At first he thought it was Jesus but then he saw the severe countenance of its face. The Lord revealed through a word of knowledge that this was a religious spirit. This gave us the opportunity to kick him out in the Name of Jesus.

Just as with any of the other gifts, the gift of discerning of spirits works hand in hand with God's Word. A young widow, for example, had recently received the baptism of the Holy Spirit. She shared some revelations that she had written down in her spiritual diary. She felt that the Lord had spoken these things to her when she was meditation in prayer and yet she was not entirely comfortable with all of it. She asked if we would confirm whether what she was listening to was from God. Immediately I felt a check in my spirit. God reminded me that He was a God of peace but she was anxious about this whole thing. She started sharing some things that she has written down from her spiritual diary and they started out uplifting. The spirit assured her of His love for her and her family; that she was His daughter. The spirit recognized her loneliness and assured her of his continual presence. But then the messages from her spiritual journal started to slowly get off the beaten track. It drew attention to a platonic friendship that she had with a man. She was attracted to him but knew there was some unresolved problems in his life that needed to be dealt with before she could be serious about him. Like her, his spouse had died at a fairly young age. Unlike her, he was not a Christian. The spirit spoke to her to pray for him because he was preparing him to be her mate. In the meantime, he would unite them spiritually in his love if she were agreeable to this. At this point, there was a direct conflict with God's Word. God does not unite light with darkness (II Cor. 6:14-15).

She went on to explain the reason for her anxiety. When she consented to this pact, she woke up and felt she was being sexually assaulted by this spirit. This went on for a number of weeks. All the time the spirit continued to assure her that he was uniting her by his love with this man.

When we were able to show her through Scripture that this was not of God, she renounced this deceiving spirit from her life and later sought further ministry for inner healing.

GIFTS OF TONGUES AND INTERPRETATION

One of the most controversial and least understood gifts is the gift of tongues. Both the gift of tongues and interpretation are largely New Testament phenomena. Many commentators, however, have drawn attention to the prophet Isaiah who speaks of the day when God will speak to Israel in a strange language.

Nay, but by men of strange lips and with alien tongue, the Lord will speak to this people (Isaiah 28:11).

While some feel that Isaiah was referring to the Assyrians who were to later conquer the Israelites (Isaiah 33:39), Paul quotes this passage to illustrate tongues (I Cor. 14:21).

The complimentary gift of interpretation was certainly given to Daniel, as God caused a hand to write words on a wall in an unknown language (Daniel 5:25-28). This was not a word to build up the body, however, but rather a judgment on the Persian nation.[8]

While we cannot establish with any certainty that Jesus spoke or prayed in tongues, there is not any doubt that this phenomenon was part of the New Testament church. Nevertheless, many people misunderstand Paul's statements about tongues. He warns that the tongue can have a harsh note like a noisy gong or clanging cymbal if the speaker does not demonstrate love (I Cor. 13:1). It may be used out of turn (I Cor. 14:27) or at the wrong time (I Cor. 14:28), but nowhere does Paul suggest that this gift had degenerated to the human level — a product of excessive emotionalism. His plea rather was that precisely because this is a manifestation of the Holy Spirit, it should be used decently and in order (I Cor. 14:40); because God is not the author of confusion but of peace (I Cor. 14:33). As a result, Paul does not tell the Corinthians

[x]Arnold Bittlinger, op. cit., p. 42.

93

to stop using this gift. On the contrary, he encourages them to continue manifesting tongues (I Cor. 14:5a), but in a proper way (I Cor. 14:13, 28) and with a proper regard to the other gifts of the Spirit as well (I Cor. 14:5). Larry Christenson in his book, *Speaking In Tongues* rightly points out that "This is the basic framework for any biblical discussion of speaking in tongues . . . Scripture simply does not support any argument against speaking in tongues, only against its abuse."[9] As we have said before, like a tool a spiritual gift can be constructive or destructive in the hands of the user. When we understand this basic truth, our whole discussion of tongues is seen in a positive framework. Paul himself reflects this position when he confesses, "I thank God that I speak in tongues more than you all" (I Cor. 14:18). Christenson concludes, "So the answer to abuse is not disuse, but proper use. We can't deprecate the gift as such, because it is of the Holy Spirit."[10]

With this understanding, we need to recognize that there are two ways in which tongues may be manifested. The most common way is as a devotional language in prayer or in song (singing in the spirit) when there is no need for interpretation. This comes as the consequence of the baptism of the Holy Spirit. In Scripture it was often identified as a sign of the baptism of the Holy Spirit and the fulfillment of prophecy (Jn. 7:38, 39; Mk. 16:7; Acts 2:1-22).

Now in this context, Paul specifically says no one should speak in tongues without someone having the gift of interpretation present lest some uninformed stranger come in their midst and think they are mad. This is

[9] Larry Christenson, *Speaking in Tongues*, Dimension Books, Minneapolis, MN, 1968, p. 18.

[10] Ibid, p. 19.

precisely what happened to me and was my initial reaction when I attended my first pentecostal meeting a long time ago. Paul says when we speak in tongues (as a prayer language) then we only edify ourselves (I Cor. 14:4).

What does that mean? It means that speaking in tongues as a devotional prayer, spiritually builds me up in the faith. This is what Jude means when he says,

> But you, beloved, building yourself up on your most holy faith; praying in the Holy Spirit.

> Keep yourselves in the Love of God, waiting anxiously for the mercy of our Lord Jesus Christ to eternal life. (Jude 20-21)

Praying in the Holy Spirit is the same as speaking in tongues. When we are praying in the Spirit, we are speaking in an unknown language — unknown to us that is, a language that we haven't learned. Paul says, "If I pray in a tongue my spirit prays, but my mind is unfruitful" (I Cor. 14:4). In other words, the mind doesn't know what is being said. But speaking in tongues is speaking forth prompted not by your mind, but by your spirit inspired by the Holy Spirit. The speaker doesn't decide what sound will come out next. He simply lifts his voice as an act of will and the Spirit gives utterance (Acts 2:4). With this in mind, Paul says that speaking in tongues is addressed to God (I Cor. 14:2) and therefore the question of whether people understand is actually irrelevant.

Just because the tongue is not known does not mean that it is gibberish. I have heard people who have no knowledge of foreign languages praise God in Greek and Hebrew, languages I learned in seminary. Many times the Lord out of His love for us will accommodate honest doubt and allow us to hear a language we do know. The Lord allowed that to happen to a friend, a former missionary to India. While he had asked Jesus to be his baptizer in the Holy

Spirit, he still had deep reservations about tongues and the Holy Spirit honored that. In a few weeks that followed however, God allowed him to hear simple folks (who had all they could do to express themselves in their native English) praise God in perfect Punjabi and Hindi — languages he had learned as a missionary to India. This experience was enough to convince him that this was of God and receive it for himself.

Many people have initially asked the question, "Do I have to speak in tongues?" Unconsciously we put tongues in the same category of swallowing an unpleasant dose of medicine. The question itself implies that it is something to be endured rather than enjoyed. Most people like myself were initially skeptical about this phenomenon. One reason was the fear of the unknown. When you don't know you don't know. But the other reason involves intellectual pride. Tongues forces the issue. It's almost as if the Holy Spirit is saying, "Are you going to put your mind in the service of your faith and be Spirit-ruled. Or will you put your faith in the service of your mind and be intellectually ruled?" Speaking in tongues is a testimony of our need to be three dimensional men ruled by the Spirit.

Someone at a Full Gospel meeting asked David du Plessis about tongues and David gave an unusual but logical response. With a twinkle in his eye he offered the following explanation:

> In Genesis we read that the Spirit moved over the earth and God created by speaking. Then Jesus the Son of God came and He spoke. Why should thy Holy Spirit be dumb? The Father spoke, the Son spoke, why shouldn't the Holy Spirit speak? And speak in such a way that you couldn't mistake the fact that it is Him, because He doesn't use your senses or intellect. Praying in the Spirit is creative praying, He makes intercession according to the Will of God.

96

Our voice, our speech, or as the Bible calls it our tongue, is our chief means of expression and it is not coincidental that it is here that the Holy Spirit chooses to flow out first. Spiritually, psychologically and physiologically our ability to speak is central. In Proverbs we read:

> With the fruit of a man's mouth his stomach (innermost being) shall be satisfied. He will be satisfied with the product of his lips.
>
> Death and life are in the power of the tongue, and those who love it will eat its fruit. (Prov. 18:20-21)

Our ability to communicate with one another in rational speech is a fundamental part of being human. This is the part we give to the Holy Spirit.

The third chapter of James compared the tongue to the rudder on a big ship, able to control the whole vessel with very little movement, or to the bit in the mouth of a horse — a small object that controls the whole animal. The apostle James goes on to say the tongue is sometimes unruly, evil, full of deadly poison (James 3:8). He says that the tongue being set on fire with the fire of hell can defile the whole body. The question is, "Who can tame the tongue?" The answer is the Holy Spirit. And so speaking in tongues is an act of faith, as well as a building up of faith inside me. The Holy Spirit says, I want to inspire and rule the most important means of expression you have, namely the ability to speak. I also want to tame and purify that with which you sin the most — your tongue.

When I pray in the Spirit, my soul, the psychological part of me, is put in its place and prayer is said to God in perfect freedom. The prayer comes just as the Holy Spirit intends it to come. If we understand this we can better understand what Paul means when he says in Romans:

> Likewise the Spirit helps us in our weakness for we do

not know how to pray as we ought, but the Spirit Himself
intercedes for us with sighs too deep for words,

and He who searches the hearts knows what the mind of
the Spirit is, because the Spirit intercedes according to
the will of God (Romans 8:26-27).

Scripture attests to the fact that the content of tongues is
prayer (I Cor. 14:14) in the form of thanksgiving (I Cor.
14:17), or intercession (Rom. 8:27; Eph. 6:18), declaring
the mighty works of God (Acts 2:11), praising God (Acts
10:46), or simply speaking to Him (I Cor. 14:2).

A good friend of ours was driving down a road and all of
a sudden he felt impressed to pull over to the side of the
road and pray in tongues. The language he prayed in was
not the usual one he used. It seemed to him that it was an
oriental language. As he prayed, he mentally asked the
Lord what was going on. Immediately the Lord gave him a
vision of an Oriental being struck down and beaten.
The Lord revealed to him that this man was suffering for
his faith in Jesus Christ. My friend was simply being used
by the Holy Spirit as an intercessor for this man.

I have personally discovered that praying in tongues
has given me more insight on how to pray with my mind.
Before receiving this gift, I used to have more "gimme"
prayers, but now my prayers are more of praise and thanksgiving for who God is, rather than what He can do for
me. I believe this has come about because my regular
prayers are lining up more and more with the prayers of
the Spirit and therefore according to the Will of God. In
reality, praying in the Spirit puts my mind into captivity
to Jesus (II Cor. 10:5) and allows it to be renewed and
transparent to the things of the Spirit.

In ministering to God's people we not only pray with
the mind but also with the Spirit. Usually when we minister
and counsel people, one member of the team leads and

asks questions while the other prays quietly in the spirit. As such, this is an effective ministry of intercession. When the Lord gives the anointing to speak out with the expectation of an interpretation then the giver and the listener are both edified. In this case, the gift of tongues along with the gift of interpretation is equal to prophecy. Many times an explanation is in order for those who might not understand. But we need never apologize for the way He uses us to speak. Both tongues and interpretation are an important part of ministering to the body of Christ.

All nine gifts of the Spirit are made available to meet the needs of the body of Christ. We need to be willing vessels for these gifts, asking God for them, and exercising them for the building up of His body.

Chapter 5

The Authority to Forgive Sins

One of the keys to exercising our authority as believers for the world, for kingdom living, and for the building up of the body of Christ is the release of forgiveness in our lives to those who have sinned against us. The word "forgiveness", like the word grace, has become so much a part of the Christian jargon. We bandy these terms about without knowing what they really mean. In a way we are like the three blind men who were asked to identify an elephant. One of the men grabbed hold of his trunk and said, "Obviously, this is a snake . . . " Another grabbed his tail and said, "No, this is a cord." And finally the third wrapped his arms around the elephant's foot and said, "I know what it is, it's a tree."

That is about the way I felt in this area of forgiveness. As a seminarian going to postgraduate school, I thought I knew everything there was to know about forgiveness. I knew, for instance, that God forgives my sins. When I repent of them, Jesus' blood both covers and remits them. He also forgets them. But there was a dimension of forgiveness that I had never learned except in the school of the Holy Spirit and the study of God's Word. I discovered that as a believer, I was commanded to forgive. I even had the authority to forgive. Through the practical application of this forgiveness, I began to see how it can change and heal lives, deliver people and build them up in their faith. In counseling thousands of Christians, I also discovered the reason why they weren't getting victory in their lives. The reason why they were hurting and wounded was precisely because they were totally ignorant of their authority (or simply unwilling) to forgive and release forgiveness to those people who sinned against them.

In chapter twenty of the Gospel of John, verses 21-23, Jesus addresses His disciples as the resurrected Christ. Before He ascends to the Father, He breathes on them and commands them to receive the Holy Spirit. With the resurrected life of Jesus now residing in them, He makes them aware of the authority that they have.*

If you forgive the sins of any, their sins have been forgiven; if you retain the sins of any, they are retained.

Some of you might be saying, "So what?" This is a powerful statement for all believers. It implies a tremendous responsibility. If you remember in the gospels (Mt. 9:2ff; Mk. 2:1ff; Luke 5:18ff), Jesus was teaching in a home in Capernaum. It was so crowded that some people carrying a paralytic could not get in, so they used a little ingenuity (it is not recorded how the owner of the house felt about it). They climbed to the roof, tore it apart, and

---

*Even taking into account John's schematic approach to the gospels, I believe along with many scholars that this incident marks the time the disciples received the born-again experience. It was only after Jesus ascended, at the time of Pentecost, that the Holy Spirit fell upon them in a new way.

lowered the paralytic down on his stretcher. Jesus marvelled not at the faith of the paralytic, but at the faith of the men who brought him to Him. What is the first thing that He says to the paralytic? He didn't say, "Be healed." He said, "Your sins are forgiven." Jesus, undoubtedly through a word of knowledge, knew that this man's healing was being blocked by his need for forgiveness. What was the crowd's response? They started grumbling. It was probably coming from the professional religious groups like the Pharisees. At any rate, they said, "Only God can forgive sins." Who was this Jesus, anyway, who dared to exercise the authority of God? Jesus responded to this criticism by saying, "What is easier to say: 'Your sins are forgiven' or to say to that man 'Be healed.'" He wasn't denying that He had God-given authority to forgive sins and that it was a supernatural thing: God's will was being done on earth as it was in heaven. But understand this: this same Jesus who had that God-given authority to forgive sins is telling His disciples (John 20:23), is telling you and me, that we have the God-given authority to forgive sins against us. This is a supernatural, healing, cleansing, reconciling, delivering event backed by the Holy Spirit. It is not simple mental gymnastics. It is something unconditional. It's not simply saying, "I'll forgive you if you shape up or forgive me." Jesus, who unconditionally forgave His tormentors while He was on the cross — "Father, forgive them for they know not what they do" — is asking you and me to do the same. This is a God-given authority available only to believers indwelt by God's Spirit.

That means only Christians can forgive sins against them. I emphasize this because some may have read Eric Segal's book, *Love Story* or have seen the film based on the novel. The main theme, you will recall, sounds rather catchy: "Loving someone is never having to say that you are sorry." In one sense this is a lot of sentimental baloney. In another sense, he's right. If all we have to say is 'I'm sorry" (and God doesn't enter the picture) it has no healing, reconciling power or effect. If that is all you can say, you might as well not say it. But if you're a believer in Christ, you can say, "I forgive you" and a supernatural event takes place. God's reconciling power enters the picture. God's will is being done on earth as it is in heaven; and that is what Jesus taught us to pray in the Lord's prayer. The Lord spoke to us in a prophecy and He said, "What do you think I was doing with my disciples? Do you think I was teaching them only about kingdom living? Part of kingdom living is forgiving; I was forgiving them and healing them and teaching them to heal and forgive one another."

Now, some of the hardest statements that Jesus ever made are in this area of releasing forgiveness to those who have hurt us, to those who have sinned against us. In turning to the eighteenth chapter of Matthew, we find that the whole chapter is devoted to forgiveness and reconciliation. In verse 21, however, Peter asks Jesus how often he should forgive his brother who sins against him. He wanted to know what seems to be a reasonable number of times? Seven times? Peter undoubtedly thought that he was being magnanimous. Seven times seems to be enough, doesn't it? In some of the Hebrew writings (the Talmud), one of the great rabbis suggested that if you forgive someone three times that was sufficient. Three times and you're out, just like in the old ball game. So here Peter is saying, "How about seven times?" and Jesus astounds him by replying, "I do not say to you seven times, but seventy times seven." For you mathematicians, how much is that? Four hundred and ninety times, isn't it? Now what is Jesus saying here? Is he replacing one number with a bigger number? Is He saying, "Delores, you hurt me once and I'm going to mark it on the blackboard or note pad and eventually when I get to 490 offenses, I am finished with you, Delores! No more forgiveness." I think some of us could add up that many sins against us from our loved ones in one day, or at least in one week. Is Jesus saying that after a person sins against you 490 times that there is no more forgiveness? No, of course not, for with Jesus, forgiveness isn't a matter of mathematics. We need to live together in the forgiveness of our sins.

Jesus follows His dialogue with Peter with a parable:

> For this the kingdom of heaven may be compared to a certain king who wished to settle accounts with his slaves (v. 23).

Now, when Jesus talks about the kingdom of heaven or the kingdom of God, He is saying "this is the way God, the Father, looks at things." Forgiveness of sins is at the very center of God's Will, God's reign, God's kingship. Jesus proceeds to tell His hearers the way God thinks through this parable. He describes a king who wanted to settle accounts with his slaves. There was one slave who owed him ten thousand talents. In the margin of my Bible it says ten million dollars in silver content, which is a lot of money even in these inflationary days. As we read on in verse 25, the slave didn't have any means of repaying the debt and so the king was going to sell him along with his wife and children and all that he had in repayment for the debt. The man pleaded and asked the king to have more patience until he could repay it and the king had compassion on him and forgave him that debt. Now isn't this exactly what God has done for us? He has forgiven our debt to sin and the devil has no legal right to us. We are under no condemnation in Christ Jesus (Romans 8:1, 2). Jesus took the debt of sin and judgment upon himself.

So the king in our parable forgave the debt of the

slave. But this same slave whose debt was forgiven, encounters another slave who owed him 100 denari. A hundred denari is the equivalent of $18. See the disparity here – ten million and eighteen dollars. This slave, who was forgiven of his debt, grabbed this other slave by the throat and said, "Pay me what you owe." And the slave asked for the same kind of compassion that this other slave had received. But he didn't offer any. He asked time to pay, but the slave whose debt had been forgiven was unwilling to do even that. Instead, he threw his fellow slave into prison. Now some of the other servants saw this incident and they reported what happened to the king. The king grew angry and he summoned this uncompassionate slave and asked him why he didn't have mercy towards his fellow slave, just as mercy was shown to him. Moved with anger, the king threw him to the torturers until he would repay all that he owed. Jesus added His own conclusion to the parable by saying, "So shall my heavenly Father also do to you, if each of you doesn't forgive his brother from his heart." That's a hard statement. Coming from Jesus it seems even more bizaare. I once asked Jesus after reading this passage, "How could He be so hard. I thought He was a loving God," and Jesus replied, "It is because I love my people that I am hard in this area. Forgiving other people is the outworking of your forgiveness unto salvation, my forgiveness of you. When you deny forgiveness for other people, you deny your own salvation and your need for forgiveness." He then promptly gave me a picture of how this works. He said, "You know, my son, you are my vessel for forgiveness. As such, you are like a hose connected to a faucet. And when you release forgiveness for other people, the Holy Spirit, the living waters, flowing through you also releases forgiveness for yourself."

Releasing forgiveness for other people and receiving forgiveness for yourself are all one piece. When you refuse to forgive other people, you are refusing the same forgiveness for yourself. You are actually cutting off your own water. You are telling the Holy Spirit "that's enough, I don't need the forgiveness for myself." Jesus emphasizes this again and again. Consider Matt. 6:14ff: "If you forgive men for their trespasses, your heavenly Father will forgive you, but if you do not forgive men, then your Father will not forgive your transgressions." You see, we don't have an option to forgive, we are commanded to forgive people who have transgressed us and sinned against us. When the disciples asked Jesus "How shall we pray?", Jesus showed them how by reciting the Lord's prayer. Some of us have prayed this prayer practically all our lives and we've never thought much about it; especially the part where it says "forgive us our trespasses as we forgive those that trespass against us." He taught this prayer as the way to pray but this isn't only the way to pray, it is a very practical way to live also. "Forgive us our trespasses, forgive us our debts, forgive us our sins as we forgive those that sin against us." That's how He taught His disciples to pray. We are His disciples and when we refuse to forgive people we are burning the bridge we have to cross over. A pompous general once approached John Wesley with this statement, 'I never forgive." John Wesley said, "Well, I hope you never sin." He was aware of the fact that receiving forgiveness and releasing forgiveness were all part of one process. We need to release forgiveness in order to receive it. There are many Christians who are not receiving it for themselves, precisely because they are not exercising their authority to forgive sins against them.

As Christians, it is in our own self interest to forgive people who have hurt us. There are many people that are emotionally wounded by others and they say, "Oh, I couldn't possibly forgive him for all that he has done to me." Usually I explain to them what I'm sharing with you. Releasing forgiveness is an act of will, an obedient act that is willing to overrule hurt feelings and emotions. The Bible tells us that we are to bless those who persecute us and pray for those that despitefully use us. We are called to put on a heart of compassion, kindness and humility, making allowances for one another, forgiving each other just as the Lord has forgiven us (Col. 3:12-13). By contrast, in the occult world there is no such thing as forgiveness or blessing. There is simply a replacing of one curse with another. We as Christians are given the authority to bless and forgive. We are called to be open ended vessels and rivers for God's forgiveness, we are to freely give it to others who have sinned against us.

Releasing forgiveness to others isn't only an important gift from God which allows us to receive forgiveness for ourselves. It also prevents us from being emotionally crippled and tortured. Verse 34 of Matthew 18 gives some insight as to what can happen when we don't choose to forgive people who have sinned against us. It says, "The Lord moved with anger, turned him (the unforgiving slave) over to the torturers until he was able to pay all that was owed him." Did you know that there are many of God's people who are experiencing needless torture in their lives? They have actually opened themselves up to living on the raw edge of their emotions, because they have not chosen to forgive people who have hurt them. In Ephesians 4:30-32, we see some of the kinds of torture we go through emotionally when we do not choose to forgive people.

> Do not grieve the Holy Spirit of God, by whom you were
> sealed for the day of redemption (v. 30).

First of all, when we don't forgive, we grieve the Holy

Spirit. What follows is the emotional trauma and torture we go through.

> Let all bitterness and wrath and anger and clamor and slander be put away from you, along with all malice (v. 31).

> And be kind to one another, tender hearted, forgiving each other, just as God in Christ also has forgiven you (v. 32)

There are far too many of God's people who are the walking wounded. They are living on the raw edge of their emotions because they have not chosen to forgive people. The result of unforgiveness is that bitterness, resentment, self pity (Satan's baby sitter) and depression creep in on them.

Many of us think that we have arrived in our spiritual walk, because we no longer engage in any overt sins of immorality, but we need to understand as we walk in the Spirit that God is trying to clean up our sinful attitudes and motives as well. The sins of the flesh are just the tip of the iceberg. We are supposed to be a Spirit led people, but more often than not we are led by our emotions. We are crippled not so much by other people hurting us as by our sinful reaction to people who have hurt us and sinned against us. If this is the case, how can we be led by the Spirit if we are crippled emotionally with attitudes of bitterness, resentment, anger and so on? How can we be open to the gifts of the Holy Spirit flowing through us to meet the needs of another person? How can we witness and make disciples if we are consumed by and in bondage to our emotions? It is very hard if not impossible. Only forgiveness can release us from our emotional fixation on people that have hurt us, and free us to be God's people for the world and body of Christ.

There is something else that we need to know with respect to forgiveness. In Ephesians 4:26-27, Paul warns:

Be angry and yet do not sin; do not let the sun go down on your anger, and do not give the devil an opportunity.

Did you know that when we refuse to forgive, we not only live on the raw edge of emotions, but we can give the devil opportunity to work on us? II Corinthians 2:10-11 says basically the same things:

But whom you forgive anything, I forgive also; for indeed what I have forgiven, if I have forgiven anything, I did it for your sakes in the presence of Christ, in order that no advantage be taken of us by Satan, for we are not ignorant of his schemes.

What kinds of schemes, what kind of opportunities are we giving the devil when we refuse to forgive people who sin against us? Let me give you a few clues to some of his schemes so you won't be ignorant as Paul says.

As we counsel and minister to couples, sometimes we find ourselves in a tennis match. Not a real one, of course, but accusations are made and are bounced off each other just like a tennis ball. She'll say, for example, "The reason I'm bitter is because of what he did to me." Or, "You'd drink, too, if you had a wife like that." One of Satan's schemes is for us to live our lives continuously on a balance scale.

On one side of the balance scale is hurt and on the other side is blame. Most people can always rationalize their hurt. Satan will give them every reason in the world for being the way they are because of what someone has done to them. His scheme is to have people living continuously on the hurt-blame-hurt-blame scale. Living like this will never heal the hurt or solve the problem, just intensify it. What recourse is there but to share the hurt with other people. The person who is hurting will say, "Hey, Suzy, did you know what so and so did to me?" Pretty soon there is another person sharing the hurt-blame-hurt-blame scale. More people get involved, take up sides, get involved in the hurt parties' offense and pretty soon a large body of believers are affected. (See Heb. 12:14-15). We can fall prey to this scheme if we don't choose to forgive. but along comes Jesus and He says, "Hey, wait a minute. You don't have to live that way anymore. Just choose to forgive. It doesn't matter whether you're one hundred percent right and he or she is one hundred percent wrong. Forgive him. It doesn't matter whether he shapes up or you shape up — forgive him. Don't live your life on a hurt-blame-hurt-blame scale. Live it in me."

Another scheme that Satan has when we don't choose to forgive is even more subtle. He usually whispers it in your ear. If you're really listening, you can hear him say, "Keep the peace." "Keep the peace." That doesn't sound too harmful, but eventually what happens is that you get the pieces. Satan would like you to bury your problems and hurts. But you know the Bible says he is a liar, a deceiver of the brethren and this is one area where he is just that. Because you never bury your problems dead, you bury them alive and eventually unresolved problems and hurts are going to come up and haunt you.

When I share this message, the Lord always gives me the opportunity to practice what I preach. We had a neighbor who was a professed agnostic and, of course, because we were Christians, she didn't appreciate us. In fact, she seemed to be looking for an opportunity to criticize us. Most of the criticism was focused on my German short-haired hunting dog. Before she moved in, I had constructed a dog pen partially hidden by a few honeysuckle bushes. Unfortunately, my dog, on occasion, would bark when she would have company on her patio. More often than not, I would take the dog into the house. But she grew angry about this. There were times I would try to make amends. I would do everything but ask forgiveness. I would say, "Joyce (not her real name), I have some extra manure for the garden, would you like some?" Her response would usually be an emphatic "No!" Then one day, I came to the conclusion that it was a hopeless situation. Maybe I should simply avoid her to keep the peace. But feelings of resentment were definitely rearing their ugly heads toward her. My neighbor was also bitter towards me. There was already a root of bitterness in her life even before the dog incident, but now it was getting stronger and it was focused on me.

Finally, the day came when the Lord got through to me. The next day I was going to teach on forgiveness and the Lord said, "You had better practice what you preach." And so feeling uneasy and squeamish, I went out in the yard ready to meet and tilt windmills with my neighbor. Swallowing my pride, I addressed her as she was stooped over her garden. She whirled around with hatred and bitterness on her face, like a lioness ready to pounce and chew me up (as well as out). But then the Lord gave me words to say, "Joyce, I've been going all over the country trying to meet people's needs, and I haven't met yours. Would you forgive me?" You should have seen the countenance on her face change. Even though she was an unbeliever, she melted with those words of reconciliation.

All the lines on her face softened. I said, "As soon as I can get time, I'm going to put the dog pen way in the back and down the hill where the dog can't see anyone and bark. Would you give me time to do that?"

"Yes," she replied. It was a beautiful experience. Any resentment I may have had promptly left me. But it also provided me with a lesson about getting things resolved immediately, without delay.

A lot of times when we try to bury a problem, it becomes harder to resolve. Why? Because unreconciled problems are like eggs. The longer we wait, the harder it is to get back to it. Like that egg, it starts to stink. Such putrifying emotions as pride, bitterness, resentment and self pity come into our lives. That's why we shouldn't listen to Satan's lies and let the sun go down on our anger.

There is another satanic scheme of which we need to be aware. If we sin long enough in a given area: spiritually, emotionally, morally, we are inviting a spiritual force to attach itself to us and program us. If, for example, we refuse to forgive people who have sinned against us, we not only live on the raw edge of our emotions with resentment, bitterness, self-pity or depression, but we are inviting the spirits of resentment, bitterness, self-pity or depression to attach themselves to these emotions. This might blow your mind, but it is a real possibility. There are sinful attitudes of unforgiveness that God wants to clean up in our lives. The choice is ours, we need to choose to forgive; otherwise, we are opening ourselves up to spiritual harrassment and oppression. Again, these are just some of the schemes that Satan uses to render God's people powerless and useless. By choosing to forgive, we give him no opportunity to ensnare us with his schemes.

There is also something else that we need to consider in this area of forgiveness. In Matthew 18:18, the chapter on forgiveness and reconciliation, we read the following:

Truly I say to you, whatever you shall bind (or forbid) on earth shall have been bound in heaven; and whatever you loose (permit) on earth shall have been loosed in heaven.

We usually use this passage in the context of deliverance and spiritual warfare. But let me tell you that deliverance begins with forgiveness. Did you know that you can bind people by your unforgiveness? Many times we are confronted with unequally-yoked couples — one is a believer and the other isn't. There are many spiritual widows and widowers. The believing spouse prays and prays for the other to come to know the Lord also and nothing happens. You know why? The reason their prayers are not being answered is mainly because he or she is binding the non-believing spouse with unforgiveness.

By contrast, we witness people who by the simple act of forgiveness, open the floodgates of reconciliation and salvation for their spouses and families in a very short time. One woman, for example, revealed this dynamic truth in her own life. She came to us deeply wounded by the rejection she suffered from her mother. In the act of forgiving her mother, she was instrumental in reconciling three generations. All of a sudden, out of the blue (more likely out of heaven), her grandmother was impressed to call her daughter. She said, "I'm getting up in years and I need to get reconciled with you. Would you forgive me for the way I treated you all these years?" Once she became reconciled with her daughter, a chain reaction ensued. The young woman who initiated forgiveness received a call from her mother. She wanted to be reconciled and asked forgiveness for the way she had treated her daughter. In the space of a week and a half, three generations were reconciled, but that wasn't all. The woman had marital conflicts and her husband was not a Christian. As she released forgiveness towards him, her husband received salvation and inner healing for his own life. This all happened because she dared to exercise her authority to forgive.

Another woman who came for ministry started to describe her husband in the kindest terms possible. And even in the kindest terms possible, he turned out to be gross. He thought, for example, that it was all right to engage in adultery as long as he let his wife know about it. As we started praying for her husband, she said, "You'll never get my husband in this place unless it's feet first." I said, "Let's engage in spiritual warfare for your husband," and we did. One of the first things we did was forgive him for the way he acted towards his wife, for his unfaithfulness and his selfishness. We then loosed the spirit of salvation in him and bound the spiritual forces that were motivating him. We could do this because she was one flesh with him and had a convenantal relationship with him through Jesus whether he wanted to recognize it or not. We also asked the Lord to give her a submissive attitude, so that her husband according to I Peter 3:1 would be won without a word. Lo and behold, much to the amazement of the wife, that man received the message of Christ the following week as he came for ministry. That man was no longer bound by any unforgiveness on the part of his wife. And the Holy Spirit, who loves to confirm his faithfulness, knocked on that man's door. Do you see why Jesus commanded His disciples to forgive one another? Conversely, do you see why Satan doesn't want us to exercise this authority? He would love to have us live on the raw edge of our emotions and bind us as well as other people by our unforgiveness.

I never realized the full dimension of God's forgiveness until I ministered to one particular woman. The incident with this woman was like a branding iron searing my spirit. It was as if God were saying to me, "I want you to remember this for the rest of your life." It started with a phone call from a lovely Christian friend inviting me to come over to her place. I knew by her voice that she was deeply disturbed. After finishing some other business, I made a pastoral call and found her weeping at her kitchen table. Her words shocked me at first. She said, "I no longer love my husband. He has destroyed whatever love I have for him." Then she proceeded to tell me why. The rejection and loss of respect that they had for each other had eroded their relationship to such a degree that they had not had a physical relationship for a year and a half. Her husband had been harsh and highly critical of her and the family. That afternoon, as a symbol of the total destruction of that love, he not only mowed the lawn, but, out of spite, mowed down her lovely flower garden. In describing the event, she repeated her litany of despair, "I no longer love my husband. He has destroyed whatever love I had for him."

Hopefully optimistic, I was about to argue, "Oh, surely, you must have some love for your husband," but the Holy Spirit spoke to me and told me to agree with her. At first I didn't know where He was leading me, but as I was obedient to Him, He suddenly gave me the right words to speak. So I said, "I agree with you. Emotionally, you don't have any more love for your husband. You admitted that. He has destroyed your love. But do you believe that Jesus still loves your husband and forgives your husband?" She thought about that for a long while and before she responded, I interjected, "Well, let me tell you that God's Word says that while we were yet sinners, He loved us. The Bible says that we are to love our enemies. And right now, your husband is your worst enemy. Now tell me this Jesus that loves us while we are yet sinners and asks us to love our enemies and even forgive them too – is He in you?"

115

"Yes, He is," she replied. "I'm a born again Christian."

"If that is the case, are you willing to let Jesus in you love and forgive and plant a seed of His love for your husband?" There was what I call a pregnant pause. I say pregnant, because God was giving birth to a resource she didn't realize she had.

Then she started to pray, "Father, you know I no longer have any love for my husband. He's destroyed that love, but just as you have forgiven me for my sins, I choose to forgive him for his sin against me. I ask that you would plant a seed of your love for my husband in my heart . . . " She finished the prayer and I left not thinking too much about what was going to happen. Three days later, she called me and with a mixture of awe and excitement said, "Praise the Lord! God has given me a new love for my husband, and what's more, he has made him my lover." I was stunned and just as excited as she was. I suddenly came face to face with the supernatural power of forgiveness. We weren't playing games. We weren't engaged in mental gynmastics. We touched the throne room of God.

Since that time, countless Christians have shared the same tremendous release in their lives when they choose to forgive people who hurt them. By exercising their authority to forgive, they opened the door for God to heal them and perform mighty miracles. Before you move on to the next chapter, I invite you to do the same.

Chapter 6

The Authority to Heal the Inner Man

In our study of man, we discovered that the Word of God says that we are tripartite or three-dimensional persons: body, soul, and spirit. Jesus is interested in healing our total person so that we may be spiritually-led people who have a soul and live in a body. When we are born again, Jesus regenerates the spirit, and as we walk in the Spirit, God begins the process of renewing the mind.

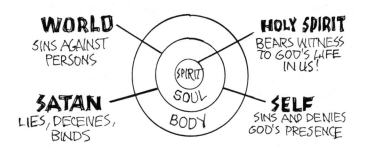

The mind is like a computer, or rather, the computer is fashioned after the human mind. Like a computer, the mind can be programmed by four things: 1) the Holy Spirit, 2) the self, 3) the world, and 4) Satan.

The Holy Spirit, speaking through our spirit, programs our mind. Many times, the Scripture likens the human spirit to a lamp:

> The spirit is the lamp of the Lord searching all the inner most parts of his being (Proverbs 20:27).

> For thou dost light my lamp. The Lord, my God, illumines my darkness (Ps. 18:28).

God fully intends us to be spiritual men and women ruled by the spirit — inspired by the Holy Spirit — and His Word. He wants to reprogram our minds so that we can hear His voice, because Jesus, the Living Word, says, "My sheep hear my voice." Paul had to constantly remind the Christians in his day to set their minds on things above, on the things of the Spirit (Romans 8).

> For those who are according to the flesh, set their minds on the things of the flesh, but those who are according to the Spirit, the things of the Spirit. (v. 5).

> For the mind set on the flesh is death, but the mind set on the Spirit is life and peace. (v. 6).

> because the mind set on the flesh is hostile toward God; for it does not subject itself to the law of God, for it is not even able to do so; (v. 7)

> and those who are in the flesh, cannot please God. (v. 8).

> However, you are not in the flesh, but in the Spirit, if indeed the Spirit of God dwells in you, but if any one does not have the Spirit of Christ, he does not belong to Him. (v. 9).

> So brethren, we are under obligation not to the flesh, to live according to the flesh. (v. 12).

118

For if you are living according to the flesh, you must die; but if by the Spirit, you are putting to death the deeds of the body, you will live. (v. 13).

For all who are being led by the Spirit of God, these are sons of God. (v. 140.

For you have not received a spirit of slavery leading to fear again, but you have received a spirit of adoption as sons by which we cry out, "Abba, Father." (v. 15).

The Spirit Himself bears witness with our spirit that we are children of God. (v. 16).

The "flesh" that Paul is talking about is not simply our physical drives but our attitudes, motivations, and emotions which prevent us from being Spirit-led men and women. The mind for many Christians is the last bastion of idolatry that needs to be conquered, redeemed and healed by Jesus and led in the service of the Spirit.

Paul affirms the futility of letting the self — the mind be the be-all of our life (Ephesians 4).

This I say therefore and affirm together with the Lord, that you walk no longer as the Gentiles walk, in the futility of their minds. (v. 17).

Being darkness in their understanding, excluded from the life of God, because of their ignorance, because of the hardness of their heart? (v. 18).

and they having become callous have given themselves over to sensuality, for the practice of every kind of impurity with greediness. (v. 19).

But you did not learn Christ in this way, (v. 20)

if indeed you have heard Him and have taught in Him, just as truth is in Jesus. (v. 21).

that in reference to your former manner of life, you lay aside the old self, which is being corrupted in accordance with the lust of deceit. (v. 22).

> and that you be renewed in the spirit of your mind (v. 23)

> and put on the new self which, in the likeness of God has been created in righteousness and holiness of the truth (v. 24).

In this day and age there is a flood on the market of pop-psychological, self-help books encouraging us to engage in introspection to know ourselves. But the question is: by whose standards and by what power? The self that is deceitful above all things? Our peer group? Consensus morality? Paul himself refused to engage in introspection based on the self or the world, because of the sin factor, the self deception, and hurts caused by sin.

> But to me it is a very small thing that I should be examined by you, or by any human court; in fact, I do not even examine myself.

> I am conscious of nothing against myself, yet I am not by this acquitted; but the one who examines me is the Lord (I Cor. 4:3-5).

The renewed mind needs to reckon the self dead. This comes as an act of will and faith. Jesus explained this another way when He said, "whoever has found his (soul) life shall lose it, and whoever loses his (soul) life for my sake will find it" (Matt. 10:39). The mind with its emotions by itself isn't bad. But when we are controlled and dominated by one or more of the following things: despondency, anxiety, self pity, resentment, pride, hate, criticism, rebellion, then we cannot be Spirit-led. When the Holy Spirit ceases to lead, emotions and intellect will lead. The self needs to be ruled by the Spirit because the self by itself always chooses sin and death. The self chooses sin against itself and against other people. By sin of self, I mean not so much breaking the rules, but willfully breaking relationships with God and other people. By sin of self, I mean sinful attitudes which stem from unforgiveness, pride, and unbelief in a loving, compassionate, forgiving God.

The Lord and His Word are really the only standard and basis for measuring ourselves. In this respect, Paul chides the rebellious people among the church who try to measure themselves with themselves or each other.

> For we are not bold to class or compare ourselves as some of those who commend themselves: but when they measure themselves by themselves, and compare themselves with themselves, they are without knowledge (II Cor. 10:12).

God and His Word are the only things that truly search and examine us. Paul was only echoing what the psalmist knew centuries before:

> Search me, God, and know my heart; try me and know my anxious thoughts; and see if there be any hurtful way in me, and lead me in the everlasting way (Psalm 139:23-24).

By sins of the self, I mean choosing not to forgive and love, using people as things, not caring enough to confront people with their needs to be healed and reconciled. By sin of self, I mean choosing to hold onto our hurts to justify the way we are, instead of choosing what God wants — for us to be whole, forgiven, redeemed, reconciled.

The Lord spoke to us one night and revealed a deeper dimension of sin that we had never comprehended. He reproved us with these words:

> I want to purify your attitudes and motives, your relationships with Me and the community of believers. In the days ahead I intend to confront you with your sin of pride; the pride of holding your hurts to yourself, the pride of self pity, the pride of resentment, the pride of not looking to Me to heal your hurts.

On another occasion, He said:

> Your life is a walk of faith and obedience to My Word.
> When your circumstances and people draw you away from
> Me and you take counsel of your fears, this is a sin, for
> without faith, it is impossible to please Me.

Most Christians feel that they have made it in their
spiritual walk when they refrain from certain kinds of sins
of immorality. But God wants to deal with our sinful
unloving attitudes; our reaction to things and people, our
motives that seek to glorify the self rather than Him.
The apostle James picks up on this in the following
passage:

> You ask and do not receive, because you ask with the
> wrong motives, so that you may spend it on your pleasures
> (James 4:3).

Paul speaks to the same thing in Philippians 2:1-8:

> If therefore there is any encouragement in Christ, if there
> is any consolation of love, if there is any fellowship of the
> Spirit, if any affection and compassion, (v. 1)

> make my joy complete by being of the same mind, main-
> taining the same love, united in spirit, intent on one
> purpose. (v. 2)

> Do nothing from selfishness or empty conceit, but with
> humility of mind let each of you regard one another as
> more important than himself. (v. 3)

> Do not merely look out for your own personal interests,
> but also for the interests of others. (v. 4)

> Have this attitude in yourselves which was also in Christ
> Jesus, (v. 5)

> who, although He existed in the form of God, did not
> regard equality with God a thing to be grasped. (v. 6)

> But emptied Himself, taking the form of a bondservant and

being made in the likeness of man, (v. 7)

And being found in appearance as a man, He humbled Himself by becoming obedient to the point of death, even death on a cross. (v. 8)

This is the kind of attitude that God wants to build in us — a humility of mind before men and God that is willing to give up its rights, personal interests, privileges; and to love and forgive unconditionally. A mind that is willing to understand God on His terms.

One New Year's Eve, the Lord spoke these words to us:

Don't trouble yourselves when people fail to understand. Just love them, don't argue with them, just love them and let Me do My work. Don't get in the way of My work. Let Me use you when, where and how I choose to use you. Don't program Me; let Me program you, and what joy we shall have together, for you shall experience My peace and I shall be blessed for using you.

. . . So My children, do not resist the resiliency, the vitalness that I am building into your life, Let the process take hold, so that I may pour my Spirit into the new wineskins. I am replacing the old wineskins — the past, the things that you hold onto, that were so dear to you, that limited work in you — and replacing it with new wineskins that will hold the new wine of the new year. In the coming year, you will have to be elastic and resilient (as new wineskins) so that you will hold all the new things (new wine) that I intend to put into your life — a new faith, a new hope. Let Me expand your world. Let Me give you a new understanding of how I'm going to work in your life. Don't resist Me. Trust Me.

The mind isn't only influenced by the self, which is to be reckoned dead, but also by the world. That includes people in the world. Sin of the self not only causes hurts to the inner man, but the world's sins and other people sinning against us can affect us as well. Paul warns us to not be conformed to this world but be transformed by the renewal of our minds that we may prove what is the Will of God (Romans 12:2). He also commands us to let our minds dwell on whatever is true and honorable, right, pure, lovely, of good repute, anything of excellence or worthy of praise (Phil. 4:8). The world is concerned with all kinds of pollution (e.g. water pollution, air pollution, etc.), but one of the most insidious kinds of pollution, and one that people aren't aware of, is mind pollution.

A friend of mine shared the truth of this from God's perspective. He and I were driving a few teenagers home from a youth rally and one of the young men mentioned that he had gone to see a certain movie, R-rated and of questionable taste. As we debated the advisability of going to such a movie, the young man defended himself by saying, "I don't think that movies can hurt me. All they do is remind me of the stuff that Jesus redeemed me from." My friend, Joe, who was only a year old in the Lord, gently interjected, "You know, I used to feel the same way. But one day as I was reading a questionable novel, the Lord spoke to me and He said, 'Joe, would you want your younger brother (7 years old) to read that novel? Would you have let him see that movie that you saw last week?' And I answered, 'No.' The Lord asked me why, and I said, 'Because he's just an innocent kid, he's just a child.' Then the Lord answered, 'Joe, you are my child. I want you to be even more innocent than your baby brother.' " That is God's divine intention for all His children, regardless of age. We are to be as wise as serpents and innocent as doves. We need to guard our eye gates and ear gates and dwell on Jesus, who fulfills whatever is true, honorable, pure, and worthy of praise.

Because the soul is like a computer, there are many people that have souls damaged by what they have experienced in the world. Some, for example, have polluted and damaged their minds by feeding on pornography. In addition, the mind can also have wounds from other people and hurtful experiences. One woman could not forget a hurtful experience as an 8-year-old. She fell out of a loft in a barn. As she fell, she grabbed a rope and held on approximately twenty feet from the ground. In fear she cried out and saw her father some distance away. He glanced up at her and laughed, which had a traumatic affect upon her. Eventually he strolled over to her and rescued her, but from that time on, she did not trust any man, including her husband. We talked about her father and his cold attitude toward her, and her lack of trust in him and feelings of rejection. We later asked her about her feelings about God. Not surprisingly, she described her relationship to God in the same way. Unconsciously, she had transferred her experience with her earthly father to that of her Heavenly Father. Like her earthly father, God was distant and not necessarily trustworthy. But as she was able to forgive her dad, we asked Jesus to heal her of that hurt memory and give her new understanding of His Father's love. The hurts and lack of love that she received from her father hindered her from receiving the love of God; her memories needed to be healed and reprogrammed by Jesus.

Another way that the mind may be programmed is by Satan himself and his demonic cohorts. The Bible says that Satan put it in the mind of Judas to betray Jesus. Satan comes as a thief and robber. He comes as a liar and deceiver of the brethren. He comes to destroy and tear down and even bind. Paul assures us that we are involved in a spiritual warfare (II Cor. 10:3ff).

For though we walk in the flesh, we do not war according to the flesh. (v.3)

For the weapons of our warfare are not of the flesh, but

divinely powerful for the destruction of fortresses. (v. 4)

We are destroying speculations and every lofty thing raised up against the knowledge of God, and we are taking every thought captive to the obedience of Christ. (v. 5)

The fortresses and the lofty things are the work of Satan. He would like nothing better than to have us preoccupied with our hurts, memories, temptations, sins of the world or sins against us. He would also like to have us to be bound (harrassed and oppressed) in the human psyche.

While the Holy Spirit deals directly with the human spirit, Satan likes to deal directly with the mind (the psyche). Much of present day interest in soul power (especially telepathy, psychic science, as a scientific work or in the realm of cults and the occult, e.g., yoga, scientology, zen) are not only humanistic endeavors but Satan's diversionary tactics to spur people to be gods unto themselves. Psychic phenomena motivated by Satan are direct counterfeits of revelatory gifts of the Holy Spirit. While Satan, for example, wants us to use ESP (power of the soul), the Holy Spirit wants to give us His gift of a word of knowledge. Satan wants to substitute the wisdom of the world for God's wisdom. The apostle James points out the difference between the two (James 3:13f).

Who among you is wise and understanding? Let him show by his good behavior his deeds in the gentleness of wisdom. (v. 13).

But if you have bitter jealousy and selfish ambition in your heart, do not be arrogant and so lie against the truth. (v. 14)

This wisdom is not that which comes from above, but is earthy, natural, demonic. (v. 15)

For where jealous and selfish ambition exist, there is disorder and every evil thing. (v. 16)

126

But the wisdom from above is first pure, then peaceable, gentle, reasonable, full of mercy and good fruits, unwavering, without hypocrisy. (v. 17)

And the seed whose fruit is righteousness is sown in peace by those who make peace. (v. 18)

Satan not only wants us to live soulishly, he also continually tries to jam our spiritual airwaves with demonic forces. Many years ago when the Voice of America broadcast the message of freedom to the Iron Curtain countries, the Iron Curtain countries retaliated and jammed the airwaves with their own frequencies. Satan tries to do the same with our minds. One time, several members of our staff were sharing a Counseling in the Spirit Seminar. While one member was sharing the introduction and premise for inner healing, another suddenly had a vision of snakes rising up between one person and the next. God revealed to him the words weren't getting off the ground. There was a heaviness in the air. Satan was interfering with the reception of the message. We stopped speaking and immediately prayed and took control over the situation and our friend saw a huge sword come through the whole room and cut off the heads of the snakes. Immediately the heaviness was lifted. Later as we were sharing the Word of God, our friend had another picture of the Word as a sword dividing the things of the spirit and the things of the soul described in Hebrews 4:12. As the sword of the Word divided the spirit and the soul, a snake (representing Satan) dropped out from between the soul and the spirit. God's Word is the offensive weapon that can do away with Satan's power.

Besides trying to block the Holy Spirit and His word from penetrating the human psyche, Satan often binds us emotionally. We have already touched on this in our chapter on forgiveness and we will deal with it more extensively in the following chapter on deliverance. We need to reiterate, however, that Satan's game plan is to bind us emotionally by our sins, the sins of the world, and the sins of our forefathers. In every case we are not only to exercise forgiveness and ask for forgiveness but also as Scripture says, Lay aside these encumbrances and the sin that entangles us and run the race that God set before us, fixing our eyes on Jesus the author and finisher of our faith (Hebrews 12:1-2). Most people cannot crawl, let alone run, precisely because they are bound. But Jesus, the author and finisher of our faith, has made provision for our deliverance from past and present bondage, be it rebellion, anger, rejection, lust, condemnation or whatever, so that we can be free to do His will and fulfill our divine destiny.

There are many of God's people who are wounded by their own sins (sins of self), unconfessed sins, the sins of the world, and satanic attacks. Only Jesus can fully heal, redeem, and reprogram (renew) their minds. Only Jesus' soul was also offered as a sacrifice. It was grieved to the point of death (Matt. 26:37-38). His soul was an offering for sin and it says that the Father was satisfied with the anguish of His soul (Isaish 53:11-12). So there is an answer to the programming of the soul by the world, the flesh, and the devil. In Jesus, God can heal the soul and restore it (Psalm 23:3; Psalm 41:4), and allow it to prosper (III John 2).

As I was trying to share this concept of inner healing with a group of people, some of whom were psychologists, the Lord showed me in a very graphic way the difference between how He heals the memories and how men (including humanistic psychologists and psychiatrists) attempt to heal the human mind. First he showed me a picture of a man drowning in a polluted ocean. Along comes a psychologist swimming in the same polluted water to the rescue. The Lord said that through his soul power, the psychologist can carry the man for awhile or he can even teach him how to swim (the equivalent of coping). But eventually both can get tired.* The Lord went on to remind me that both still had to contend with the denizens of the deep, like the barracudas of sin and the sharks of Satan and demonic forces. But along comes Jesus in the Gospel boat and He invites both men to come out of the water (the atmosphere of sin and death and man's futile psychological struggle to redeem himself). He wants to redeem them and even, by faith, teach them how to walk on the water (to be in the world but not of the world).

The Lord has sent thousands of people to us who have undergone all kinds of psychological and psychiatric treatment. Only Jesus, the wonderful counselor, was able to meet their needs and heal them. Somehow, inner resolve and knowing the problem does not heal it. The apostle Paul knew that when he confessed:

> For I know that nothing good dwells in me, that is in the flesh, for the wishing is present in me, but the doing of the good is not.

> For the good that I wish, I do not do, but I practice the very evil that I do not wish (Romans 7:18-19).

Paul, as we have mentioned before, recognized the civil war that is within. The old man — the self with its sins and death wants to do its own thing. He was simply echoing what the prophet Jeremiah some 400 years before stated: the heart is deceitful above all things, desperately wicked; who can understand it. Paul asked the question, "Who will deliver me from this body of death?" And he proceeds

---

*The fact that the fields of psychology and psychiatry have a higher incidence of suicide than any other profession would seem to indicate that they get more than tired, they simply give up.

to answer it for himself. "Thanks be to God, through Jesus Christ our Lord" (See Romans 7:24-25).

Many people have confessed that through strong inner resolve they thought that they had overcome some of their problems, only to find with a change of circumstances that they were still there. A family counselor, for example confided that she thought that she had resolved all her problems when she divorced her husband, but since she had established a relationship with her co-worker, the problems had come back to haunt her. Again she was attesting to the fact that knowing the problem wasn't enough to heal it — no more than knowing that you have cancer is going to heal you of the cancer. Many people, because of the deep hurts, have stuffed their problems in inner recesses of their subconscious minds, and some are totally unaware that their problems still exist.

I counseled a man who was having marital problems. The Lord revealed to me that he had a deep hatred of women because he was wounded by women in his life and deeply hurt by one woman in particular. When I shared this word with the man, he did not receive it. He felt everything in his life had been resolved. He felt he had no problem with his concept of women. I knew he was telling the truth as he understood it; he was pretty straight-forward and wasn't the type to hold back anything. In fact, many times he was brutally frank about himself. With this in mind, I asked him if he were willing to let Jesus identify it even though he couldn't. As I laid hands on his forehead, I prayed, "Jesus, You are the same yesterday, today and forever. You were there throughout John's life. Bring to his memory this truth and incident." Immediately the Lord did, and tears started flowing from his eyes. He was amazed because he did not know that hurt was still there, but Jesus did. He wanted to heal him and have him forgive that woman and the others so that he would no longer be crippled by the events of the past. Jesus does not want us to cope with things, or stuff things or engage in some sort of psychological lobotomy. He wants to heal and deliver and set us free from our problems (brought on by sin) and our hurts.

Is all that I have said so far meant to be an attack on psychology and psychiatry? The answer is yes and no. Yes, when humanists deny the element of sin and the demonic and try to have people believe that the human mind can heal itself. Yes, when they try to deny moral and spiritual values. No, when they recognize that not all guilt is false guilt. No, when they recognize that Jesus and confession of sins and forgiveness are powerful agents for the healing of the inner person.

We have watched Jesus minster to many dedicated Christian counselors — counselors who had a handle on the problem but couldn't cure it until Jesus healed them. In their struggle to categorize, to use men's best ideas and give a name to the problem, they found that there was only one name that could possibly heal them, JESUS.

In recent years psychologists and psychiatrists have openly admitted that there is a crisis going on in the field of psychology and psychiatry. Dr. O. Hobart Mower, a research professor of psychology at the University of Illinois, in his book, *The Crisis in Psychiatry and Religion,* makes the following assertion:

> The concept of sin is far more workable than the amoral sickness diagnosis that psychology and psychiatry have employed. Despite some pretentions and affirmations to the contrary, the fact that psychoanalysis, on which modern dynamic psychiatry is largely based, is in a state of virtual collapse and imminent demise.[11]

What this man is saying is that psychotherapy's attempts to remove guilt, and treat sin as sickness and guilt as false guilt have not worked. Why? Because much of the psychological problem stems from unconfessed and unresolved sin which has brought on real guilt.* This is in complete agreement with God's diagnosis:

> If we refuse to admit that we are sinners then we live in a world of illusion and the truth becomes a stranger to us. But if we freely admit that we have sinned, we find God utterly reliable and straight forward – He forgives our sins and makes us thoroughly clean from all that is evil. For if we take up the attitude "we have not sinned," we flatly deny God's diagnosis of our condition and cut ourselves off from what He has to say to us (I John 1:8-10, Phillips).

God's diagnosis is sin, and we therefore not only have guilty feelings, but we *are* guilty. Guilt, far from being a psychological bad guy (a detour to be avoided), is God's signpost that leads us back to the Heavenly Father for repentance, forgiveness and total healing.

According to Dr. Mower, many psychologists and psychiatrists are abandoning the sickness approach to psychological problems and are looking toward moral and and religious answers. The crisis in religion, however, is that the religious people have bought his false psychological premise.

> The religious people are caught up and bedazzled by the same preposterous system of thought as that from which we psychiatrists are just recovering.[12]

---

[11] Dr. O. Hobart Mower, *The Crisis in Psychiatry and Religion,* An Insight Book by D. Van Norstrand Co., Inc., 1961, p. 51. Karl Menninger, MD in his book, *Whatever Became of Sin* (Hawthorn Book Pub., N.Y., 1973) also calls attention to this same fact that many psychological problems have their roots in sin.

*Any false guilt with its feelings of rejection and condemnation can, more often than not, be attributed to Satan's lies and Satanic bondage.

[12] Ibid, p. 52.

In his book Dr. Mower proceeds to discuss the various psychological disorders and pinpoint their cause in sinful attitudes and broken relationships. Is it any wonder then that a psychologist in the Twin Cities offers his clients three choices. He tells them, "I could use psychoanalysis and you might just be with me the rest of your life. I can also use Gestalt method and we'll get all your problems out in the open, but I can't cure them. Or you can meet Jesus and be out of here this afternoon." Now this might seem arrogant or even flippant, but that is not the case. It means that when those people invite Jesus as their Savior and Lord and Healer to forgive them for their sins and remove their real guilt, this same Jesus is going to walk out of the counselor's door with them and continue that work as the outworking of their salvation. Jesus through His Holy Spirit is the only one that can reprogram and heal the mind and set it free from inner hurts and the guilt of sin and supply the truth and authority which can counteract Satan's lies.

After people have sought forgiveness for their sins, forgiven those who have hurt them, exercised their authority to deliver themselves from spiritual bondage and broken any curses from the past (we will discuss this in the chapter on deliverance), we anoint them with oil for the healing of their memories. We ask Jesus to heal their memories even to the time when they were in their mother's womb. Many times, we ask them to express a prayer of faith, such as the following:

Heavenly Father, as You are healing my memories I submit my mind to Your Spirit within me, I ask You to renew my mind according to the promises of Your Word so that I might have the mind of Christ and believe as You believe and love as You love and forgive as You forgive and understand as You understand. Amen.

Just as the mind can be wounded or hurt, so also can the spirit. The Old Testament uses the word "heart" for the spirit. In both cases, it refers to the inner spiritual man that has been wounded. Earlier in our ministry, we had observed that there were many people who have forgiven people who hurt them, but there was no joy in their lives. While they may have had mountain-top experiences, they usually dwelt in the valley of sorrow and sadness. This lack of joy showed in their countenances. The promises of Jesus, "I have come that your life may be full," was not a reality for them. The joy of the Lord was not their strength because they were wounded in their spirits as well as in their memories. There are many scriptures that touch on this, such as the following:

> A joyful heart makes a cheerful face, but when the heart is sad, the spirit is broken (Proverbs 15:13).
>
> A joyful heart is good medicine, but a broken spirit dries up the bones (Proverbs 17:22).
>
> The spirit of a man can endure his sickness, but a broken spirit, who can bear (Proverbs 18:14).
>
> Like a city that is broken into and without walls, is a man who has not control over his spirit (Proverbs 25:28).

There are people who have no control over their spirit simply because their spirit is broken. The fruit of the Holy Spirit, especially joy, doesn't remain in them because they leak. They can't contain the joy of the Lord because they are wounded.

How do people get wounded in their spirit? The answer is in the same way they have been hurt in the human psyche. Many times, people suffer broken relationships in the form of rejection or betrayal or are wrongfully accused; some received punishment in anger and frustration. Regardless how people have been wounded, the Lord promises to heal His people.

The Lord is near to the broken hearted and saves those who are crushed in the spirit (Psalm 34:18).

He heals the broken hearted and binds up their wounds (Psalm 147:3).

Jesus is the fulfillment of the prophecy of Isaiah 61. He has come to set free those who are downtrodden (Luke 4:18; Isaiah 61:2). He made provision for this on the cross, too, and we need to appropriate this by faith.

When we began this ministry of Jesus, the Lord dramatically revealed to us through visions and prophecy what was happening to people as we anointed them with oil for the healing of memories and a wounded spirit. On one such occasion, a spirit-filled psychologist friend of ours came to visit us. At first we thought that he wanted to talk shop. But he assured us that he wanted inner healing. He shared with us that for years he had struggled to resolve psychologically the problems in his life and in the life of his family. While he had a handle on some of the problems, he still had feelings of rejection and a poor sense of self-worth. His mother and alcoholic father were divorced at a time when he was still very young. Very little love was expressed through either of his parents. His mother later remarried and more rejection came into the picture through the lack of love from his stepfather. At age 14, he went to a church camp and experienced the reality of Jesus, a born-again experience. But this joy was short-lived. When he tried to share his new found faith, his stepfather, a nominal Jew, slapped him across the face. In later years, saddled with the problem of rejection, he found it hard to reach out and love his wife and children. The end result was that the whole family was hurting.

As we asked the Lord to let the gifts of the Holy Spirit be manifested in us to meet the need of our brother in Christ, the Lord revealed through a word of knowledge that our friend's problem was rooted in his family as a spiritual inheritance. He not only had feelings of rejection, for example, but was bound by the cord and spirit of rejection and fear of rejection. He simply needed to take authority and be delivered of these problems and be set free. As he did this and forgave his father, stepfather, mother and others who hurt him, and asked forgiveness towards those people whom he had hurt, he found a complete release as if a heavy weight came off him. The passage in Hebrews 12:1-3 became real to him:

> Therefore since we have so great a cloud of witnesses surrounding us, let us also lay aside every encumbrance, and the sin which so easily entangles us, and let us run with endurance the race that is before us, fixing our eyes on Jesus, the author and perfecter of our faith, who for the joy set before Him endured the cross despising the shame, and has sat down at the right hand of the throne of God.

He found he was no longer encumbered by the weight of sin and sins against him. He found himself no longer encumbered by spiritual forces of rejection and fear of rejection. Before he dealt with these things in his life, he could not even crawl, let alone run and fulfill his divine destiny. But Jesus wasn't done with him. In the process of anointing him with oil for the healing of memories and a wounded spirit, he was able to literally fix his eyes on Jesus, the Author and Finisher of his faith. In a vision, he saw Jesus standing around a table with His disciples. Before them He held out a chalice and, addressing the psychologist, told him this chalice represented his spirit. Our friend observed the chalice and noticed that it had a deep gash in it. As we anointed him with oil for the healing of his spirit, Jesus put His hand over the deep gash and healed it and set it on the table.

The following week, the psychologist brought his wife

for ministry. As Jesus ministered to her and delivered her from many of the same problems, the Lord gave this psychologist another vision. He saw the same vision that he had seen the previous week — Jesus around the table with His disciples. Only this time, Jesus held a broken communion plate. Jesus revealed that this broken communion plate represented his wife's wounded spirit. As we prayed for healing, Jesus fused that broken plate together and laid it right next to the chalice which represented the psychologist's spirit and said, "Now you can both serve me." True to His Word since that time, the psychologist and his wife, as well as his whole family, have a tremendous prophetic and counseling ministry. Two of his daughters and their husbands have studied for the ministry. The Lord has promised them all a dynamic ministry together. That was the divine intention of Jesus for them. He has a divine intention for all of us. But first we need the authority to heal the inner man — authority in Christ Jesus, the Author and Finisher of our faith, so that we can forget the past and press on to our high calling.

Chapter 7

The Authority to Heal the Outer Man

Part I — His Will to Heal

There is a parable concerning two little fish who met a frog beneath a rock. "Don't you know you're in great danger, little fish?" croaked the frog. "No!" the little fish cried. They became frightened. The frog continued to tease them. "Don't you know fish can't live without water. You better find a water supply quickly or you'll die." The little fish swam to their mother in great distress. "Mother, the frog says if we don't find water quickly, we'll die. Mother, what's water?" "I don't know," confessed the mother fish who was agnostic. "I never heard anything about water. Let's go and ask the otter." "Water, my dear?" laughed the otter. "Why, you live in water. That's what you breathe."

As Christians we are living in the healing and saving waters of God. This is so whether we believe it or not. Jesus said that the kingdom of God is in your midst. His kingdom includes healing, salvation, deliverence, His miracle working power. Paul says in Him we move and have our being. He reminds the Corinthians that their bodies are the temple of the Holy Spirit. The God who counts even the hairs on our head cares about every detail in our life. In faith we can either absorb this truth or in unbelief and/or ignorance live beneath our privilege as Christian men and women of God. Until recently, the church has bought the lie of the devil and been (or at least felt like) a fish out of water in the area of divine healing.

Yet, if we glance over the gospel accounts, we discover that divine healing occupied over half of Jesus' ministry. Two thirds of Luke, the physician's gospel, cover Jesus' ministry of healing. After Jesus read the scroll of Isaiah 61, which described the Messiah's ministry, He laid aside the scroll and said, "Today, this is being fulfilled in your hearing" (Luke 4:18). Somehow those present had difficulty believing the hometown boy was the anointed one who came to fulfill Isaiah's prophecy. Oh, they heard that He had healed a man in Capernaum, so they asked Him, like a trained seal, to prove Himself and do a repeat performance. And Jesus told them He couldn't do anything just as Elijah couldn'd do anything in the old days because a prophet was without honor in his home town. In other words, they didn't believe He had the authority as the Son of God. This had been the problem in the Lord's house. The church has put a limit on what God in Jesus Christ can do by unbelief or ignorance or just plain poor theology. Too often when we mention the word "healing" we think about something like a tent meeting and an Elmer Gantry type of faith-healer who exploits the masses. But this is precisely because the church and the people haven't

139

taken this ministry seriously. In this vacuum, Satan has come in and cheapened the word and ministry of divine healing.

Yet healing is an integral part of the cross and the will of God. Consider the following passages:

> And when evening had come, they brought to Him many who were demon possessed; and He cast out the spirits with a word, and healed all who were ill,
>
> in order that what was spoken through Isaiah, the prophet, might be fulfilled, saying, 'He Himself took our infirmities, and carried away our diseases' (Matthew 8:16-17 comp. Isaiah 53:4).
>
> And He Himself bore our sins in His body on the cross, that we might die to sin and live to righteousness; for by His wounds you were healed (I Peter 2:24).

Someone commenting on this passage in I Peter put grammar aside and said, "If we *were* healed that means we *is* healed." We need to quit apologizing or begging God for healing and simply claim it for ourselves because it already has been done on the cross for us. Just as we need to appropriate by faith, salvation, the baptism in the Holy Spirit, forgiveness and deliverance so we need to appropriate healing which Jesus has made available from the cross. Jesus taught His disciples to pray, "Thy will be done on earth as it is in heaven." This, of course, is part of the Lord's prayer. We need to know that God's Will is complete wholeness in heaven. And by inference, we need to pray for wholeness on earth because that is His Will. It is with this understanding that the apostle John prayed for Gaius:

> Beloved, I pray that in all respects you may prosper and be in good health, just as your soul prospers (III John 2).

In the Gospels, we read that Jesus gave His disciples the authority to proclaim the gospel power over demons and heal diseases. He first gave this authority to the twelve (Luke 9:1-2), and then to the seventy (Luke 10:1-9). In both of these accounts, the authority to heal was a vislble sign that the kingdom of God was present. After His resurrection, He commissioned them again to preach the gospel and promised that healings would be one of the signs of those who believe (Mark 16:18).

Along with salvation, healing is basically an expression of God's compassion and mercy. Jesus, who represented the heart of God, was moved to compassion to heal the lepers. When He looked at the crowds who followed Him, He was moved by compassion and He healed their sick (Matthew 14:13-14). When the two blind men cried out for mercy, He had compassion and healed their eyes (Matthew 20:29-34). His compassion was not only for the lost sinner, but also for their sickness, which was a result of the curse of the law and the fall of men. Therefore, Jesus became a curse for us by dying on a cursed tree (Galatians 3:13).

Jesus promised also whoever believed would do greater works than He because He was going to the Father (John 14:12). In other words, we are called to be this instrument of His compassion especially as we build up the body of Jesus. Several years ago, at a Bethany Fellowship Conference in Minneapolis, Larry Christenson shared the story of a pastor and one of his parishioners in California. She called up her pastor and asked, "Do you believe in James 5:14?" He responded, "Of course, I believe it. What does it say?" She said, "It says here if you're sick, you should call the elders of the church and they'll come over and anoint you with oil." "Oh," he said, "I don't believe that. That's not for our age." "Well," she said, "I believe in it and I want you to come over and anoint me." "No," he said, "I don't believe it." She said, "I don't care if you don't believe in it or not, I believe in it and I'm a paid-up dues member of your congregation and I expect you to come and anoint me with oil." It was pretty hard to argue with that kind of logic. He went to her home and went through his litany of doubt. He said, "I still don't believe in it. It isn't for this age." She said, "Never mind, you anoint me with oil, and I'm going to be healed." And that is exactly what happened. She had the faith and believed God's Word even though her pastor didn't. I'm sure that her pastor's theology took a beating that day which, hopefully, marked a new beginning for his ministry.

In recent years, the church has been recovering its ministry of healing. We are discovering that Jesus is Lord not only over our soul and spirit but our body as well. Jesus who intends to render the spirit, body and soul complete before His coming (I Thessalonians 5:23) is the same yesterday, today and forever. Many Christian doctors and psychiatrists are challenging the church to rediscover this ministry and this authority. Dr. Richard C. Cabot, for many years a professor of social ethics at Harvard Medical School, and a leader in medical and social education, said that the minister (I would add any believer) could be doing 75 percent of the healing work of the physician, and could do some of it better than the physician, if he knew his business.[13]

At this point let me interject that we as Christians shouldn't make healing, health and bodily comfort an end in themselves. We needn't be so worldly that we forget that we are pilgrims and have our divine citizenship and destiny in heaven. From the point of birth, the body is gradually wearing out and unless Christ comes, physical death will overtake us. We, therefore, need to look forward

[13] Alfred Price, *Healing, The Gift of God,* St. Stephens Episcopal Church, Tenth St., Philadelphia, Penn., 1910, p. 9.

to the time when we will put on our spiritual bodies. As a pastor, I have prayed with many an old saint who was ready to go and receive that ultimate wholeness that can only come with the face to face encounter with Jesus.

When our time comes, we should fall like a ripened apple falls to the ground when it reaches maturity. It has fulfilled its God-given destiny. But we should not be like an apple that falls in the spring because a worm got into it. I believe from the testimony of Scripture that it is reasonable to expect physical health and vitality to do God's work and fulfill our divine destiny as disciples of Christ. Sickness and the pain suffered from sickness is no virtue in itself. It is basically due to the fall of man and the curse of law. Jesus redeemed us from the curse of the law and there is no sickness in Him. He is not the author of sickness, Satan is.

This is not to deny that God can use pain and sickness for His purpose. One day as I was struck down with the flu and was trying to fight the good fight of faith, claiming healing in the name of Jesus, the Lord spoke to me that although He was not the author, He allowed it to happen because it was the only way He could get my attention. He wanted me to rest in Him and minister to Him. God allowed sickness to come on Job as a test of his faith. In the first chapter of Job, Satan addressed God and said the only reason why Job is righteous and faithful to God is because God has blessed him. Take that hedge of protection and you will see him curse you to your face. What follows is that Job's friends end up condemning him of his sons' sins and despite moments of affirmation (I know that my Redeemer lives), Job ends up attempting to justify himself. God used that infirmity to let Job die to himself, his theology, his ideas of what God can and cannot do. When he is confronted with the sovereignty of God, he repents and humbles himself before the Lord. But in the final episode, God heals him and blesses him twice as much.

God allows many trials and tribulations to refine us. He prunes us so that we bear more fruit and put on the righteousness and character of Christ. His word alone is supposed to correct us and reprove us. But when we get to the point where we are willing to let God do His work in us, we need to be well enough to do the works of Christ.

Many people, when they discuss healing, inevitably bring up Paul's thorn in the flesh. Three times he prayed to be delivered from it and God's answer was "My grace is sufficient for you, for My power is perfected in weakness (II Corinthians 12:7-9). Some people speculate that this thorn was a physical disability, or moral temptation or persecution. I am more inclined to take the reading at face value. The thorn in the flesh is said to be a messenger of Satan to buffet him. The purpose of the buffeting was to keep him humble. It could conceivably have been spiritual harassment through persecution. But regardless of what it was, it did not incapacitate Paul to fulfill his role as apostle to the Gentiles. On the contrary, Paul says he was spurred on to work harder than any of the apostles.

It is my observation, and Scripture seems to support this, that most sicknesses have very little redemptive significance. When Jesus says to take up your cross and follow him, He is not referring to sickness so much as persecution and suffering for righteousness' sake; accepting trials and the discipline of the Word as a means of character building. Consider the following passages:

> But if when you do what is right and suffer for it you patiently endure it, this finds favor with God.
>
> For you have been called for this purpose since Christ also suffered for you, leaving you an example for you to follow in His steps. (I Peter 2:20b-21)

While this passage describes suffering with Jesus, it moves on to the promise of healing because of His suffering on our behalf.

> and He Himself bore our sins in His body on the cross that we might die to sin and live to righteousness; for by His wounds you were healed. (I Peter 2:24)

Apart from our suffering for righteousness' sake and trials and tribulations that come our way, I believe the overwhelming testimony is that the perfect Will of God is healing for His people.

When we consider physical healing, we need to take account of four major factors: 1) healing hid in Christ, 2) healing through forgiveness (reconciliation of the inner man), 3) healing through deliverance, and 4) healing to the glory of God.

What do I mean by healing hid in Christ? The Bible tells us that we have died to self and our life is hid in Christ (Col. 3:3). Faith witnesses to the fact that whether we are sick or well there is only life in Jesus. There is no death in Him, no sickness in Him, no bondage in Him, no curse in Him. There is simply total wholeness in Jesus. Having said this, we have to recognize that many Christians have not received total wholeness in their life. That almost seems a contradiction in terms, doesn't it? As Christians, we need to understand that whether we are successful or unsuccessful in our attempts at claiming healing, we always have healing in Jesus whether it is evident or not. Just as our life is hid in Jesus, so our healing is hid in Jesus. Faith appropriates what is hidden in the spirit and makes it become evident in the natural world. But many times we lack faith, or maybe there is unforgiveness, or spiritual bondage which blocks healing or perhaps God simply wants to take that person home. In His sovereignty, He alone has authority over the day of death (Ecclesiastes 8:8). As believers, we must recognize that ultimately His will is not thwarted by our inability to release faith or factors that hinder faith from being released, or even death itself. The Word of God assures us that He is the God of the living, and He is faithful even when we are faithless, because He cannot deny Himself (See II Tim. 2:12-13).

Several years ago, another pastor and I were called to minister to a wife of a dentist. The whole family were born-again, spirit-filled believers. She had a strange blood disease that brought her to the point of death many times. As we prayed for her the Lord revealed to us there was a need for forgiveness in her life. She quickly responded and forgave several members within her family. The Lord also revealed that there was a spirit of infirmity that was a part of the family inheritance. We dealt with that. The wife seemed to improve and her condition stabilized. This lasted for one and a half years, then she had a relapse. She had gone to several Kathryn Kuhlman miracle meetings and had been on the prayer list of several men with nationally-known healing ministries with no results. People in her prayer group prayed for her, but her condition grew worse and worse and she landed in the hospital. Several of us pastors visited her and prayed for healing and claimed it with her. Her parish priest and other pastors, including myself, left with a great sense of peace. Two days later as I was meeting with our staff, we heard the news that she had died that morning. I was stunned and I said, "Lord, I am not leaving here until I find out what happened. What did we do wrong?" I must say I felt burdened down and a complete failure. Then the Lord spoke through one of the elders who had gone there the day before and had anointed her with oil. He undoubtedly was feeling just as bad. The Lord addressed him and said, "You did exactly what I told you to do, my son. You anointed her with oil and claimed the promises of My Word and I healed her, but I chose to take her to Myself. She has suffered enough. You should see how radiant and happy she is. Do not have any regrets. I prepared her heart . . . " As soon as the Lord said, "I have healed her and I chose to take her to Myself," we all became aware of the sovereignty of God who knows the length of our days and numbers them (whether they be short or long), who wills to heal and also knows the fragility of our faith. His sovereignty encompassed all of that. The weight and burden, along with the judgment that I had, fell off me (and I am sure the others) and was replaced with an awesome feeling of peace, the peace that passes all understanding. Logically it did not make sense. Here was a woman who at age 31 was taken in the prime of her life. Here was a husband who was without a wife. Here were four children without a mother. The Lord continued to speak to us and assured us that He had not abandoned the husband and his children. He had a plan for them all. He mentioned that the costly hospital and doctors' bills would be paid (because of his wife's chronic condition, he could not get her insured). Four months later God's Word proved true. All the bills were paid through a government agency and friends. At the same time, the Lord laid it on the heart of a woman in a prayer fellowship to take care of the children until he prepared the heart of a woman who would become his mate. One year later, this is precisely what happened. It was one of the most beautiful and edifying Christian weddings I have ever attended, with all four children participating in it.

From incidents such as these, I have learned that we need to be faithful with the promises of God's Word. No matter what happens, we need never lose heart or feel condemned for our seeming failures. While God's sovereignty validates His promises, it even goes beyond them;* He will not be thwarted from His divine intention. In the eleventh chapter of Hebrews, there is a long list of Old Testament heroes who died in faith and did not receive the promise, but God gave them a better promise:

> All these died in faith, without receiving the promise, but having seen them and having welcomed them from a distance, and having confessed that they were strangers and exiles on the earth. (v. 13)

> But as it is, they desired a better country, that is a heavenly one. Therefore, God is not ashamed to be called their God; for He has prepared a city for them. (v. 16)

We who are under the New Covenant have the promises made available through the cross. The kingdom of God is in our midst, as well as in our hearts, and yet God still has a better promise that can only be completed as we fall asleep in Jesus and make our final abode in heaven. The apostle Paul who was vitally alive in the spirit and claimed the promises of Jesus still longed for that day when he would be at home with the Lord (II Corinthians 5:1-8). As citizens of heaven and sojourners in this world, we need to be as free and loose as Paul about remaining here on earth and fulfilling our divine destiny and still long for the better promise to be with the Lord.

While God's will and His promise is to heal, His sovereign will is for us not to question our faith or anyone else's faith or engage in any prolonged introspection and continually ask the question, "Why?" When we do, we are always in danger of getting out of balance; of losing

---

*While God promised, for example, to anihilate the Moabite nation, in His sovereignty, He allowed a Moabite to become a heroine of the Jewish nation and part of the royal lineage of King David. While He promised to destroy the city of Nineveh, in His soveriengty, God spared the people because of their repentance. Even Jesus recognized God's sovereignty when He said, "Only the Father knows the time of My second coming."

sight that God is the healer; of limiting His sovereignty by our faith or His promises. We are simply to be faithful with the measure of faith we have and move from faith to faith knowing full well that even though we have the mind of Christ we see in the mirror darkly, but someday face to face.*

The Lord spoke to me a few years later about this healing hid in Him with respect to my mother. We had prayed for her for the healing of Parkinson's disease. Numerous prayer groups in the body of Christ had prayed for her. Every time I would come and visit her in the nursing home, I would anoint her with oil for healing. Even as she grew incontinent and could not speak, I used to bring my guitar and sing songs at the side of her bed. The Lord told me to praise Him for her healing and we did just that as a family. This went on for two years. Then she died three days after her seventy-third birthday. At first I began to question my hearing of God's voice. I questioned my faith. In tears of grief, I cried out to the Lord that maybe I should not speak in prophecy anymore if I were so far off the mark. The following morning, the Lord spoke through my wife these words of comfort:

My son, do you not know that I understand your grief for I, too, lost a beloved earthly parent. (It is not recorded, but you know it is true, otherwise, I would not have needed to assign my mother's care to someone else. As the eldest son of a widow, I had that task to do.)

My son, My obedient son, you prayed according to My will, and in My name. Do not choose not to speak again. For there are many things I would choose to speak through you. You have heard my voice and heard my words and spoken them even though you did not always understand them. This sickness was not unto death, but

*Jesus, Himself, although He could do no miracles in His own home town because of unbelief, was still faithful in ministering healing to the few.

149

unto healing and life hid in Me. I received her to Myself
and healed her and she chose to remain with Me when I
showed her what her death (or her life) could accomplish;
though she hesitated knowing your grief. I ask you now
to give Me that grief and let me turn it to good, that you
may truly comfort your family with My words, inspired
by the One who is called the Comforter . . .

I cannot begin to describe the peace that I felt at that time.
God showed me that all His people are destined for healing. There is no sickness unto death;* that is for unbelievers. He either heals them now visibly on earth or
gives them total healing which is hidden in Christ. So our
seeming failures are not failures with respect to God. His
sovereign will to heal should be used neither as a means of
condemning ourselves (for our lack of faith or other
peoples' lack of faith), nor as a cop-out for not exercising
our faith and claiming these promises of healing.

A second factor that enters into the healing of the
outer man is the healing of the inner man. Unforgiveness
or unforgiven sin can not only block the flow of His
healing power, but can directly result in physical sickness.
Many sinful attitudes, for example, such as anger, bitterness, resentment can affect us not only spiritually and
psychologically but also physically. A doctor at Mayo
Clinic confided, "We can deal with 25 percent of the
people who come to us by physical instruments of science.
Seventy-five percent, we do not know what to do with
because they are passing sickness of their minds and their
souls to their bodies. It is more important to treat the man

*Of course, this doesn't deny physical death. Yet, it is interesting to note that
Jesus, knowing that Lazarus is already dead, denies that he has a sickness
unto death because of the Father's promise of resurrection and wholeness.
Hence, while some people use this term, we need to be aware that, after the
cross and resurrection, the state of death (sting of death) and even the place
of death (Sheol) are transformed for believers. (See 1 Thes. 5:10 and 1 Cor.
15:55.)

than the disease. That is why I am interested in spiritual healing and why I believe it is of the chief function of the church to heal the sick and say unto them that the kingdom of God is come nigh unto you."[14]

Paul in chastising the Corinthians calls to their attention that the reason that many are weak and sick and some have died is because they have not rightly discerned the body of Christ. The Communion that symbolized their unity with Christ and each other only brought judgment upon them. The glorified Christ revealed to the apostle John that the false prophetess Jezebel because of her immorality would be cast on a bed of sickness (Revelation 2:22). God, speaking through the prophet Micah, warns that Israel will be struck down and made sick because of their sins (Micah 6:13).

A woman attending one of our marriage enrichment seminars was bent over with arthritis. She was bitter and resentful towards many people who had hurt her, especially her husband. Because of her longstanding unwillingness to forgive, she was also bound by the spirit of bitterness and resentment. As we dealt with the spiritual bondage and asked her to forgive her husband and others for the hurts they had caused, her whole body started to straighten up. God began pouring out His healing power to her in the act of reconciliation and forgiveness. Many times when I teach on forgiveness and have given people an opportunity to release forgiveness to those people that have sinned against them, many report physical healings.

King David testified to the truth of this need to be cleansed from sin (Psalm 32). When he did not confess it before God, it affected him physically.

> How blessed is he whose transgression is forgiven, whose sin is covered. (v. 1)

> How blessed is the man to whom the Lord does not impute iniquity, and in whose spirit there is no deceit. (v. 2)

[14]Ibid, p. 8.

> When I kept silent about my sin, my body wasted away
> through my groaning all day long. (v. 3)

> For day and night thy hand was heavy upon me; my
> vitality was drained away as with the fever heat of summer.
> (v. 4)

The Psalm speaks to the emotional stress and strain which affects us in our sin. It is what my Pentecostal friends call "Holy Ghost miserables." This is the result of the old self within us (which by faith is to be reckoned as dead) in conflict with the new man. Sin can produce a psychological and physiological chain reaction. In other words, sin can affect us emotionally, which in turn can affect our metabolism or cause a chemical imbalance and lower our resistance to disease. Doctors confirm that more than 80 percent of our diseases originate psychosomatically; that is, they start with emotions. I would go farther than that and say they originate from sin or sinful attitudes, such as the sin of unforgiveness.

David in our Psalm offers the answer to sin and sickness — confession and agreement with God about our sin.

> I acknowledge my sin to Thee, and my iniquity I did not
> hide; I said, I will confess my transgressions to the Lord,
> and Thou didst forgive the guilt of my sin. (v. 5)

> Therefore, let everyone who is godly pray to Thee in a
> time when Thou mayest be found; surely in a flood of
> great waters they shall not reach him. (v. 6)

> Thou are my hiding place; Thou dost preserve me from
> trouble, Thou does surround me with songs of deliverance.
> (v. 7)

As soon as we repent of our sins, He delivers us from Satan's darts and opens the doorway for healing.

There is another factor that we need to consider in the area of healing of the outer man — healing through deliverance. Sometimes in addition to the prayer of faith, and dealing with sins in our lives, we need to exercise our authority to break curses and to renounce an evil spirit which has manifested itself physically.

As Jesus and His disciples descended from the mountain, they were suddenly confronted with a father pleading for his son's healing. What a contrast. The disciples had a mountain-top experience with Jesus. They had been enraptured by the glory of God and had seen a glimpse of Jesus' glory; and now they were face to face with the nitty-gritty realm of the demonic (Matthew 17:14; Mark 9:14-28; Luke 9:37-42).

> When they came to the multitude, a man came up to Him, falling on his knees before Him saying, (v. 14)
>
> "Lord, have mercy on my son, for he is an epileptic and very ill, for he often falls into the fire, and often into the water. (v. 15)
>
> And I brought him to your disciples and they could not cure him." (v. 16)
>
> And Jesus answered and said, "Oh unbelieving and perverted generation, how long shall I be with you? How long shall I put up with you? Bring him here to me." (v. 17)
>
> And Jesus rebuked him and the demon came out of him and the boy was cured at once. (v. 18)

Here, what looked like an epileptic seizure proved to be a demonic spirit that was binding the boy.

In Jesus' encounter with a woman, Luke the physician, (14:11-13), tells us that the sickness was caused by a spirit.

> And behold there was a woman who for eighteen years had a sickness caused by a spirit; and she was bent double, and could not straighten up at all. (v. 11)
>
> And when Jesus saw her, He called her over and said to her, "Woman, you are freed from your sickness." (v. 12)

153

> And He laid His hands upon her and immediately she was
> erect again, and began glorifying God. (v. 13)

Frankly, until I discovered this for myself, I always felt that it was the so-called mentality of that age which could not distinguish between sickness and evil spirits. At least that is what I was taught in seminary. But praise God, the Holy Spirit is always ready to confirm His word.

In the case of the woman who had arthritis, for example, the Holy Spirit had shown to us as we were ministering to her that because of her unforgiveness towards other people, she had become emotionally bitter and resentful. This emotional bitterness and resentment caused metabolic disorder in her body and allowed arthritis to set in. Because of choosing not to forgive and the sin of unforgiveness, she opened herself to spiritual bondage. As a result, she not only had to receive inner healing, be forgiven and release forgiveness, but she had to be delivered from the spirit of bitterness and resentment before she was totally healed.

A young man, considered a manic-depressive person, had extensive examinations by doctors and psychiatrists who concluded that he had a metabolic disorder. Every time he would be in a warm climate, he would have a personality change. Thoughts of suicide came to him whenever he experienced heat. As a partial answer to the problem, he moved from a southern state to a northern climate and seemed to function quite well when it was cold. But he was a prisoner to climate. During the summer months he would fall back into deep depressions. As we prayed in the spirit, the Lord showed me that he did indeed have a metabolic disorder. But the metabolic disorder was a result of an occult curse that had run down through his mother's family. The evil spirit was using this metabolic disorder to keep him captive. In Jesus' name we broke the curse of the occult and renounced the

154

demon and sentenced it to the wastelands of the world. Then God healed him.

Through incidents such as these I have discovered that sickness can affect the total person, body, soul and spirit. And Jesus, who is Lord of all, is the only one who can heal and unite the whole person.

Not all sickness is due directly to sin and spiritual bondage, however. Because sickness is still a curse to mankind, sometimes Satan still uses it as an access point to afflict the righteous. Sometimes our shield of faith is down and Satan, like a roaring lion, catches us unawares. The Bible describes him as a destroyer, a devourer, a thief. He is constantly trying to deny the promises of God. For this reason, God's word encourages us to be alert, to fight the good fight of faith which brings glory to God.

The ninth chapter of John recounts the healing of a blind man. Like the friends of Job, the disciples ask Jesus if the man or his parents had sinned. Jesus denied that either was the case.

As He passed by, He saw a man blind from birth. (v. 1)

And His disciples asked Him saying, "Rabbi, who sinned, this man or his parents that he should be born blind?" (v. 2)

Jesus answered, "It was in order that the works of God might be displayed in him." (v. 3)

We must work the works of Him who sent Me as long as it is day; night is coming when no man can work. (v. 4)

While I am in the world, I am the light of the world. (v. 5)

This same Jesus who is no longer physically in the world, now dwells in us all and still wants to be healing light for the world through the faith of his people.

Several years ago, my wife was able to give testimony to the glory of God when she was giving birth to our son Jonathan. When she was in labor, toxemia set in. In simple terms, the baby was not getting enough oxygen. As I understand it, the normal heartbeat of a child within the womb is 160-180 per minute. Doctors are concerned when the heartbeat gets down to 120. Our child's heartbeat was 80. I could feel the uneasiness in the labor room as the doctors and nurses were constantly checking the heartbeat. Hours before we had prayed a prayer of dedication. We had already confessed that it was His child. We thanked Him for the privilege of being parents and stewards of His creation. Our doctor, who was a general practitioner, called in a specialist. He suggested a Caesarian operation, but I could tell that he felt it was already too late for the baby. In fact, he came over and told me in the best bedside manner that I could expect either to lose my wife Grace, or baby, or both. In either case, there was a good chance that if the baby survived, he would be retarded.

I wish I could tell you that the faith of the Lord flooded my heart and I prayed a prayer of faith. I can't! But as I started praying in tongues, I knew the Lord wanted to bolster my faith through the prayers of His people. I immediately left the labor room and called a friend to start praying and ask members of her church to pray on a prayer chain for Grace and the baby.

While I was calling, the doctors gave my wife an injection to try to counteract the toxemia, which abated immediately. This amazed the staff, particularly a Benedictine nurse. After eight months of observation of toxemia cases, she called my wife and explained to her that she had never seen toxemia abate that quickly after an injection. She said that it usually would take 30 minutes or more. She then asked, "Do you suppose it was a miracle?" Grace assured her that it was and began to share more of what happened, to the glory of God.

While people were praying for her, she felt like her body was being bathed in God's love. In addition, one of the members of our staff received a word of knowledge from Acts 3:16 to confirm the healing of Jonathan.

> And on the basis of faith in His name, it is the name Jesus, which has strengthened this man whom you see and know, and faith which comes through Him, has given him this perfect health in the presence of all.

Just as Peter testified to the miracle-working power of Jesus to heal the lame man, so Grace had an opportunity to testify to the healing of our son. Far from being retarded, Jonathan is a bright and animated boy. Praise the Lord!

Chapter 8

The Authority to Heal the Outer Man
Part II — The Faith to Appropriate Healing

Most people believe in divine healing. Yet it is not enough to believe in healing. We need to appropriate healing by faith for ourselves. To illustrate this, suppose a man comes into a church and he suddenly keels over on the floor. Someone asks if there is a doctor in the house, and a doctor comes on the scene. He examines the man lying on the floor and then he says, "This man is dying of malnutrition and he has only 30 minutes to live." So various people in the congregation scurry about and procure some food: The doctor speaks to the patient who by now is conscious and says, "Do you believe if you take this food you will live?" The man responds, "I do believe if I take this food I'll live." He persists in saying this, "I believe unequivocally that if I take this food I'll live." Twenty nine minutes and fifty seconds later in midsentence, he says, "I believe . . ." and falls dead. What went wrong? His belief was right and the food was good. He believed that the food would make him well. The problem, of course, was that he never appropriated this food for himself. By the same token, many people believe in God and His works. (The demons believe in God also and they tremble because they know their end is near.) But they have never received by faith the living bread of life, Jesus, for their Savior or Healer. They remain spiritually dead or physically ill.

Just as Jesus had already made provision for salvation, the Baptism in the Holy Spirit and deliverance, so he also has made provision for healing. But this needs to be appropriated by faith. Jesus, for example, marvelled at the faith of the centurion who believed that Jesus would heal his servant (Luke 7:1-10). He told the woman with the issue of blood that her faith made her well (Luke 8:48). But how do we exercise faith? In order to exercise faith, we first need to know what faith is. The writer of Hebrews gives us a definition of what faith is:

> Now faith is the assurance (or substance) of things hoped for, the conviction (or evidence) of things not seen. (Hebrews 11:1)

So many times, we think we have faith but all we have is hope. Faith is not hope, nor hope faith. The substance or the reality of healing is in faith. It is evidence or conviction of things unseen. In other words, faith not only believes, but appropriates and receives as evidence what God had already provided for on the cross. This includes healing, salvation, provision, and all six-hundred-some-odd promises with God's Word. It is unseen because it is in the spiritual realm. The rhema type of faith says, "I have it now." Jesus sheds further light on this way of faith (Mark 11:22-24) and how this rhema faith, the gift of faith, can be appropriated.

> And Jesus answered, saying to them, "Have faith in God. (v. 22)

> Truly, I say to you, whoever says to this mountain, 'Be taken up and cast into the sea,' and does not doubt in his heart, but believes that what he says is going to happen, it shall be granted to him. (v. 23)

> Therefore, I say to you, all things for which we pray and ask, believe that you have received them and they shall be granted you. (v. 24)

Jesus commanded His disciples to have faith in God. In the Greek, it says we are to have the faith of God. Faith that will move mountains must come from the God who makes the mountains. We need to have the God-kind of faith. How do we attain Godly faith? The Word of God says that Jesus is the high priest of our confession. We need to profess or confess before God with Jesus as the high priest of our confession that His word is true. Faith activated by confession claims into the material world what has been made available in the spiritual world. It says, "Your will be done in my body as it is in heaven." In terms of healing, it involves "believing" God's healing before we already receive it. Does it mean that we deny our sickness or the symptoms? No, but by faith we look to Jesus, the Author and Finisher of our faith, and not to our sickness. This is totally different from Christian Science, which denies the reality of sickness and sin. As Christians, pain, sin and suffering are real, but we don't put our faith in them. We don't even put our faith on healing; rather we put our faith in Jesus, who heals. Faith says, "By Your stripes, Jesus, I am healed. I thank and praise You for it, Jesus."

This is precisely what my wife did a few years after we were married. When she was eight years old, she contracted polio, both the bulbar and spinal types. The right side of her body was completely paralyzed; the other side only partially. Fortunately, in her southern Iowa farm com-

160

munity, they believed in prayer. God honored their prayers and faith and the paralysis stopped just above and below the vertebra containing the nerves to the diaphragm. Paralysis there would have necessitated her being in an iron lung. The young student pastor who went to visit Grace felt God's glory and presence in that room. I don't know if this falls in the category of kissing and telling, but after years of therapy, the only noticeable effect of that polio is her slightly lopsided pucker when Grace kisses me.

About 12 years later, possibly as a result of this polio came petit mal seizures. They started out as long headaches that later became blackouts. One day as she was driving me to a little country church to preach, she had a blackout and the car went out of control. I reached out and grabbed the wheel as we spun around two or three times. I managed to put my foot on the brakes and remain on the road. An EKG test indicated that she needed medication. The doctor prescribed Dilantin for her and told her that she would have to take it for the rest of her life. In addition, she would not be able to drive until the seizures were under control.

After our marriage, God slowly but surely began to show us through books and His Word that He does want to heal his people, but we needed to pray with a specific purpose for it. While I was pastoring two churches in the north central part of Wisconsin, I received notice that a Presbyterian church in Manitowoc, Wisconsin, was having a healing mission with Father Alfred Price, an Episcopal priest, as the main speaker. I had heard Father Price before at seminary and I must confess that he was not well received by some of our faculty. But for me, the message of healing was a breath of fresh air. Alfred Price was at that time a spokesman for the Order of St. Luke's, an organization founded by Gaynor Banks, whose sole purpose was to bring the healing ministry back into the

Church. As I listened to Alfred Price and saw hundreds of people come forward to receive healing, I suddenly was impressed with the compassion of Jesus. I saw the difference between compassion and sympathy. When Jesus showed compassion, He did something about it. He never offered sympathy because sympathy is powerless to do anything. The miracle and healing episodes of the gospels took on new meaning. I came away from that conference with an inner resolve to take this ministry more seriously.

As I shared the way I felt, my wife began meditating on the scriptures on healing. Soon she started building up her faith by personalizing them and claiming these promises for herself as she talked with God. At the same time, not to be presumptuous, she was faithfully taking her pills. Finally, one day she looked at the bottle of pills; there were six left. Soon she would have to have another prescription filled. Once more she requested healing for her epilepsy, that God's will would be done in her body as it is in heaven. The Lord suddenly impressed her in her spirit that she wouldn't need them any more. The gift of faith, the rhema, God-type faith came to her. Her faith activated by her confession of God's Word had brought into existence what was already done on the cross.

Confessing healing is not much different than confessing Jesus as our Lord and Savior (more about this in another chapter). In fact, it's much easier because once we have Jesus as our personal Savior, we have His faith to receive healing (Romans 10:9-11).

> That if you confess with your mouth Jesus as Lord and believe in your heart that God raised Him from the dead, you shall be saved. (v. 9)

> For with the heart man believes, resulting in righteousness, and with the mouth he confesses, resulting in salvation. (v. 10)

> For the scripture says, 'Whoever believes in Him will not
> be disappointed.' (v. 11)

Verse eleven is a promise and we need to hold onto the promise in terms of salvation and healing.

Many times, we need to persist in our confession of faith, just as the widow (Luke 18:1-8) persisted till she won justice from the unjust judge. God is not unjust, but He does want us to build up our faith so that we have strong spiritual muscles. When we persist in our prayer of faith, confessing Jesus as our healer, we are building up our faith. In the process, Jesus and His Word go beyond head knowledge into our hearts: which, in turn, ignites the gift of faith.

We not only need to persist and persevere in our prayer of faith to build up faith, we need to fight the good fight of faith. Why do we need to fight? Because while God's will is to heal us and to not disappoint us by His Word, Satan wants to discourage us and disprove the power of God's Word.

I never realized the full implication of this until I asked several believers in the body of Christ to pray for my mother whose body was being ravaged with Parkinson's Disease and hardening of the arteries. As the two women were praying for my mother, one of them was given a vision of my mother in bed. She saw a light hovering over my mother. They continued to pray and some more light started to enter her body. But immediately she saw demons coming on the scene, surrounding her, trying to rip off the healing that was taking place. They persisted in praying for her and felt they themselves were being beaten up by demonic forces. Pleading the blood of Jesus Christ, they cried out to the Lord and the demons not only left them but in the vision fled from my mother. From that day forward, she never had to contend with any more pain.

I share this with you because we need to know that in the unseen spiritual world there is a war going on. While we can claim the promises of God's Word, Satan and his cohorts are trying to lie to us and discredit the effective power of the cross and the prayer of faith. Daniel prayed interceding on behalf of the Jews in captivity and received an answer to his prayer twenty-one days later. The angel of the Lord told him that his prayer had been heard the very first day, but the answer did not come because he was delayed by the prince of Tyre. The prince of Tyre was undoubtedly a prevailing satanic spirit. The angel enlisted the help of the warrior angel Michael to help him fight off this spirit so that he would be able to deliver the message. God has given us the faith and power in Jesus to fight that fight of faith.

As a pastor, I soon learned that the prayer of faith isn't only a good tool for the individual, but also for the body of believers. Believers are called to exercise their faith and authority for each other. Jesus not only recognized the faith of individuals, He also honored the faith of groups of people who had faith for others. When four men transported a paralytic on a stretcher, they couldn't approach Jesus in a house because of the crowd around Him. Undaunted, they got onto the roof and tore it apart and lowered the man down to Jesus. Whereupon, Jesus marvelled at their faith. That's persistence! And their faith undoubtedly sparked the faith of the paralytic who obeyed Jesus' command to take up his bed and walk.

As soon as I caught hold of this truth, I started asking people to pray with me for members that were sick. The thing that amazed me is that the seemingly least-spiritual people in the congregation became excited and involved. They started asking me (sometimes telling me) to not forget to pray for such and such a member. Some of the same people who had conveyed obliquely that I could never meet their needs as pastor became enthused. I soon discovered why. People were getting healed and word got around that "something was happening." That something was the healing power of Jesus.

Sometimes God's faith rests with no one but Himself. In His divine sovereignty, He simply chooses to heal. In this case, He usually works from the outside in. Jesus confronted the father whose son needed deliverance and asked him, "Do you believe?" And the father responded, "I do believe, help my unbelief" (Mark 9:24). In many areas in foreign missions, especially where the gospel is preached for the first time, there are usually signs following the Word of God. God heals the unbelievers as a demonstration of the power of the gospel and His compassionate love for them. An evangelist friend, for example, who held a crusade in India would start with perhaps only 100 people the first night. But because of the healing that took place, it was not uncommon for him to have 100,000 in attendance the following night simply because the gospel is power.

Paul attests to this when he says:

> For the kingdom of God does not consist of words, but in power. (I Corinthians 4:20)

> For we are not like many peddling the Word of God but as from sincerity, but as from God we speak in Christ in the sight of God. (II Corinthians 2:17)

Several years ago, as I watched Kathryn Kuhlman's miracle service, I unexpectedly found myself healed of a curvature of the spine. God in His graciousness healed me without my asking for it. I was choosing to be a spectator and God decided I should be a participant. I felt what seemed like an electric current down my spine and my back straighten up. I believe God allowed this to happen to show me that it is ultimately His faith that heals. I must say I was humbled by this experience.

Years later, the Lord spoke in a prophecy about faith and confirmed what I have already shared with you.

There is a distinct and awful tendency among my people to blame one another for illness, especially prolonged or recurring illness. While I said to various ones whom I healed, "Your faith has made you whole," for others it was the faith of friends, or even my own faith which was the agent for healing. So do not hesitate to pray, believing for what you know to be My will (that which is in heaven) even though you may have prayed before, for faith comes by hearing and hearing by the Word for wholeness as well as salvation. And if you are the one in need of healing, do not receive condemnation for asking again for prayer (verbal prayer which you can hear) for by it I will build faith.

When you pray for others, pray in secret also, but let them know of your prayers (and my answers through you) that their faith may be built up. But let me guide the sharing lest you be guilty of parading your piety before men or inflating your own ego. Let the sharing be in such a way that it is a part of building up one another in love.

In addition to the prayer of faith confessing and claiming the promises of God, God sometimes bestows on us a special anointing for healing. There are times, for example, when God has used me as well as many others on our staff to command and speak healing. With the anointing, God says, "Be healed," and the person receives healing. In this case, the gift of faith, the rhema is already present. There is no need to pray a prayer of faith; there is no delay between promise and fulfillment.

At a Full Gospel Businessmen's meeting, the Lord spoke to my wife and told her to lay hands on a young girl and she would receive healing for her epilepsy. The girl was restored immediately. A man, after receiving inner healing, complained about a dislocated disc in his back. As I prayed over him, the Lord again assured me that he was going to heal him. I could feel power coming from my arms and hands and this 240-pound man seemed to shake and was slain in the spirit. Again God healed him.

We need to add here that when God gives a word of faith as a command, the person who is seeking the healing knows it, too. I say this because several years ago there was a front-page article about a so-called faith healer who told a family that their daughter was healed of diabetes. As an act of faith, he advised them to throw away the child's insulin. As a result, the child died. This, of course, was not the faith of God, this was presumption. The gift of faith was not there in the form of a command. While the child's healing was still hidden in Jesus, the man had no right to suggest that the child's insulin be thrown away. One member on our staff had diabetes and the Lord promised that He would heal him. He claimed that promise, but he kept taking his insulin until one day his body reacted to the insulin. Then and only then, did he realize that the rhema, the gift of faith, had come.

God's faith not only works through individuals, Himself, and the body of believers, but also works through various ministries.

> Is any one among you sick? Let him call for the elders of the church, and let them pray over him, anointing him with oil in the name of the Lord.
>
> And the prayer offered in faith will restore the one who is sick, and the Lord will raise him up; and if he has committed sins, they will be forgiven him.
>
> Therefore, confess your sins to one another, so that you may be healed. The effective prayer of a righteous man can accomplish much. (James 5:14-16)

As an elder of the church, I, along with other members of the staff, often use oil to anoint people for both inner healing of memories, wounded spirits, and physical healing. As I am obedient to His Word, the Lord continually reminds me of that authority.

A young woman from the Twin Cities, for example, came up to our headquarters in St. Cloud by bus. As I picked her up at the bus station, I noticed that she was blind. She explained that she had lost her sight at birth. Born prematurely, she was put in an incubator with too much oxygen. The oxygen burned her eyes out. In later years, she had undergone cosmetic surgery and had plastic eyes installed. She had come to our ministry center to receive inner healing. As we finished ministering to her by anointing her for healing of her memories and her spirit, she asked us to anoint her eyes. I gulped along with my prayer partner because what she was asking was not the natural process of restoration for healing, but a miracle, something from nothing. With tears in both our eyes, we dutifully anointed her eyes for healing and forgot about it. Three weeks later she phoned us and informed us that she was able to see light from darkness. She had gone to hear Evangelist Morris Cerullo and while the service was beginning, in the act of worshipping the Lord, she started to see light from darkness. A few months passed by and my wife and I were invited to her house for dinner. When we were there we marvelled how capable she was as a homemaker. She seemed to have everything under control. We soon learned that that was part of her problem. For some twenty-six years she was able to cope with not seeing. She read and typed in braille and played the piano and organ and had a beautiful singing voice. She had a responsible Civil Service job. Her life was fulfilled as a blind person. While she felt the Lord was urging her to seek miraculous healing for her eyes, she was, at the same time, fearful about seeing because it was an unknown world for her. And so my wife and I started praying for her that she would no longer have any fear about seeing; that her faith would not be blocked by fear. As I raised my head, her artificial eyes suddenly tracked properly for the first time and she looked me in the eyes and said, "Denis, I can see you; I see what you look like." I had never described myself to her nor had she asked. God, somehow through a vision, had revealed that to her. Then the Lord gave a prophecy through my wife:

My daughter, like any father, I love you and I desire to bless you. Do not take the counsel of your fears. I desire that you see and I am preparing your heart to receive the miracle that I have for you which will glorify Me.

A few weeks later she shared that she felt pressure behind the plastic eyes. She also mentioned that when she would dream, her dreams would correspond with her everyday life when she was awake. This meant that her dreams were never visual. They oriented around sound and touch. But just recently, she started to have visual dreams and see colors and people's faces, things that she had never experienced before. The Lord was fulfilling what He had promised. He was preparing her heart to see.

God's special anointing and gift of faith for healing and miracles has become more evident in these last days. It is a part of the signs following when the Word is preached. It is given sovereignly through such well-known ministries as Morris Cerullo and the late Kathryn Kuhlman and through vessels who lay their hands on the sick such as Oral Roberts, as well as to the ones who receive it. Regardless of how it is done or by whom it is done, it is done as an expression of His compassionate heart towards His people.

God is healing His people. His healing is not for our sake alone, but for His own sake. He desires His people to be well so that as freely as they have received from Him, they may freely give and exercise their authority to heal. He has made His faith available for us so that we might glorify Him in our bodies as well as in our spirit and in our soul.

Chapter 9

The Authority to Deliver from Spiritual Bondage and Break Curses

Several years ago at an interdenominational meeting, I recall a Roman Catholic priest and sister who were embarrassed to read in print what Pope Paul VI had said about the reality of the devil. They were embarrassed because as far as they were concerned, Satan and demons were something out of the dark ages. They felt that demons and Satan as described in the Bible account were the ancient world's understanding of things. They were taught to reinterpret and demythologize these things and classify them under the category of psychoses or neuroses. I must confess before I became spirit-filled, I felt the same way. Maybe I was not quite so radical, but in terms of awareness and importance, the idea of, as well as the reality of, the demonic came somewhere between the 130th and 140th things to be reckoned with in my walk

171

with God. But let me set the record straight, Satan is real. To borrow Hall Lindsay's book title, *Satan Is Alive and Well on Planet Earth*, he is well only when Christians don't understand that he is a real adversary and we have authority over him in Jesus Christ.

The general public was laughing at the idea of Satan a few years ago but there has been such a great revival of the occult that people aren't laughing any more. In fact, a feature story on Satan and satanic worship made the cover of *Time* magazine a number of years ago. According to Anton LeVey, the head of the Satanic Church, there are more than ten thousand churches in the United States where people worship the devil. Sybil Leeke, who considers herself a witch, says there are more than 20,000 witches in America. In recent years, "The Exorcist" and many similar films have come on the scene. There seems to be a fascination with the occult and the demonic even though people come out of the theater as they did at the showing of "The Exorcist", horrified, nauseated and even physically ill.

What are we to make of all this? For one thing, it is not a nice, neat subject. It is kind of incompatible to anyone whose idea of the church is something cozy and orderly. In the Gospel of Mark, the demon-possessed man in the synagogue must have upset the liturgy for that morning. The Gadarene demoniac in the Gospels wasn't exactly a tourist attraction either. In fact, people avoided the place where he lived among the tombs. But Jesus didn't. He came to set the captives free. He visited him and delivered him from the demons just as He did others on numerous occasions. And when He was through with His earthly ministry, He told His disciples that He would give them authority over the demons. As Christ's followers, we need to recognize that the demonic forces today can only be met by the power of people walking in God's spirit, not in theological debates or religious programs we can affirm mentally. In Ephesians 6:12, Paul reminds us "we are not fighting flesh and blood, but against persons without bodies, the evil rulers of the unseen world, those mighty satanic beings and great evil princes of darkness who rule this world, and against huge numbers of wicked spirits in the spirit world (Living Bible). Elsewhere, He says "the Gospel I preach is not talk, it is power . . ." (I Cor. 1:18f; I Cor. 4:20; II Cor. 11: 3-4). He could have just as easily added . . . the only power that will defeat the forces of evil.

Oh, I wish I would have known that when I was fresh out of seminary or graduate school. I wish I had known my adversary and my authority as a believer when I had my first little church on an Indian Reservation. Many evangelists and pastors came to this reservation and left frustrated by the bound up hearts of the people living there. Many, like myself, were not able to recognize the oppressive demonic activity that pervaded the community. Although I believed God's Word was true and preached Christ-centered messages, I was blind to the spiritual realm of the demons and the authority I needed to exercise over them. Even though over one quarter of Jesus' ministry was spent in deliverance, somehow I bought the lie of the so-called modern scholarship that denied the reality of the demonic. But it wasn't too long after I asked the Lord to fill me with His Spirit, that I was suddenly made aware of the reality of the demonic. The Lord made sure that there was no doubt in my mind about the adversary when He sent certain people along the way who needed this ministry of deliverance.

One of my first encounters came at a Woman's Aglow meeting where I was an advisor. While I was seated listening to the speaker, the Lord drew my attention to a woman across the room whom we'll call Evelyn. Evelyn, I was to learn later, had been in and out of mental institutions. Her hair was matted and she looked like a man in drag. There was a certain devilish grin about her that made me feel uneasy. I quickly turned my attention away from her and absorbed myself with the rest of the meeting and the main speaker. At the end of the meeting, a lovely, well-dressed woman spoke to us about her friend that needed ministry. She felt that she needed deliverance. My first inclination was to say, "Deliverance from what?" And then right behind her I saw that her friend happened to be the same woman I had felt uneasy about earlier in the meeting. Another pastor and myself started to speak to her and then without provocation, the most masculine basso profundo voice responded through her and said, "I'm not going to leave this woman." I must admit, the hair on the back of my head stood up and I started to panic. I felt like the man who told his pastor, "Pastor, I have good news and bad news. The good news is I have the devil on the run. The bad news is that he is running after me."

Right then and there, I wanted to run. But then miraculously, the words of I John 4:4 flooded my soul, "Greater is He that is in you than he that is in the world." With these words, I suddenly felt a tremendous up-welling of the living waters of the Holy Spirit. With this up-welling I started to feel the confidence and authority of God. I heard myself cover the meeting place and ourselves with the shed blood of Jesus, bind Satan, and ask the demon to name himself. This was quite a big step for a minister who used to kid some of his more conservative Pentecostal friends for their slaughterhouse religion. But then, right before my eyes, the demon in her started to say, "No, no, not that!" I discovered the truth of the old Pentecostal song, "Power in the Blood." As it turned out, there were many demons attacking and controlling that woman: alcoholism, witchcraft, a religious spirit, rejection and fear of rejection, anger, hatred, rebellion, condemnation, suicide and so on. But there was one demon that named itself who would not leave. After a couple of attempts at expelling him, we asked the woman whether she wanted to be delivered of this demon and have Jesus as Lord of her life. Her response shook me again, because she said, "I'm really not sure about Jesus. But I've seen him (referring to the demon of lust) and he is beautiful. He has told me to wear these rings and if I came here for help that I would die."

After she reluctantly gave us the rings, I explained to her that Satan and his cohorts are liars and deceivers of the brethren. Then I asked her if she were saved; if she had the reality of Jesus in her life. She exclaimed that she was a churchgoer and was baptised and confirmed in her church. But it was quite obvious that while she had the form of religion, she did not have God's Spirit. I went on to explain that Jesus warned His disciples about delivering people. Once the house, their inner spiritual house is cleaned out from demons, it needs to be filled with Jesus. Otherwise, the demons would come back with seven more companions and the person would be seven times worse than before (See Matthew 12:42-45). This experience with this woman and the possible consequence of her being partially delivered without receiving Christ left me in a cold sweat. It also left an indelible impression on me to always make sure where a person is with Christ before I would minister with them for deliverance.

As my pastor friend explained the plan of salvation, she persisted in exclaiming, "I thought I was a Christian, I believe in God, I was baptised and confirmed. I've done many things for the Church." We shared with her that the Bible says even the demons believe in God and they tremble because they know their end is near (James 2:19). Besides, it isn't what she has done or can do for the church that counts, it is what God has already done for her through Jesus Christ.

For a while, it seemed that the woman was reluctant about wanting to be delivered from this demon of lust. It looked like we were at an impasse until her friend spoke up and pleaded with her to receive Christ. She said God had a plan for her and her husband, and He would heal their relationship with each other. That was apparently just the thing that needed to be said. We didn't know it, but her friend knew that she and her husband were estranged. As soon as we led her through the sinner's prayer, we claimed her as a new child of God and with her assent, we rebuked the demon of lust only to find more demons crying out. One, in particular, in a high-pitched voice cried out in desperation, "Where will I go? I've been in her for thirty years." It was a religious spirit. But it brought up a good question, "where should he go?"

In the New Testament, the demons in the Gaderene demoniac asked to be sent into the pigs. Jesus complied with their request. One of the things we have discovered is that demons are legalists. By that, I mean they need to be sent to a particular place and told by whose authority you do it – which is to say in Jesus' Name. Early in the game, when they would be cast out without any particular direction, they sometimes would come back and try harassing me or someone else in the ministering group. I can recall after I had ministered to another woman, I woke up with something – a demon – choking me around the throat. All I could do was plead the blood of Jesus and immediately it left me. One demon threatened that if he were expelled from a person, he would enter another person down the block whom we knew was living for the devil. We told him he could not. Jesus mentioned when demons are cast out, they wander in the dry places. For that reason we usually command them to go to the wastelands of the world in Jesus' Name.*

From my early attempts at ministering deliverance, I learned that I not only need to make sure that the person was hooked up to Jesus, but that they took an active part in their own deliverance. Today, we usually ask the person who is receiving ministry to renounce for themselves, with us leading them, the spiritual forces that are binding them; and in the Name of Jesus sentence them to the wastelands of the world. There is a tendency within Christian circles, especially in the area of deliverance, to do ministry to and for an individual instead of with the person. The person receiving ministry is left in a passive role. While the demons may know that we as a ministering body have authority over them, it is important for them to know that even the person that is bound, claims this same authority. When we minister with the people, therefore, we are put in a position of agreeing with them (Matthew 18:20). This in turn puts the demons on the run and eliminates any long, drawn-out battle.

As Christians, we need to understand that we are on the offense; not on the defensive. The best defense is a good offense. When the Bible speaks of the church against whom the gates of hell shall not prevail (Matthew 16:18), it doesn't mean that we're cringing behind the gates of hell. What this passage is saying is that the people of God are on the offense. By the

*Scripture seems to attest to the fact that there is a certain place in hell where evil angelic forces are chained — a place called Tartarus, where they remain until Judgment day (See II Peter 2:4 and Jude 6). For that reason some feel justified in sending the demonic forces to the pit or dark dry places to be chained until judgment day.

authority of Jesus, we are walking over the gates and setting the captives free. This was and still is a part of Jesus' ministry through His people. Contrary to some people's understanding, deliverance is not a specialized kind of ministry done by people who somehow have some special gift from God. There is no deliverance ministry as such, simply the ministry of Jesus which is available to all of God's children who know their authority (See Mark 16:17). God even told us, "I deliver you from the deliverance ministry." At first, we thought that meant that we were through with deliverance. He assured us that was not the case. He simply wanted to reveal to us that this is not an office, like pastor, teacher, apostle, evangelist, prophet; it is the authority of every believer over Satan — just as we are called to fulfill the great commission, witness to His presence, forgive others, etc.

One demon spoke out of a woman and asked why I was smiling and my response was simply, "Because the battle is already won." When we were discovering our authority as believers, many times the demons tried to pull rank on us. On one occasion, the demon spoke out and said, "Don't you realize I am an angel." Satan and his cohorts who try to pose as angels of light are always trying to throw their weight around. In I Peter 5:8, we read that "he prowls about like a roaring lion seeking someone to devour." The Christian needs to realize that by the authority of Jesus (the Lion of Judah), Satan is a toothless, whipped pussycat. The more confidence we have in Jesus' authority, the less fight he puts up. We've found that in most of the ministry and counseling situations that there are little or no demonic manifestations. In our earlier bouts with demons, their outward manifestations were primarily for our benefit, to assure us that yes these things do exist. The Lord also instructed us not to talk with the demons or have them name themselves and give honor to them. He said, "If you want to know who they are, just ask me and I will tell you (through a word of knowledge)." And that is precisely what we do.

A woman who received the baptism in the Holy Spirit and was in a local women's full gospel fellowship prayed that there would be nothing in her life that would prevent her from giving herself totally to God. She prayed something to the effect that if there were anything in her life that prevented God from working in her, that He would reveal that to her. She had no sooner made that petition, than some loud dissonant voices came out of her mouth. It seemed that whenever she would try to praise God, she would be interrupted by moaning and wailing voices. This went on for a week. Needless to say, it scared her out of her wits. She had people pray for her and then in desperation she called us. As we prayed and asked her to renounce these spiritual forces that the Lord had already revealed to us, I could see her body stiffen. She was expecting to have these demons manifest themselves again. I assured her that she didn't have to worry about that because in Jesus' Name the battle had already been won on the cross. By the authority of Jesus, she needed to bind Satan and renounce the spiritual forces. She needed to make it a part of her confession to Jesus the High Priest and we, acting as the body of Christ, would agree with her. She did that and after it was all over, I could see the relief and wonder on her face as if to say, "Is that all there is to it?" The answer is, "Yes."

Certain authors on this subject like to talk about the degrees which people are afflicted by the demonic; namely, harassment, oppression, and possession. While there are certainly degrees of affliction, Jesus is more concerned with setting us totally, completely free, regardless of the degree. I personally refrain from these categories simply

179

because they are not all mentioned in the Bible. The word "possession" has an obvious bad connotation. The implication is that the person possessed has no control or will to extricate himself from the demon's hold and therefore must be passive in his deliverance. But the demoniac who had a legion of demons in him was still able to bow before Jesus and worship Him. The word "possession" comes from the King James translation of the Greek word which means "to demonize". For this reason, I personally prefer the word demonized. This takes in all the categories and degrees of spiritual bondage.

How do people get demonized in the first place? In ministering to thousands of people, we find that many times, people get under spiritual bondage through repeated sins. For example, if a person submits to lust he opens himself to that spiritual force of lust. If he submits to pornography, he submits to the spirit of pornography, and so on. Sin enslaves, and who is the enslaver? Satan himself.

Spiritual bondage goes beyond simply moral sins. Many times, people are bound by their sinful attitudes. For example, if a person refuses to forgive people that have hurt him, then he not only has the emotional problems of bitterness and resentment and self-pity, but also the spiritual bondage of the spirits of bitterness and resentment and self-pity. According to the Word of God, there is no neutral ground in the spiritual realm. We have a choice of life or death of partaking at the table of the Lord or the table of demons (See I Cor. 10:21). We either side with the world of darkness or the world of light.

People also become demonized through traumatic experiences in their life. This is especially true in non-Christian families. In one particular instance, for example, a husband and wife with their son came for ministry. They were deeply concerned over their son's behavior. They had been Christians for a number of years and spirit-filled and yet were not getting any victory in their lives and especially in their son's life. As we prayed for the gifts of the Holy Spirit to be manifest, the Lord gave my prayer partner and me knowledge of some of the problems in their lives and in the life of the son. But the Holy Spirit revealed there was one problem peculiar to their son. This was confirmed as they went on with the discussion of how their son would never stick to any job and how he, at age 17, could not settle down. Although he had a very tender heart for the Lord and his parents, somehow from the very earliest time he would have the urge to run away from home. The Holy Spirit prompted me to ask them whether he had been sick or had a crisis happen to them before they were Christians. The mother said, "Yes, he had multiple sclerosis when he was three and was at a point of death for quite some time." According to the Holy Spirit, that was the point of attack when he received a spirit of restlessness. In Jesus' Name, we bound Satan and took authority over it. That young man received deliverance from restless spirit and other evil influences in his life and was able to finish his schooling. He went to Bible school, studying to become a minister of the Gospel.

In another case, a young man was afflicted with a spirit of rejection when he was born prematurely and confined to an incubator for several weeks. As a child, he was always wanted. He received affection from both his parents, and yet he grew up feeling rejected. Because of this, he had great difficulty in receiving love and offering love. He compensated for his poor sense of self worth by driving himself to achieve in school and later on in his work. But because he was in bondage to the spirit of rejection, the more he achieved, the less satisfied he was with himself. The more his parents and friends expressed love for him, the less he felt loved. It was a no-win situation. All that love and all those achievements were like water being poured through a sieve. He was never satisfied. He never had enough. And this is true of anything demonic. You can never satisfy a demon. Finally there came a point in his life when he received Christ. That experience more or less put a lid on things so that he could cope with his life situation. As he grew in his walk with God, he discovered that Jesus does not want us to just cope, He wants to deliver us completely from evil influences. And that is precisely what happened when he received ministry and was delivered of the spirit of rejection.

Some people are also demonized when their will is lowered or deactivated through drugs, hypnotism or psychological methods of passivity. Many people we have counseled that have come from the drug culture have confessed that the deeper they got into the drug scene, the more they were aware of satanic forces. Some even saw them, heard them, and were even asked to worship Satan or to do some heinous crime. Others were told to take their life. One woman who had undergone hypnosis for therapeutic purposes, became deeply depressed and wanted to take her life. In all these instances, their will was put in a passive state. One young man whose mind was literally blown from LSD trips, amphetamines and barbiturates, kept seeing visions of lions coming after him. Although he had received Christ as his Lord and Saviour, Satan was like that roaring lion (I Peter 5:8) trying to devour him. As we stood against the demonic forces that were harassing him, especially the demon of pharmocology (drugs), the vision left him. We prayed also that God would heal his mind and allow him to thirst and hunger for God's word. God honored that prayer. He graduated from Bible college and became co-pastor at a New Testament Charismatic church.

182

The occult and various forms of Eastern religions provide another open door to the demonic. The Old and New Testaments are replete with warnings against involvement in the occult.

Consider the following:

Do not turn to mediums or spiritualists, do not seek them out to be defiled by them, I am the Lord your God.(Leviticus 19:31)

There shall not be found among you anyone who makes his son or daughter pass through the fire, one who uses divination, or one who practices witchcraft, or one who interprets omens or a sorcerer, or one who casts a spell, or a medium or a spiritist, or one who calls up the dead. For whosoever does these is detestable to the Lord; and because of these detestable things the Lord your God will drive them out before you. (Deuteronomy 18:10-11)

And when they say to you, "Consult the mediums and wizards who whisper and mutter," should not a people consult their God? Should they consult the dead on behalf of the living? (Isaiah 8:19)

Now the deeds of the flesh are evident which are: immorality, impurity, sensuality, idolatry, sorcery, and things like these, of which I forewarned you that those who practice such things shall not inherit the kingdom of God. (Galatians 5:19-21)

Many people define the occult in a rather limited way. They recognize that spiritists and overt worship of the devil is something to be avoided, but they fail to see any danger in the more popular ouija board, horoscopes, waterwitching and palmistry. While some of this is what we call lollipop-stuff, it still is in the realm of the occult. It's like candy with poison in the middle. Many people get involved out of sheer ignorance, but this in itself is no excuse. If I were ignorant of traffic signals and I ran a stop sign, I could still hurt someone or get killed. The same thing is true of dabbling in the occult. These so-called harmless things are part of Satan's subtle bag of tricks to prevent people from seeking God's guidance through His word and Spirit. The same is true for the Eastern forms of religions (Yoga, TM, etc.) that promise peace of mind. Many of the initiation rites are prayers of obedience to gurus, and gods which are in reality demons. If Satan cannot get people to worship him directly, he will let people get fascinated with soul power.*

One young college student, who was studying to be a teacher of transcendental meditation, confessed to us that she was looking for peace of mind and escape from memories of an unhappy childhood. In her initial encounter with TM, she felt that she was getting help. The TM course was offered at a religious school under the guise of being non-religious. She began to wonder, however, when she was given a mantra (special prayer) and encouraged to offer prayers to gurus and Hindu gods in their initiation rite (Puja).

When you're hurting, you tend to overlook a lot of things: Like everything that Satan does, he offers something that looks like the real thing, but somewhere there is a hook in it. When you swallow the bait, you pay the price. This young woman paid the initiation price of $125 and as she got deeper into it, her peace of mind turned into mental depression and spiritual oppression. She felt driven to take her own life, but then a spirit-filled friend of hers led her to Christ and encouraged her to seek inner healing from her past hurts and deliverance. Jesus provided that peace she was looking for and enabled her to forget the past and press on to her high calling.

*Soul power includes such things as ESP, telepathy, clairvoyance.

There is one final area where Satan has a legal access, and that is through "cords of iniquity". This involves bondage through spiritual inheritance. Here are just a few passages that speak of this phenomenon:

> You shall not worship them (idols) or serve them, for I the Lord, your God, am a jealous God visiting the iniquity of the fathers on the children on the third and fourth generations of those who hate me, but showing loving kindness to those who love me and keep my commandments. (Exodus 20:5-6; Deuteronomy 5:9-10)

> The Lord is slow to anger and abundant in loving kindness, forgiving iniquity and transgression; but He will by no means clear the guilty, visiting the iniquity of the fathers on the children to the third and fourth generations. (Numbers 14:18)

> Ah, Lord God! Behold, Thou hast made the heavens and the earth by Thy great power and by Thine outstretched arm. Nothing is too difficult for Thee, Who showest loving kindness to thousands, but repayest the iniquity of fathers into the bosom of their children after them, O great and mighty God. (Jeremiah 32:17-18)

> For the ways of man are before the eyes of the Lord, and He watches all his paths. His own iniquities will capture the wicked, and he will be held with the cords of his sins, he will die for lack of instruction, and in the greatness of his folly he will go astray. (Proverbs 5:21-23)

> For I see that you are in the gall of bitterness and in the bondage (cord) of iniquity. (Acts 8:23)

From these many references, we see that sin can bind not only us, but also visit and bind to the third and fourth generations. Just as there is a genetic inheritance, there is also a spiritual inheritance (some blessings, some iniquities) which is passed on from generation to generation.

King David experienced a cord of iniquity in his life that visited to the third and fourth generation. When he murdered Uriah and took Bathsheba as his wife, the prophet Nathan reproved him and revealed this cord of iniquity that was to be a part of his spiritual inheritance. (II Samuel 12:9-11)

> Why have you despised the word of the Lord by doing evil in His sight? You have struck down Uriah the Hittite with the sword, have taken his wife to be your wife, and have killed him with the sword of the sons of Ammon. (v. 9)

> Now, therefore, the sword shall never depart from your house, because you have despised me and have taken the wife of Uriah the Hittite to be your wife. (v. 10)

> Thus says the Lord, 'Behold, I will raise up evil against you from your own household; I will even take your wives before your eyes and give them to your companion, and he shall lie with your wives in broad daylight. (v. 11)

This prophecy was fulfilled to the letter. David's son by Bathsheba died at birth. Absalom, his son, killed his step-brother Amnon for seducing his sister Tamar. In an attempt to gain the throne of Israel, Absalom was killed in battle and later another son Adonijah is killed by Solomon. In the third generation, the kingdom was split and scripture says there was constant war between Rehoboam and Jeroboam (I Kings 14:30).

At some time or other, we have all observed for ourselves how little Johnny so-and-so acted like his Dad or Mom. He manifested certain character quirks or attitudes. Usually we wrote that off as a learned response or environmental model. In other words, Johnny was simply imitating Dad or Mom. If he had a temper, we assume that he picked it up from Mommy and Daddy. But this is not necessarily so. We have observed first-hand that many adopted children would still take on some of the characteristics of their biological parents. Many psychiatrists and psychologists have confirmed this. Underlying many environmental models and genetic inheritances are the spiritual inheritances.

Our first encounter with this came when a spirit-filled Christian policeman was sharing his problems at our summer camp in the north woods of Minnesota. He mentioned that he had been an alcoholic and hadn't had a drink in eight years since he came to know Christ. His whole family as far back as he could remember on his father's side had a drinking problem. Even though he had victory in this area of his life, he seemed to have the alcoholic mentality. At times, when the pressures were great, he did have a craving for a drink, but he would pray to Jesus for help. As far as he was concerned, he had this under control. His main problem was continual respiratory problems and hoarseness in his throat. He had prayed for healing and asked others to pray for him with no results. He also happened to mention that his eight-year-old son also had respiratory ailments. We prayed and asked the Lord why this man had not received his healing. The Lord spoke in a prophetic word that this man was suffering under a curse of alcoholism that had come to his great, great grandfather who hated Him. We then asked the Lord what we could do about it. The Lord answered and instructed us to use the authority we have in Jesus Christ to break the curse — this cord of iniquity — and renounce the spirit of alcoholism that had used that cord to oppress him. As we did this, the most incredible thing happened. The policeman was instantaneously healed of his respiratory problem. But that was not all. We were to learn later that his son, who was 300 miles away in Minneapolis, was healed at the same time. The cord of iniquity had manifested itself physically. The policeman's craving for drink disappeared and he no longer was one step away from being a drunk. God delivered him totally.

Since that time we have learned that the cord of iniquity is a form of curse and scripture tells us that "Christ redeemed us from the curse of the law, having become a curse for us — for it is written, 'Cursed is every one who hangs on a tree' — in order that the blessing of Abraham might come to Gentiles so that we might receive the promise of the Spirit through faith (Galatians 3:13-14)." The apostle John shares that when there is a new heaven and new earth, there will be no more curses (Rev. 21:1-22: 3). But, obviously, until that time, there are curses with which we need to contend. Jesus, who died on the cross and became a curse for us, has also given us the authority to break curses.

While many people can lose their deliverance through outright disobedience, there are many more whose deliverance is incomplete because they haven't dealt with the cords of iniquity or spiritual inheritance which allows the demons direct access to them. In a sense it's similar to a child being delivered from his mother's womb. In order for the delivery to be complete, the umbilical cord needs to be cut and tied. Likewise, in order for the spiritual deliverance to be complete, the cords of iniquity need to be cut and tied (sealed) by the shed blood of Jesus.

Many times, as we have broken the cords of iniquity in the name of Jesus, either we, or the people ministered to, will have visions of the cords being cut. On one occasion, a young Christian woman who had received ministry for herself brought a mother and her 15 year-old daughter for ministry. The young daughter held her three-week-old child which was born out of wedlock. After asking for the gifts of the Holy Spirit to be manifested in our lives, the Lord revealed there were cords of rejection, lust, and rebellion in that family's life. As we discussed this with the mother, all of a sudden her defenses went up and she said, "I don't have a problem." The Lord revealed otherwise. In fact, she was going to a psychiatrist for help. The spirit of rebellion in her motivated her to question our integrity and our authority to set the captives free. She continued to question us and express her doubt and unbelief concerning what Jesus could do in her life. I politely informed her that we weren't here to defend ourselves or the ministry of Jesus, we were here to simply proclaim it. Obviously, she was not ready to receive it. Her daughter was, however, and I asked her if she would be willing to let her daughter's life be a testimony to what God can do. She hesitated and then grudgingly agreed. As we encouraged her daughter to exercise her authority as a believer and began cutting cords by the power of Jesus, my partner John Davison, who was praying in the spirit, had a vision. In the vision, he saw a big, two-handed sword cutting these cords. At the end of these cords was material that looked like garbage. As soon as the sword cut them off, out of the center of these cords were streams of water representative of the living waters of the Holy Spirit. As we anointed her for the healing of her memories and a wounded spirit, the Lord gave John another vision of the young girl with hands raised before the throne of God, rejoicing and praising Him. Alongside her was her mother, sad, head down, and hands tied behind her back, obviously completely bound by the cords of iniquity and spiritual forces. What a contrast. We could see the contrast on earth (in the natural realm) as the young daughter radiated the love of God and the mother scowled and looked miserable. John was given the privilege of seeing it in heaven in the spirit. As they departed, we prayed for the mother and the Lord assured us that in His own time, He would soften the heart of that mother and prepare her heart to receive all that He had for her. Praise God!

In dealing with people involved in the occult or with a cord of the occult, we have discovered that there is the threefold curse of poverty, sickness, and death to be reckoned with. By death, I mean violent death, early death, sometimes suicide (or attempts). In Deuteronomy 28, there is a list of blessing of those who follow God and curses of those who follow other gods. The list basically falls in these above three categories. One person was brought for ministry by a Roman Catholic charismatic prayer leader. She had been institutionalized several times in her 26 years and was presently under psychiatric threatment as a manic depressive patient. Her spirit-filled companions, with their joyful and hopeful expressions provided a contrast to her sullen, wild-animal appearance. Her hair nearly covered her eyes as if she wanted to hide from us.

As we prayed in the spirit, God showed us that among the numerous problems in her life, there was a cord in the form of witchcraft. In sharing things about her life and family, she bore witness to the curse of the occult background. She related how her father died in a car accident. One uncle had hung himself. A greater number, including herself, had made several attempts of suicide. She was partially deaf. Several members in her family had chronic sicknesses as well as bouts with tuberculosis. Her immediate family had lived in abject poverty and she in her depressed and oppressed state could not hold a job. When we asked her about her involvement in the occult, she mentioned that she was involved in witchcraft. Many members in her family had dabbled in fortune telling, ouija board games, seances, water witching, etc.

In all my years of ministry, I had never seen a woman more rejected by her family. In addition to the occult, cords of rejection, alcoholism, fear of rejection, rebellion, anger, hatred, lust, depression, self-pity, resentment, bitterness had come down through her family. We asked her to commit her life to Christ and led her through her deliverance. Immediately, her whole countenance changed, she began to take on the same joy and hope of her companions.

The transformation was as if God had done plastic surgery on her. Her hearing dramatically improved. God promised her that He would make her healing complete as she continued to walk in His ways.

According to Deuteronomy 28, countries as well as individuals can be under a curse. One country in particular with its worship of 330,000 idols seems to have had a history of being under the curse. No matter how much foreign aid that has come to it, it still seems to have no prosperity. That country of course, is India. Poverty, sickness, and death have been the rule rather than the exception and yet the most prosperous and wealthiest state in India has been the state of Kerala, which has the highest percentage of Christians. Coincidence? I think not.

Even people with no occult background who consult fortune tellers, astrologists, or have their palms read, are subjecting themselves to a curse. Scripture instructs us that the steps of man are ordained by God (Prov. 20:24). When we look elsewhere for direction and guidance, we are denying the blessing and the promises of His word. The guidance that comes from some place else usually seems harmless enough. Satan, by design, makes it that way. The deeper a person is involved with the occult and the more he puts his trust in it, the more enslaved he becomes to it. Involvement with the occult is not unlike experiments made with frogs. When you put a frog in hot water, he immediately tries to leap out. But if you start him in a cool pot of water and gradually increase the heat, he'll stay in there and eventually boil to death. That is precisely what happens with sin and the occult world. It seems harmless enough, but there is always a price to pay. There is always a hook in it. One woman paid a price that cost her two marriages and untold damage to her third one. Years ago, she had her fortune read. She made a practice of it, because she thought it was fun. One day the fortune teller predicted that she would have unhappy marriages. She commented to us, "I guess that fortune teller was right, because that is what happened to me." But then we told her that the only reason the fortune teller was right was because she agreed with the predictions. What she agreed upon was a curse. She was shocked at first, but then she agreed with us to break this curse, repent of her past sins, and receive inner healing. When she got hooked up to the promises of God, she saw first-hand the blessings of Christian marriage.

We are not only affected by either the curses or blessings that come from breaking or following the covenant that we have with God in Jesus Christ, but also by what we say or what other people say by the power of the word. While we will elaborate on this in greater detail in a later chapter, we need to touch on this in the context of curses. Many Christians would be horrified to learn that they have been laying curses upon themselves or members of their family or friend by what they say or don't say. Scripture tells us there is power in the word. Death and life are in the power of the tongue (Proverbs 18:21). We can curse people by what we say. The apostle James calls the tongue an unruly evil full of deadly poison whereby we bless God and curse men (See James 3:8-11). That is why Jesus makes such a harsh statement in Matthew 12:35-37:

> The good man out of his good treasure brings forth what is good; and the evil out of his evil treasure brings forth what is evil and I say to you, that every careless word that men shall speak, they shall render account for it in the day of judgment. For by your words, you shall be justified, and by your words, you shall be condemned.

Paul warns the Ephesians in the same manner:

> Let not unwholesome words proceed from your mouth, but only such a word as is good for edification according to the need of the moment, that it may give grace (blessing) to those who hear. (Ephesians 4:29)

In Psalm 109, there is an interesting statement that graphically speaks of how words affect us, be they a curse or a blessing:

> He also loved cursing, so it came to him and he did not delight in blessing, so it was far from him.
>
> But he clothed himself with cursing as with his garment and it entered into his body like water and like oil into his bones.
>
> Let it be to him as a garment with which he covers himself, and a belt with which he constantly girds himself. (vv. 17-19)

In dealing with curses, we need to recognize that the opposite of a curse is a blessing. A blessing involves the creation and promise of something good. Salvation, forgiveness, eternal life, the abundant life, health, and longevity fall within this category. A curse, as we have seen, involves something destructive. It bespeaks evil, injury, sickness, and doom. In the Old Testament, the prophet Balaam was asked by the Moabite, King Balak, to curse the Israelites, but God would not let him (Numbers 22). Joshua put a curse on whoever would rebuilt the city of Jericho (Joshua 6:26). Heil of Bethel in the days of Ahab suffered the consequence of that curse when he rebuilt Jericho. His youngest and the oldest sons died (I Kings 16:34). Curses are used regularly in the occult and pagan world in order to have power over another person. Because there is no forgiveness or salvation, the occult world usually reverses a curse with another curse. Jesus, on the other hand, not only promised and became a blessing for those who would receive Him and obey Him, but also encouraged His disciples to bless those who curse them and pray for those who despitefully use them (Luke 6:28).*

Many people come to us for ministry and they remember vividly that their father or mother said that they would never make it financially or in their marriage. Not surprisingly, they became what their parents said they would be. One beautiful young Christian wife had a difficult time in committing herself to her husband. When we asked her about her early life, she mentioned that her dad wrongfully accused her of consorting sexually with boys. He accused her of being the equivalent of a prostitute. What happened was that in the accusation, he was also cursing her and making it a fulfilled prophecy. Later on in her high school years, she felt almost a compulsion to do the very thing he foreordained for her. In spite of her strict upbringing, she ventured into all kinds of immorality and met her husband, who had the same problems. Both eventually received Christ and felt convicted by the Holy Spirit to get married. But her problem of commitment to her husband wasn't resolved until the curse that her father put on her was broken in the name of Jesus.

Another couple came for ministry and in the course of conversation, the Holy Spirit revealed to me that there was a curse on the husband. The man complained that he failed in every business venture that he entered. With bitterness, he reflected on how his mother was right about not trusting him with money and how he would never

---

*The only place recorded where Jesus cursed anything was when He cursed a fig tree. He cursed it because it did not bear fruit. The result was that it withered and died. He used this curse to demonstrate a point of faith and the power of the word (Mark 11:12-14, 20-23). Nowhere, however, does it say He cursed people.

make it as a businessman. That was it! In terms of our confessions, we are either agreeing with Jesus, the High Priest of our confession, or Satan, who comes to destroy and steal. Parents who are in a position of authority can either allow Satan to curse their children or Jesus to bless them.

Christians not only have the power to break curses, but also are protected from them as they put on the whole armor of God (Ephesians 6:3f). When they stand firm, girded with the girdle of truth (people of integrity), the breastplate of righteousness (no unforgiven sins or unforgiveness), shod with the gospel of peace (no axe to grind, no fear or worry), taking up the shield of faith (no doubt or fear) and the sword which is the word of God (confident trust in the word), they are invincible against Satan's darts. The word of God says, "A curse without a cause does not alight (Proverbs 26:2)" An evangelist friend of mine shared the truth of this word in an incident that happened to him in a midwestern city. While he was speaking at a Full Gospel Businessmen's meeting, some members of a witches' coven tried to break up the meeting. They threatened to put a curse on him, in this case a curse of cancer. He answered and repelled their threats with Holy Spirit boldness. He reminded them that Jesus is Lord of his life. He is the Greater One — greater than he that is in the world, than he that is motivating and ruling them. Because Jesus is the greater one, he had the whole armor of God to protect him. There was no known sin in his life for which he had not asked forgiveness, nor anyone he needed to forgive and so any curse that they put on him would bounce back on them. This boldness left them dumbfounded. One of the witches was so convicted that she received Christ on the spot. The rest left in an array of confusion.

This incident simply demonstrates the authority we have over demonic forces and curses. Satan is a defeated foe. We need to recognize our authority to be delivered

195

from his power (if he has any over us) and break curses that he may put upon us. Like the Israelites who were given the promised land, all authority has been given to us. We need to exercise that authority and possess the land.

Chapter 10

Fellowship and Ministry to the Lord

Many of God's people have tried to do the works of God without understanding that the works of God are only a by-product of our fellowship and ministry to Him. They are interested in the acts of God instead of the God who acts. They have the wrong priority and are put in the impossible place of making a sovereign God a servant of their faith. The common theology of today is so man-centered that it is easy to forget that it is only when we are saturated with the glory and presence of God that we can do anything. Jesus said it succinctly: " . . . without me you can do nothing." He reminded His disciples that He was the vine and they were the branches. They could not bear fruit without Him (John 15:1-8). The Bible further teaches that we are bought with a price. We are, therefore, to glorify God in our bodies and in our spirits which are God's (I Corinthians 6:20). It stands to reason, if we are to be healed and delivered, we need to present our body to Him. Similarly if we need a miracle or healing, we need to be in touch with the miracle worker. The word of God says, "Submit therefore to God; resist the devil and he will flee from you" (James 4:7). Too often we dwell on resisting the devil. But it is only as we do the first part – submit to God and fellowship with Him that we have the power and authority to resist the devil and send him running.

But how do we fellowship with Him and minister to Him? I believe there are three major ways that we accomplish this: prayer, worship, and obedience to His word.

In the Gospels, especially in Luke's account, we see Jesus constantly praying to the Father, seeking to know His will; constantly reminding His disciples that He only does what He sees His Father do. And it's amazing that in spite of all the spectacular miracles (and maybe because of them), the disciples never asked Him how to do miracles. They asked Him how to pray. Perhaps it was because they somehow knew that everything He did and everything that He was had a direct bearing on His communion with the Father through prayer. We all need to recognize that for ourselves.

I believe it was Dwight L. Moody who said, "I have so much to do today I have to spend two hours with the Lord in order to do it." Several men and women of God have echoed this same truth. Prayer is more than the pause that refreshes, it is the energizer, the spiritual gas that keeps God's men and women going. When we work by the power and authority of the Spirit, we can accomplish more in one minute than we can in a whole day, week, or month in the flesh. In a prophecy, the Lord spoke to us in this manner:

> Let the oil of my Spirit move through you lubricating, empowering, cleansing, directing.

That can only come with fellowshipping with the Lord in prayer. The prayer that we are talking about is not the back-against-the-wall prayer life that we sometimes get into when the going gets rough. The prayer life that I am talking about is the constant reporting-for-duty type of prayer that submits to God all that you have, including your ministry. It is also prayer that seeks to understand and know the will of God; and, once knowing and understanding, seeks to please Him and love Him. It is prayer that visits with God, listening and talking with Him. One day as I prayed for direction, guidance and a special breakthrough in the ministry, the Lord responded with these words:

> My son I love you and bless you. I know that you are hungry and eager to do my will, but my will for you is to wait on me. Yes, you have been faithful in the little things. In many ways you have been unselfish. I know you better than you know yourself. I seek obedience and you are rendering my life-giving love to many people who come to you. I, too, am impatient with the world. But there are many factors that you don't know about that make it impossible for me to act in my special way right now. Revival comes when people seek My Face and hope in Me. Rest assured that time is soon.

Seeking His Face, waiting on Him are all terms that speak of our fellowship with Him through prayer. If you read the history of revivals you find that they come about through prayer. It is preparation not only of the harvester's ministry but for God to work in secret upon the people who are to be a part of the harvest. Charles Finney, the great evangelist of the mid 1800's was a man of prayer. He also had as his special intercessor a man called Father Nash. When that man would pray, bars would close and people would come under conviction. They could be found weeping the streets. It was as if God had come down in a cloud.

The presence of God was felt in the town and area for which he was interceding. When it was time for Finney to preach, the harvest was ready. It was like picking ripe fruit. Charles Finney himself confessed:

> Unless I had the experience of prayer, I could do nothing. If even for a day or an hour, I lost the spirit of grace and supplication, I found myself unable to preach with power and efficiency or win souls by personal conviction.[15]

John Hyde, known by his co-workers as Praying Hyde, was a missionary to India. Through the power of prayer, he was instrumental in leading great revivals in the Punjab region. In his everyday walk with God, he prayed that God would give him an opportunity to bring one person a day into His kingdom. Eventually God put it in his heart to pray for two, then three and then four a day and God honored that prayer request as long as he lived.[16]

When a reporter asked Katherine Kuhlmann how she prepared for her miracle services, she said, "I don't prepare, I have to be ready all the time." She was expressing the truth that we have to affirm for ourselves. God calls His people to be ready all the time as they fellowship with Him and seek His face.

Several years ago I was privileged to attend a Billy Graham School of Evangelism. More than anything else, I was impressed by the amount of prayer that went into the ministry. To an outsider it would seem that the Crusade itself was the whole thing. But fully two-thirds of the time was spent in prayerful preparation prior to and as follow-up after the Crusade. Pearl Goode for many years was ap-

[15] Basil Miller, *Charles Finney,* Dimension Books, Bethany Fellowship, Inc., Minneapolis, Minnesota, 1942, p. 40.

[16] Francis McGaw, *Praying Hyde,* Dimension Books, Bethany Fellowship, Inc., Minneapolis, 1970, p. 51.

pointed by God as the primary intercessor for Billy Graham and his ministry. The Lord would provide money for her to follow Billy Graham and his team and she would lock herself up in a motel and pray for revival and the anointing of the message. From the whole experience of the School, I came away with the understanding that God does not anoint organizations or methods so much as He anoints praying people who minister to God.

Fellowship through prayer not only energizes us and provides the power and authority of God to minister, but refocuses our ministry on Him. The Bible says, "Seek ye first the kingdom of God and His righteousness; and all these things will be added unto you" (Matthew 6:33). "These things" can mean ministry as well as provision. When the ministry of Jesus, be it healing, deliverance, witnessing, becomes an end in itself, it becomes an idol to God. You might wonder "Why?" Because without prayer — submitting ourselves, and all that we do for Him — we end up building our own kingdoms and taking the glory to ourselves. God will not share His glory with anyone; no matter how small or how great the ministry, no matter how noble or God-inspired it started out to be.

Our fellowship with God through prayer reminds us that we are His instruments — precious instruments — but His instruments nonetheless, to be used by Him, when and where He wills. My wife was in a Bible Study when she received a word from the Lord which humorously demonstrated this truth.

Oh my people, you are my tools. You can do nothing by yourselves, but only as you let me use you and move in obedience to My command. If I put you on the shelf for a time, stay there. For how can a carpenter use his tools if they are running about in the carpenter's shop? I do not use a chisel to do the work of a saw, nor a hammer that of a plane. You do a poor job at best when you do the work to which I have not called you, and you are unavailable when and where I do need you.

At these words, they all burst into laughter with the picture of all sorts of tools with legs running about trying to be helpful while Jesus was tackling the one He needed just then.

There is another key to fellowshipping with the Lord and that is through worship, more specifically, through worship and praise. The Bible instructs and exhorts us 555 times to worship and praise the Lord. Obviously, this is one of the most important features of our walk with God.

While many people lump praise and worship together, we need to recognize that although they go together, they are distinctly different. Praise is primarily an expression of the soul while worship is an expression of the spirit. Mary expresses this distinction at the time of the Annunciation:

My soul exalts (magnifies, makes great) the Lord, and my spirit has rejoiced in God my Savior. (Luke 1:46-47)

While praise is centered on what God has done or is doing, worship is centered on God Himself. Worship goes beyond praise to appreciation, love, and finally to adoration. It is the release and expressing of our love to God. Jesus remarked to the Samaritan woman that God is Spirit and those who worship Him must worship Him in Spirit and in truth. He went on to stress that this is what God the Father seeks.

Both praise and worship minister to God and prompt Him to release His power. Scripture witnesses to this. While the disciples were in prayer in the upper room, the Holy Spirit fell upon them as tongues of fire. What follows is that they were worshipping and praising the Lord in different languages, and the anointing came upon Peter to preach, with thousands coming to know the Lord. Paul and Silas were imprisoned in Philippi and as they were praising and worshipping the Lord, God added His basso profundo voice in the form of an earthquake and they were set free to witness to the prison guard. As Isaiah was praising and worshipping the Lord, he received his call and the authority to be a prophet for God and minister to His people (Isaiah 6). Young David in praising and worshipping the Lord in the presence of Saul was able to temporarily put to flight the demonic forces that were tormenting the king. King Jehoshaphat prayed to God to intervene on behalf of His people against the onslaught of the Moabites, Ammonites and inhabitants of Mount Seir. The Israelites were greatly outnumbered. As the king humbled himself before the Lord, God answered his prayer request through the prophet Jahaziel. God assured them that the battle was not theirs, but His. All they had to do was go forth and praise the Lord for the victory. They would not even fight, rather they were simply to stand still and watch God win the battle. The outcome of this strategy was that as they praised God, the enemy became confused and destroyed each other. The victory was won through praise and worship (II Chronicles 20:1-30). It is interesting to note that the tribe that led Israel in praises was the tribe of Judah, whose name means "praise." Praise (and worship) needs to come first in our lives as we battle against Satan and fight the good fight of faith.

Many times after a teaching on healing, deliverance or forgiveness, people will be healed and delivered in the act of worshipping and praising God. One frightened man, for example, came for ministry. Among other things, he had a spirit of fear. This spirit, of course, lied to him and told him if he came to us for ministry, he would die. The man was so bound by this fear, it was difficult for him to share with us his other problems, so the Lord prompted us to worship and praise Him. In the act of praise and worship, the man fell to the floor, curled up in a fetal position, and we literally praised the demon out of him.

You might wonder why there is so much power in praising and worshipping the Lord. The answer is that praise and worship directs our attention, and therefore our faith, to the greatness of God and His authority to do all things. David blessed the Lord in the sight of all the assembly with these words:

Blessed art Thou, O Lord God of Israel, forever and ever.

Thine, O Lord, is the greatness and the power and the glory and the victory and the majesty, indeed everything that is in the heavens and earth; thine is the dominion, O Lord, and Thou doest exalt Thyself as Head over all.

Both riches and honor come from Thee, and Thou dost rule over all, and in Thy hands is power and might; and it lies in Thy hand to make great, and to strengthen everyone.

Now, therefore, our God, we thank Thee, and praise Thy glorious Name. (I Chronicles 29:10-13)

In this passage, David calls attention to the fact that praise and worship are rooted in recognition that God is sovereign. He has dominion over all things. It follows then that we can only praise and worship God to the extent that we believe He has control over all the circumstances and events in our lives. Our fellowship with God, through praise and worship, brings both mind and spirit under deep conviction that God is Victor, Saviour, Healer, Deliverer, Provider, our All in All. Because of his deep conviction of the greatness of God, Paul, while he was imprisoned, encouraged the Christians to praise God in all things. Praise and worship, then, is faith in action that says God is in control, regardless of the circumstances.

Praise and worship not only proclaim the greatness of God, but magnify God in us. They draw us into Him and Him into us. We enter His courts with praise (Psalm 100:4).

He inhabits the praises of His people. The psalmist confessed:

> I will bless the Lord at all times. His praise shall continually be in my mouth.
>
> My soul shall make its boast in the Lord; the humble shall hear and rejoice.
>
> O magnify the Lord with me and let us exalt His name together. (Psalm 34:1-3)

Having made this claim, he acknowledges that God delivered him from his fear (v. 4). Praise is a magnifying glass that makes God big in me. Praise takes my eyes off the problem and magnifies Jesus in my life. The Psalmist, depressed with his situation, asks himself, "Why is my soul cast down? Hope in God" (Psalm 43:5). Because he knows that God will come to his rescue, the psalmist vows that he will praise the Lord while he lives (Psalm 146:2). Does this mean even when we are feeling miserable or defeated? Yes. This is when praise becomes a sacrifice — a sacrifice of our feelings, pride, understanding, etc. Praise and worship take us beyond our feelings and circumstances. As an act of will, they remind us that we are to live a life based on faith in God.

Prayer and worship (praise) are two ways of fellowshipping with and ministering to God. But these two steps should lead to the third step which is the most important of all — obedience. If we are to have fellowship with God, we need to be obedient to the promptings of His Holy Spirit and His word. The people of Israel struggled in the wilderness for 40 years. Because of their disobedience, they never entered the Promised Land. King Saul lost not only his authority as king, but also his life because of his disobedience. Eli, the priest of the temple, along with his whole family, was cut off from the priestly office because of disobedience to God. The prophet Amos, as a spokesman for the Lord, reproved the people of Israel for their disobedience. It was not enough for them to go through the perfunctory motions of worshipping God. God wanted them to be obedient to His word. In Ephesians 5:17-18, Paul reproves the church with these remarks:

So then do not be foolish, but understand what the will of the Lord is and do not get drunk with wine for that is dissipation, but be filled with the Spirit.

"Be filled" is a command and in the Greek it has a sense of continuation. So Paul is saying here, "Don't get drunk, but continue to be filled by the Holy Spirit." How do we continue to be filled? Through obedience and our desire to do God's will. In Galatians 5:25, Paul again says the same thing, "If we live in the Spirit, let us walk in the Spirit." The Greek word that he uses for walking has the sense of the military order — hup, two, three, four. By implication he means disciplined obedience. We reach a point in our lives (the sooner the better) when God desires to give us His marching orders and maintain His Lordship over us.

Imagine how impossible it would be if we were in the army and we ignored the commander's instructions on how the battle should be fought. Or better yet, consider a coach of a football team marking the X's and O's on the blackboard and figuring out a game plan to beat the adversary, but certain team members decide to follow their own game plan. They run when they should block and block when they should run. God as the commander-in-chief and Lord of our life has a terrific plan for winning the battle against sin and Satan's schemes. His plan requires disciplined obedience to bring glory to Him. While God may allow young Christians to get away with disobedience and even use rebellious vessels to do His work out of compassion for those who have a need, ultimately, He pulls in the reins. He reminds us, "Who are you working for? Me or you?"

The apostle Peter explains his new-found boldness and anointing before the Sanhedrin with these words, "We are witnesses to these things and so is the Holy Spirit . . . whom God has given to those who obey." We have already stated that the Baptism of the Holy Spirit is received by faith. Is this a contradiction? No, the answer is that faith receives the Holy Spirit, while disciplined obedience maintains it!

David Du Plessis tells the story about an evangelist who would come into a particular town once a year. A certain man came forward to recommit his life and asked to be filled by the Holy Spirit. No sooner did the evangelist leave town than the man continued to be harsh with his wife, cuss his kids, and walk in the same disobedience as before. The second year, once more he was convicted and went forward and asked to be filled by the Holy Spirit, only to backslide the rest of the year. The evangelist came the third year and again the same man came forward only to lapse back into his former ways. Finally, the fourth year, the evangelist came and ministered the Word and the man started to go forward and recommit his life. But his procession was interrupted by a woman in the back row of the church wildly waving her hands. It was the man's wife and she called out, "Preacher, preacher, it's no use. The guy leaks." There are many areas in our lives where we leak, where the living waters leak out of our life and we shorten the hand of God in our lives. The leaks may be caused by spiritual bondage or hurts that we can take authority over, but more often it is a direct result of our disobedience to the word of God and the prompting of the Holy Spirit.

There are many Christians that have sought the Baptism of the Holy Spirit with no interest in being obedient. They have dabbled in it like a person taking up a hobby. They play with it for a while and then they put it away. Paul had their counterparts in many of the early churches. He called them foolish, babes, carnal Christians. To the Roman Church, he gave this reminder:

> Do you not know that when you present yourselves to someone as a slave for obedience, you are slaves to the one whom you obey, either of sin resulting in death, or of obedience resulting in righteousness? (Romans 6:16)

In other words, there is really no grey area in our life. Neither are we masters of ourselves. We are either obedient to God and submit to His will or we are obedient to the devil and submit to his will. That is the only option we have. When Jesus says to His followers, "Come to me ye that are weary and heavy laden and I will give you rest." That sounds nice doesn't it? No obligation, right? Wrong. Because He goes on to explain how we can receive that rest, "Take my yoke upon you and learn from Me, for I am gentle and humble in heart; and you shall find rest for your souls, for My yoke is easy and My load is light" (Matthew 11:28-30). We have replaced the yoke of slavery to Satan and sin with the yoke of obedience to His will. Like it or not, we are called to be slaves, bondservants of the Lord. Ironically enough, it is only as we are obedient bondservants that we will be spiritually free.

What is a bondservant? When Paul was addressing the people of the Roman Empire and calling them to be bondservants to the Lord, they knew exactly what it meant. The Roman Empire, as it expanded and conquered different nations, employed them as slaves to do its labor. Scholars speculate that there must have been upwards of 70 million slaves in the Roman Empire. As slaves, they had no rights.

208

They owned no property. They belonged totally to their masters. Paul is saying the same thing with respect to the Christians. Just like slaves, we have no rights (only promises). We are not our own. We are bought with a price, the shed blood of Jesus Christ. Because of the importance of this role, many of the apostles introduce themselves as bondservants (slaves) and secondly as apostles (See Romans 1:1, Philippians 1:1, Titus 1:1, and Jude 1:1).* As Christians, we need to see our general calling is to be obedient and submissive bondservants. It is only after we are faithful in this calling that we can be responsible for the special high calling which God has for each of His children.

This walking in obedience to the Spirit is not an easy thing. Obedience involves going through God's boot camp where we die to self and rise up to God. In another chapter, we will talk more about this, but with the Baptism of the Holy Spirit comes the Baptism of Fire which begins to purify us and reduce us to obedient bondservants.

One day as I was worshipping and praying, asking the Lord how long I would have to wait for the ministry that He has put on my heart to come to pass, the Lord spoke these words to my wife in the next room:

Comfort him with this, I am preparing him for My use and I will use him mightily as he learns to seek Me first . . . I am

*Paul uses Jesus as the supreme example when he exhorts the Philippian Church to have this same attitude that was in Christ Jesus who although He was equal with God chose to empty Himself of all His glory . . . taking the form of a bondservant . . . becoming obedient to the point of death (Philippians 2:5-8). Because of His obedience, God highly exalted him, bringing glory to His Name (vv. 9-10). While the Old Testament makes a distinction between Jewish bondslaves (those who voluntarily indentured themselves and were released at year of jubilee) and involuntary slaves (who were usually spoils of war), the New Testament writers seem to merge the two understandings.

not slow in my preparation, though it may seem so to him. Even My Son walked with Me in perfect obedience for thirty years before I sent Him forth to minister. Then He accomplished the redemption of My people. Any one who would learn to walk with Me in perfect submission and perfect obedience, will be able to fully accomplish My purpose. Those who run ahead, or try to accomplish someone else's purpose may indeed make a big show, but it will be of wood, hay, and stubble and will be a fiery spectacle to last only for a moment when all things are revealed. I would not have that for him, but fine jewels, carefully cut, polished and set forth in the finest gold and silver settings. Be patient, therefore, as I work in secret yet a little while.

This prophetic word was undoubtedly referring to Paul's admonition in I Corinthians 3:10-15. The quality of our work, whether it is based on the foundation of Jesus Christ and the grace of God can be compared to gold, silver, precious stones, wood, hay, straw. All our work will be judged and tested by fire. The wood, hay, and stubble, which will burn up, will be the work not done in obedience to the Will of God (and therefore, according to His grace). This will be the work done in the flesh, when men try to do the works of God without the power, outside the will of God. Jesus testified to His disciples: "My food is to do the Will of Him who sent Me and to accomplish His words" (see John 4:34). Many times, the Lord has shown us that our good works done in the flesh have gotten in the way of the best works done in obedience to His Spirit.

A good gauge of whether or not we are ministering in obedience to God is whether or not we are at rest and the ministry is effortless. The prophet Isaiah promises, "They that wait on the Lord shall renew their strength; they shall mount up with wings as eagles; they shall run and not be weary; they shall walk and not faint" (Isaiah 40:31). The Sabbath rest that the writer of Hebrews talks about (4:1) is a ministry of obedience first to the Lord, that carries over into the ministry to His people. In Ezekiel 44, we read that because of their disobedience, the Levitical priests were not allowed to minister to the Lord. They were only allowed to minister to the people through the perfunctory ritual. Only the sons of Zadok who were faithful and obedient could come into the Lord's sanctuary and minister to Him. They were given special linen garments. Why? Because they were not to sweat. When we minister in the Lord and to the Lord by His power and in obedience, it is no sweat. Now this doesn't remove the possibility of hardship, or persecution for righteousness sake, but ultimately it is effortless.

We have heard the expression, "I'd rather burn out for the Lord than rust out." When we are truly moving with the approval and anointing of God, we don't have to do either; we simply shine forth. It's not frustrating busy-ness, but spirit-directed fruitfulness.

When the angel Gabriel confronted Mary with the prospect of her being the mother of Jesus, she did not quite comprehend it all and yet she said, "Behold the hand-maid of the Lord. Be it according to Thy Word." This was a confession of complete submission and obedience. With that submission and obedience, the promise of the Lord from the beginning of creation was fulfilled in and through her. In her obedience, she received the Word of God and became one with Him and gave birth to the Son of God. Now as sons and daughters of God, we are to yield our-selves to this same Word and bring forth the fruit and the works of God.

Charles S. Price, who was used mightily in the ministry of healing in the early 1930's and 1940's, speaks to the dilemma of wanting to do or receive the works of God and not being obedient to the will of God:

What use is it to pray when we still withhold our wills from Him who loves us and gave Himself for us. Many have almost screamed themselves into hoarseness and into spiritual and physical exhaustion, importuning and pleading before the throne of Grace and wondering why the answer never comes. They thought that they were waiting for God and all the while, He was waiting for them. They have desired — but have they desired the Will of God? They have asked — but has that asking been born of an operation of the Spirit within?[17]

While Mary was obedient and submitted to what little revelation she had, we who have the full revelation have little or no excuse. Jesus has revealed Himself totally by the witness of His Spirit and His written word. In this respect, Paul encourages us to study the word so that we may be obedient:

Be diligent to present yourself approved to God as a workman who does not need to be ashamed, handling accurately the word of truth. (II Timothy 2:15)

Smith Wigglesworth, another mighty man of God at the close of the 19th century, explained the secret of the power of God in his life along with the compassion of Jesus. He shared that it was instant obedience to the promptings of the Holy Spirit and the Word of God that made him a vessel for God. In this respect, he offered the following advice to young people:

You must be so soaked with the Word of God, you must be so filled with it, that you yourself are a living epistle, known and read by all men. Believers are strong only as the Word of God abides in them. The Word of God is spirit and life to those who receive it in simple faith, and it is a vivifier of

---

[17]Charles S. Price, *Spiritual & Physical Health,* Logos International, Plainfield, N. J., 1972, p. 56.

all who own its sway. Know your book, live it, believe it, and obey it. Hide God's Word in your heart. It will save your soul, quicken your body, and illumine your mind. The Word of God is full and final, infallible, reliable, and up to date, and our attitude towards it must be one of unquestioned obedience.[18]

It is my personal regret that I did not soak myself in the Word earlier in my life. Just as it is easier to train a child in the way he should go earlier in his life, so it easier to train ourselves in obedience to God's Word earlier in life. But regardless of whether we have missed this opportunity or not, we need to study that word, hunger for it, receive it in simple faith, and be obedient to it. Our motivation should always be to please God and fellowship with Him through His Word.

The release of God's power and authority in our life hinges on our ministry and fellowship with Him through prayer, worship (and praise), and obedience to His Word. All three factors unite us with the Source of all ministry — Jesus Himself.

[18]Stanley Howard Frodham, *Smith Wigglesworth, Apostle of Faith,* Gospel Publishing House, Springfield, Missouri, 1972, p. 111.

Use What you Have

One of the most obvious places to start in exercising our authority as believers is to start where we are. I say it is obvious, but in reality there are many Christians who go from conference to conference, crusade to crusade, speaker to speaker, marveling, luxuriating and basking in the light and authority of other well-known Christians. They say within themselves, "If only I had the talent of evangelists like Billy Graham or Morris Cerullo; if only I had the gift of healing like Oral Roberts, then I'd really be able to serve God." They say this little realizing that God wants to use them daily wherever they are. Amazingly, this was a problem even during apostolic times. Peter addresses the Christians in his time and exhorts them to use what gifts they have.

> As each one has received a special gift, employ it in serving
> one another, as good stewards of the manifold grace of God.
> (I Peter 4:10)

In the parable of the talents (Matthew 25:14-30), the servant wasn't punished for having only one talent, but rather

214

for not using it — for burying it.

Some years back, the Lord spoke to a group of people, some of whom were ten-talent and one-talent people, some of whom were mature in their faith and others immature.

> Oh, my children, take each day as it comes. For you are my witnesses each day. Each day you are on my mission. Regard each day as a treasure, for it is my gift to you. Do not worry about tomorrow, for that is my concern. Only be concerned about giving what you have. Each one of you will be called in the coming year. Be aware of my calling and be aware of my mission for you. You feel that some have greater missions than you, but my children, each one of my missions is important. No one is more important. No one is greater than the other in my eyes.

We need to know that the one-talent people are just as precious in the eyes of the Lord as the ten-talent people with a seemingly greater mission.

In the parable of the talents, you'll notice also that those who were faithful to use God's talents increased their talents. In a similar parable of the pounds (Luke 19:12f), the faithful servants who used their master's money were given authority over a number of cities. This same principle applies to exercising the authority and gifts that God has given to each of us. The more we faithfully use His authority and talents, the more God will increase that authority. I have personally witnessed one- or two-talent people who, because of their faithfulness in using what they had, surpassed those who had more talents, but never used them. As they were faithful in the little things, God gave them responsibility and authority to do more.

There are three basic principles that can help us use what we have. The first principle is uniting our faith with God's Word. Whether we are a one-talent or a ten-talent person, we have to start where everyone starts, with God's

Word and our faith. We need to unite our faith with God's Word because that's what God's Word tells us to do.

> Therefore, let us fear lest, while a promise remains of entry to rest, any one of you should seem to have come short of it.
>
> For indeed we have good news preached to us, just as they also (the Israelites); but the word they heard did not profit them because it was not united with faith in those who heard. (Hebrews 4:1-2)

The "rest" that the writer of Hebrews is talking about is the rest that comes with the satisfaction and fulfillment of God's promises. The Israelites who wandered in the wilderness did not receive the promise of God's Word, the land of milk and honey and their rest, because they did not unite their faith with the Word of God. The writer of Hebrews warns the Christians to be careful, lest they lose it, too.

How do you unite faith with God's Word? To begin with, the faith that the Bible talks about is always active. It is your faith that needs to be active. You need to practice using it. Visualize the Word of God as a baseball and your faith as a bat. Your faith needs to be united, needs to connect with the Word of God.

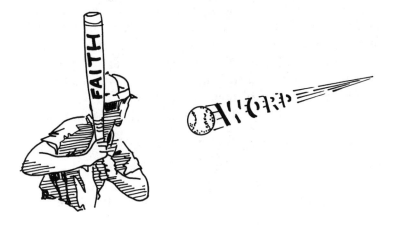

In a baseball game, a person doesn't get home runs by having a bat and a ball. He needs to do something with that bat and ball. He needs to connect the bat with the ball. The same thing is true of our faith and God's Word. Faith needs to connect with God's Word. Unlike a baseball game, God does not throw us curve balls or change-ups, He throws straight balls. He isn't tricky. In fact, He doesn't want us to strike out. On the contrary, He is a rewarder of those who faithfully seek Him. Now, a lot of people get discouraged and strike out, and blame God for their failures. They let Satan tell them that they have no faith, that the situation is hopeless. But Paul reassures us every believer has a portion of God's faith. The only question is, are we faithful in exercising that portion of faith that God has given us? Are we united with His Word? God's Word says to forgive those that trespass against us. Do you obediently exercise your faith to forgive someone who hurts you? That is a faith-builder. God commands us to share the Good News. Do you share the Good News with other people? That's another faith-builder. What happens when you lose something? Do you exercise your faith and ask God to help you find it? Or do you vent your anger and impatience? Most of us are inclined to wait for a spiritual world series and when we fail, we blame God for our lack of faith. Fred Price, pastor of one of the fastest growing churches in California, offers the following words of wisdom:

> You don't wait until the doctor tells you that you are terminal to start using your faith. You don't wait until they fire you off the job to start using your faith. You should be using your faith twenty-four hours a day. Faith is a way of life, not a panic button, to get you out of a problem. In fact, once you learn how to live by faith, you won't have panic crises, because you will "head them off at the pass," as it were, where you ought to be.

I can remember earlier in my walk in the spirit where I could have used that kind of wisdom. I was ministering and praying for a nominal Christian who had cancer. Somehow I had it all pictured in my mind that I was going to believe God for a miracle and as a result he and his whole family were going to come to Christ. Well, I prayed and took up a prayer vigil at his bedside with a couple of friends and God blessed us with His overpowering presence. But a couple days later, the man died, not of cancer, but pneumonia and I thought I'd never recover. I was so low, as the saying goes, that if I had died they'd have to jack me up to bury me. It took me three months to get to the place where I wanted to exercise my faith again. What I had was not faith, but presumption. Yes, I was acting on God's Word. But this plan came from my head rather than from God's Spirit. Undoubtedly, if I bothered to ask, He would have had me lead the man to Christ and then pray with him for his healing. How do I know that? In later years, the Lord referred to this episode in my life and brought to my attention that the Shekinah glory that we felt while kneeling before that man's bed was not only for our benefit, but his. He shared with us that this man, in his comatose state, heard us praying to Jesus for healing. He was able to make his peace with God and receive Jesus as his Lord and Savior, the healer of his soul. Nevertheless, this whole episode demonstrated how flabby and small my faith was. There was another factor that I had not considered. My faith had to contend with unbelief in certain members of the family. If Jesus could do no miracles in His hometown because of unbelief, how could I? So I struck out on God's Word. Was that God's fault? No. God's Word never changes. My faith was simply not strong enough to contend with that size of problem. That's why you and I need to "faith-it" in little things and build our spiritual muscles. Then when the day comes we can hit that home run and gain that promise of His Word.

God allowed me to hit a home run a few years later. The situation was practically the same, the man had cancer all through his system the doctors had given up all hope of recovery. He was a nominal Christian. What I did was lead him to Christ and then share with him the truth of divine healing. Was he willing to put his measure of faith, however small and newborn, on the promises of God's Word and agree with me that God's will would be done in his life as it is in heaven? The man nodded, as tears were streaming from his eyes. I anointed him with oil, and weeks later when he was examined, there was no trace of the cancer. What faith he lacked, I had because the more I practiced uniting my faith with God's Word the more I saw people getting healed in body, mind, and spirit.

Paul encourages us to work out our salvation in fear and trembling (see Phil. 2:12). Just as an athlete works out to perfect his skill, so we need to exercise our faith by uniting it with God's Word to see results. Many times this involves putting feet to our faith, either through confession or acting on it. This is what the ten lepers did when Jesus told them to walk to the temple and show the priest that they were healed. The point is when He said it, they weren't healed. They could have said, "Jesus, you're crazy, we still have leprosy." By faith they had to walk to the temple, believing that they had received and the Bible says as they obeyed His word, as they walked toward the temple, they were healed.

One of the most dramatic illustrations of uniting our faith with God's Word in terms of using what you have is when people receive their tongues as a devotional language. A lot of people initially have difficulty in receiving their tongues because they somehow think the Holy Spirit is going to circumnavigate their voice box and tongue. The truth of the matter is in order for them to receive and express what is already theirs, they need to use their voice and tongue with the belief that the Holy Spirit will provide the words. In faith, they unite their voice and tongue with the Inspired Word of the Holy Spirit and God gives them a new language to praise Him. Again we need to use what we have by continually uniting our faith with God's Word. The Lord gave a special insight to this truth as He spoke to my wife:

> Come, my child, take time with me and I will see that all the necessary things are done. Seize the time, do not let it slip away unnoticed — yet hold it lightly, too, ready to turn loose at my command. Come, feast on my Word (and on my words to you) and grow strong, not fat.

> Yes, it is possible to grow fat even upon my Word, if it is only consumed and stored up, instead of being acted upon in obedience. It is life, health, and strength when it is both eaten and exercised. Most of my people suffer from spiritual starvation, and, like starving people, need to eat and digest my Word to grow strong. But once the strength begins to flow through the body, it requires exercise (obedience) to truly strengthen the one who has been fed. Neither (spiritually) starving Christians nor gluttons are particularly useful to me. I would have you (all my people) eat what is necessary to exercise faith, then go out and do it! The more one exercises, the more he needs to eat, and the more he eats, the more he must exercise. If my Word has lost its savor, often that fact reflects a lack of exercise, while exercise whets the appetite for wholesome food.

A second principle that we need to consider in using what we have is the principle of asking. Jesus said, "You receive not because you ask not." We need to ask God how to invest our talents. We need to ask for the authority of Jesus to be manifested. We need to ask for the gifts of the Holy Spirit. Granted, a few people ask and do not receive simply because they ask with the wrong motives. Scripture confirms this (see James 4:3). But if it is clear in your heart that you want to glorify God and help build up the body of Christ, you will receive the gift and the authority to meet that need. It doesn't matter how far along you are in your walk with God. God will use you to glorify His name and minister to His people. On many occasions, when we are short on staff members to help minister, we resort to using people who have never been used before, usually people who have taken our seminars who want to be used. As we ask for the gifts of the Holy Spirit to work in our lives, inevitably, the person who has never been used before will have a vision, or prophecy, word of knowledge, etc., to minister to the person that has the need. God gives us that authority when we ask for it. On a few occasions, when we ourselves have forgotten to ask, we will go to the Lord and say, "God, what's the matter? Why aren't we making a breakthrough with this person?" And the Lord inevitably says, "You forgot to ask." God knows the need but He will not meet it until we ask. When we want to exercise our authority as a believer for ourselves or others, don't assume anything. Go to the Father and ask. Like the widow who persisted until she received justice from the unjust Judge, we need to persist in asking a just and compassionate God for His gifts and the authority to use them. Jesus said:

Ask and it shall be given to you, seek and you shall find, knock and it shall be opened to you. (Matt. 7:7)

The sense of this in the Greek is continual action. In other words keep on asking and it shall be given unto you; keep on seeking and you shall find; keep·on knocking and it shall be opened to you. When we continually do the above, then God promises the following:

For everyone who asks receives, and he who seeks finds, and to him who knocks it shall be opened. (Matt. 7:8)

The prophet Elisha followed his mentor Elijah where-

221

ever he went. When the time came for his friend to depart in a chariot of fire, he still would not be put off from following him. Finally Elijah asked Elisha if he could do anything for him before he left. And Elisha asked for a double portion of his spirit upon him Upon request, Elisha received Elijah's mantle of authority before he left. If you check with the Biblical account, you will see that while Elijah performed seven miracles, Elisha who asked for a double portion, performed fourteen. Now you might think that Elisha was a bit brash asking for a double portion of Elijah's spirit, but Jesus said the kingdom of heaven suffers violence, – it is forceably entered – and violent men take it by force – seize it for themselves (see Matt. 11:12 and Luke 16:16). Who are the violent men? The men of reckless, abandoned faith who are willing to give their all to Jesus and ask Him for His all to accomplish it.

This type of asking excludes what I call a "worm theology." You know the kind I mean – where we wiggle in the dust with a false sense of humility and say, "I'm so unworthy to be used by God. How can He possibly use me?" Of course, we are unworthy. In and of ourselves, we should eat worms and die; or better yet let the worms eat us and die. But we need to remember as God's children, bought by the shed blood of Jesus Christ, we are made worthy. In Christ, our sins are not only atoned (covered), but remitted (removed). We have the resurrected power and the Spirit of Jesus imputing and imparting His righteousness in us. Besides, as an earthly father, I wouldn't deny my child the chance to please me or minister love to someone else. Neither would our heavenly Father. Many times out of His compassionate heart, He will use immature, sometimes disobedient people to minister healing and deliverance to His hurting people. Check Paul's letters to the Corinthians and Matthew 7:22 and see if this isn't true. All we need to do is ask.

That's what I did one day. I asked the Lord in prayer, "Lord, I want Your authority to be manifested in me so that when I speak or minister in your name, people will know it is not me, but you speaking and ministering." While I was praying this prayer, another brother a mile away had a vision of me with white robes. The next day he shared it with me. My first thought was "Lord, does that mean graduation day? Are you going to take me home soon?" As the man prayed for an interpretation and understanding of that vision, the Lord revealed that it was a robe of authority. The Lord honored my request because I asked.

In the beginning stages of Okontoe's discipleship camp for youth aged 14 to 17, we were a bit hesitant about asking the Lord about their place in the body of Christ. We saw the youth on fire for the Lord, filled with the Holy Spirit. They were eager to serve Him and know where they fit into the body of Christ. As elders of the community we asked, "Lord, dare we ask you where they fit into your body? Do you desire to reveal to them what your plan is for them? What if some should feel left out?" The Lord spoke through an elder in a prophecy and encouraged us to lay hands on them and minister to them. He would reveal to His children exactly where they fit into His body. We started at 10 o'clock in the morning with a break for lunch and supper. The Lord spoke in a chain prophecy for nine hours telling the seventeen youths where they fit into His body and what His plan was for them in the coming year. One or another of the elders would receive a portion of the prophecy and many of the young people would pick it up and be used to minister and reveal to each one how they were to be used by God. "My daughter, I will use you in a minister of helps . . . My son, I anoint your hands to play music and lead my people in worship of Me . . . My daughter, I have a writing ministry for you, you will write children's books . . . " and so on.

It all happened because we dared to ask.

The third principle based on using what you have is the principle of "as freely as you have received, freely give." Jesus spoke these words to His disciples early in their walk with Him. He was commissioning them to be fishers of men, to preach the kingdom of heaven is at hand, heal the sick, raise the dead, and cast out demons, freely receive, freely give (Matt. 10:7-8). As Jesus shared His life with them, ministering healing and deliverance, they were to do likewise. They were to give what they freely received from Jesus. We are, too.

A mother asked her child why she was always falling out of bed and the child responded, "I guess I go to sleep too close to where I get in." You know that has been a problem with all of us somewhere down the line in our spiritual walk. Starting where we are doesn't mean remaining where we are. We either are moving and sharing the blessing of God or we are constantly falling out of grace in our walk with God. As we receive the blessing of God and His gifts, we are to freely give them away. We are called to invest our talents and blessings in others. In addressing the Samaritan woman, Jesus promised, "He that believeth in me, from his innermost being shall flow rivers of living waters (see John 7:38). This means if the living waters, the Holy Spirit, indwells us, we need to be channels for work and blessing, not reservoirs holding the blessing of the living God.

Years ago, I remember reading about an Italian village that had used a thousand-year-old Roman aquaduct for its source of water. In an effort to modernize, they built a new reservoir and piped the water underground to the city. Amazingly, in less than a generation the aquaduct started to fall apart from lack of use. This can happen to us in a spiritual level. When we refuse to share ourselves and be a channel for the living waters, we can quickly dry up and fall apart

The Bible says, "He who sows sparingly, shall reap sparingly; and he who sows bountifully, shall reap bountifully" (II Cor. 9:6). I'm no farmer, but I know enough to know that if you don't plant a seed, you can't expect to reap anything. Paul further adds:

> Now, he who supplies seed to the sower and bread for food, will supply and multiply your seed for sowing and increase the harvest of your righteousness.

> You shall be enriched in everything for all liberality which through us is producing thanksgiving to God,

> For the ministry to this service is not only fully supplying the needs of the saints, but is overflowing through many thanksgivings to God. (II Cor. 9:10-12; see also Luke 6:38)

Notice, as we sow abundantly, the promise is we will be enriched in everything. In the third chapter on witnessing I mentioned how I shared the ministry of Jesus with one man to the point of discipling him and how he in turn freely gave of himself to a pastor who was able to minister to 450 members of his congregation. That is the overflowing capacity that God wants to build into His people whether it be in witnessing, healing, tithing, offering love or forgiveness or what-have-you.

Many times we are waiting to receive overflowing abundance before we will give of it. But this goes against spiritual principles of God's Word. I've never been to the Holy Land, but they tell me the Sea of Galilee is something to behold. There is a special freshness about it as the breezes waft over its surface. This isn't only because of the fond memories that we might have about the Lord ministering around it, but rather because it is based on the principle of freely receive, freely give. In the north end, the sea receives water from the rivers and streams that come from the mountains and at the south end, it flows out again to form the Jordan River. The Dead Sea, on the other hand, receives from the Jordan River and other waters. There is no outlet and because of that, they tell me it is brackish and stagnant. In fact, you can smell it before you see it. In a few words, it stinks to high heaven. Now to be sure, we are called to be the fragrance of Christ, but this is altogether different than being stagnant in our Christian walk. No, the secret of Christian growth is in sharing what God has done for us. As we freely receive from God, we are called to freely give.

King Solomon, expressing the wisdom of God, shared this centuries ago:

> There is one who scatters yet increases all the more, and there is one who withholds what is justly due, but it results only in want. The generous man will be prosperous and he who waters will himself be watered. (Prov. 11:24-25)

If we want to be bankrupt in the Lord, all we have to do is hold on to what we have. If we want to be rich in godly qualities, we need to share.

Many times, we feel we may have hardly anything to offer. Just like that one-talent man, many times we emotionally and spiritually don't feel that we have it within us to share anything. We feel totally inadequate. That is the time when we need to sacrificially give of ourselves and draw on the supernatural strength of God, who helps us in our weakness. We need to start to freely give before we freely receive. For example, if we want more love in our lives, we need to offer love as a faith offering to God. If we want more encouragement in our life, we need to offer encouragement as a faith offering to God. If we want more provision, we need to offer what we have as a faith offering to God. If we want more joy in our lives, we need to offer joy to other people and so on. Sometimes we will not be giving out of our abundance, but out of our need.

Several years ago, I read a magazine article and since

then I have heard many people refer to this story. The article was entitled, "How I learned to Love My Husband." The woman who wrote the article related how she rushed into an early marriage just to get out of an unpleasant home situation. When the newness of the marriage wore off, she found out how immature, unloving and selfish both she and her husband were. The upshot of it was that she discovered she no longer loved him, but somehow she knew that divorce wasn't the answer. Knowingly or unknowingly, she started seeding love by freely offering it to her husband — a love offering she didn't emotionally have. Without being a hypocrite, she began to act as if she did love her husband, undoubtedly trusting and expecting God to give her that love. She did little things like going to the trouble of cooking foods he especially liked. She began to keep house to please him and dress to please him. She expressed herself toward him in the most loving way she could. Pretty soon he started to respond to that love. Some years later, the reality of the love bore fruit when one of her teenage sons blurted out, "Mom, all the kids say we sure are lucky because you and dad like each other so much." By faith she had constructed the outward form of love and God filled it in with the real thing. By faith, she drew on the love of God for her and her husband. It began when she freely gave of herself, of something she thought she didn't have. She had to freely give before she even received.

We need to use what we have (and sometimes even things we don't think we have). We release and increase God's power in our lives as we unite our faith with His Word, continually asking Him for His daily grace, e.g., gifts, power, authority. And as we receive that grace, we freely offer it to others.

Chapter 12

Speak the Creative Word —
The Word of Faith

In the beginning was the Word, and the Word was with God,
and the Word was God. He was in the beginning with God.
All things came into being through Him; and apart from Him
nothing came into being that has come into being. In Him
was life; and the life was the light of men. (John 1:1-4)

The apostle John has begun his gospel by describing
Jesus as the Word. As the Word, he was pre-existent with
the Godhead. When God spoke things into existence, Jesus
as the Word created it. But His creation did not end there.
When He incarnated Himself in the world, He continued
to create by speaking life to those dead in their sins. He
revealed God's love for them and His divine intention to
make them into new creatures. Before He ascended to the
Father, He breathed upon them the Holy Spirit, who, He assured them, would bring to remembrance all things and glorify
and bear witness to His (creative) Word in every believer.

Jesus is still creating today. He began His new creation in us when we heard the Word and confessed it. In Romans 10:8-10 we read:

> The Word is near you in your mouth and in your heart. That is, the word of faith which we are preaching, that if you confess with your mouth Jesus as Lord, and believe in your heart that God raised Him from the dead, you shall be saved; for with the heart man believes, resulting in righteousness, and with the mouth he confesses, resulting in salvation.

Our confession of Jesus as Lord and Savior allows Jesus, the Creative Word, to make us sons and daughters of His kingdom. We become new creatures in Jesus Christ. Jesus extends His creation through our confession. Through our confession, we become an integral part of His creation and His creative Word.

The word "confession" means saying the same thing. It means we are agreeing with God's Word and His ultimate intention. We are testifying to the promises made available to us when Jesus died on the cross. In confessing Jesus as our Savior and Lord, we are, for example, testifying and agreeing with God that we have fallen short of the glory of God. When we confess our sins, we are agreeing with God that we need His forgiveness and His cleansing. That is what it says in I John 1:9.

> If we confess our sins, He is faithful and just to forgive us our sins and to cleanse us of all unrighteousness.

The writer of Hebrews, therefore, encourages us to hold fast to our confession without wavering because God is faithful to His promises (Hebrews 10:23, see also Hebrews 4:14).

But confession isn't only agreeing with God's Word, the Bible says Jesus is the High Priest of our confession. Jesus as the Living Word intercedes on our behalf before the Father to lay claim to our confession (Hebrews 3:1). As the Living Word, He honors and vouches for the written word. In a sense, it is quite similar to the situation I found myself in on a trip. While I was visiting my father- and mother-in-law in Tucson, I had a couple of personal checks to cash (otherwise, I wouldn't have been able to get home). My mother-in-law took me to her bank and vouched for me. She assured the banker I was a man of integrity and the checks I had would be covered by the money I had in my bank. Now, Jesus as the High Priest of our confession not only vouches for our integrity but also the integrity of His Word before the Father. He can lay claim to us because we are saved and are made righteous with His righteousness. We can also lay claim to His Word because all the promises of His Word have been appropriated by His death on the cross. The Bible says He became poor that we may be rich. All the promises of His Word are stored in our heavenly bank account. They not only include salvation and forgiveness (the greatest miracle of all), but total provision for the total person (healing, deliverance, financial provision, etc.)

The Word, for example says "my God shall supply all your needs according to His riches in glory by Christ Jesus"(Philippians 4:19). When the Lord was leading me into a life of faith living without any guaranteed salaries, this passage became a very important promise that I needed to confess. As I confessed His total provision, God answered. Even before I had any established ministry, God demonstrated His love and provision by touching the heart of a person (a widow, of all people), who provided us with $5,000 on which to live while He told us to wait on Him and trust Him. Incidents like that not only increased my faith, but humbled me. From the very beginning, God made sure I knew that it wasn't my ministry to Him that would provide for my needs. It was He and He alone that

230

was my provider. In later years, the Lord spoke to us as a body about this. He said that when we would look to anyone or anything other than Him (ministry included) as a source of supply, that this was idolatry and an offense towards Him. Our eyes needed to be focused on Him and the promises of His Word. My wife, Grace, has provided some pretty funny menus now and then, but God has been more faithful to His promises than I have been in confessing them.

One day my wife and I were looking at tents at a shopping center. We were planning to go camping during the summer. On many occasions, we had borrowed a friend's tent and we were planning to do so again. So we were just looking and our eyes fell on a beautiful tent. It had all the features one could want for a family of four, but then we looked at the price. It was $200. Now that may not seem like a lot to some people, but it was a lot for us. We had always prided ourselves in our frugality and that price seemed too much; we didn't have the money anyway. Besides, we knew the difference between wants and needs, and this didn't seem to fall under the category of a need, so we forgot about it When I got home I checked to see if we could borrow the tent from my friend. To my surprise and disappointment, he was planning to use it the same time we were. There we were without a tent, and so I said, "Grace, I believe God wants us to get a tent. When some money comes in the mail, or whatever, I'm going to take it and buy a tent." I no sooner spoke this than the phone rang. The caller, a beautiful sister in the Lord said, "Denis, I'm sending you $200 to buy a tent for camping." That was just the exact amount we needed to buy that tent we were looking at. Since the person designated the check for the tent, in good conscience I couldn't buy something cheaper and pocket the rest for living expenses.

God has shown us in incidents such as these that He

not only wanted to meet our needs, but even go beyond the need. By faith we need to receive His lavish generosity. Jesus expressed this lavish abundance when He fed the 5,000. He not only met their need, but even went beyond their need. There were 12 baskets of food left over. While Jesus wants us to be content in all situations, His greatest desire is for us to confess and believe that He is the rewarder of those who diligently seek Him. We are to delight in Him and He will give us the desires of our heart (Psalm 37:4). Somehow the distinction between wants and needs no longer seems valid when our greatest desire is to please Him and He us.

Once we establish in our hearts that Jesus is the Creative Word, that He is still creating today by His Holy Spirit, our confession based on the promises of His Word becomes a dynamic, cooperative adventure with Him. We are never put in the impossible position of bending the arm of God to do our will. We simply know that we know, that we know, that it is His will to create through our confession. Jesus has purposely limited Himself to working through His body. He only acts as we agree on His Word and recognize Him as High Priest of our confession.

Our confession also involves another element. The element of faith. If I were to write this in terms of a mathematical equation it would look something like the following:

$$\frac{\text{FAITH} + \text{CONFESSION}}{\text{PROMISES OF GOD'S WORD}} = \text{CREATIVE WORD}$$

Both faith and confession based on God's Word equals the Creative Word.

Let me interject here that spiritual principles (truths) involving faith are not formulas. Spiritual principles only work as we fellowship with and relate to God, the source and medium for all faith (see chapter 10). I mention this because too many immature Christians (instead of relating and pressing on to God) reduce dynamic Biblical principles to sterile formulas. When the formulas fail, they become disillusioned with God. They wonder why it doesn't work. It does not work because the faith is not inspired by the Holy Spirit.

We have already defined faith in earlier chapters. We have established that faith is something that we live by, walk by and are justified by. It is not mental assent, but rather a gift from God. Each person has a measure of it. It is something quite different from hope, and yet quite related. We can place our hope in the Second Coming of Jesus and our reign with Him in glory. We can even place our hope in the promises of God made available to us as believers. But hope by itself will not make these promises available to us. Only faith can do it. Hope can motivate us to exercise our faith. There is hope, for example, in the universal words, "Jesus Saves,' or "Jesus Heals," or "Jesus Provides," or "Jesus Delivers." But faith motivated by that hope appropriates these promises and turns them into the Rhema Word — the word for me. Faith receives it now. Faith says, "I have it now." When I heard the message of Jesus Christ, I didn't hope to be saved someday. No, I received it right then and there and confessed it with my mouth. The Word of God says, "now is the day of salvation."

But if faith is for now, how does it come to us? The Bible says, "Faith comes by hearing and hearing by the Word of Christ" (Romans 10:17). When I heard the proclamation of the word of salvation, I made a confession of Jesus as my Lord and Savior — I heard for myself (that was the natural part); and the gift of faith became activated through the Holy Spirit (that was the supernatural part) so that I could believe in my heart (my spirit). Faith, therefore, is activated by hearing and speaking God's Word. The

233

hearing comes through proclamation, and my confession simply personalizes that proclamation in my own hearing. As a nonbeliever, this faith did not originate within me. It was a gift of God (see Ephesians 2:8). It accompanied the Word and the Holy Spirit. As a believer, however, faith resides in my regenerated spirit because the Holy Spirit now resides in it. As I speak (confess) God's word after Him, agreeing with His promises, and personalize this in my own hearing, faith acts within my spirit to produce the works of God through Jesus, the Creative Word. Even though the Word of God says every believer has a measure of faith, faith is still a gift of God. Why? Because it is the faith of God. It isn't ours to possess, but rather ours to express and confess. Faith is the Holy Spirit bearing witness to Jesus, the Creative Word in our spirit. That is why we don't base faith on healing, salvation, or deliverance. Rather we base faith on Jesus who is the Healer, Savior and Deliverer.

At the same time, it can rightly be called our faith because our spirit is the container for the Holy Spirit who is bearing witness to the Creative Word, and we through our will and confession can activate that gift of faith. We can even increase it. In II Thessalonians 1:3, Paul thanks the Lord because he saw the faith of the Christians enlarged. The more we confess our faith — the faith of God — the more our faith increases. Just as a body builder exercises to build up his strength and muscles, and the scholar builds up his mind through study, so the human spirit can be strengthened and enlarged and have the capacity to contain more faith (the God-type of faith) through continued confession of God's Word.

When we minister inner healing to people, fully half to two thirds of the time is spent getting people to know and accept what God's Word says for their particular situation and building up their faith to confess God's Word and take authority over their problem. We encourage them to make

234

positive confessions of God's Word, because His Word encourages us to hold fast to our confession (see Hebrews 4:14). Our faith and authority can only keep pace with our confession and acting on God's Word. In face of worry and anxiety, for example, we need to see that much of this arises out of doubting God's Lordship over our life. This is a sin against God and we need to repent of that and ask God's forgiveness. Then we need to confess that God is our refuge and strength, an ever present help in trouble. The peace of God which surpasses all comprehension shall guard our minds in Christ Jesus (Phil. 4:7). This allows Jesus, the Living Word, to become the high priest of our confession and seek the throne of grace for peace before the Father. By faith, our confessions establish His will on earth (the physical realm) as it is in heaven (the spiritual realm).

The truth of how faith can be enlarged was never more evident than when we ministered to one particular man. He was 58 years old, an alcoholic, with a history of occult involvement. His mother and his father, long since dead, were spiritual mediums. He had a wild look about him like an animal about to be trapped. We started with prayer and thanked God for bringing this man here. We confessed that there was no condemnation in Christ Jesus and that Jesus had brought this man to us to receive His love and righteousness. We invited Jesus to monitor our conversation and be the counselor and use us as his spiritual vessels. We asked that the gifts of the Holy Spirit would be manifested through us all so that we could effectively minister to this loved one. After the prayer, he seemed to be more settled. As we talked to this man, we saw that he wasn't a Christian. So we shared the Gospel of Jesus Christ with him and led him in a sinner's prayer and confession of Jesus Christ as his Lord and Savior. We proceeded to explain his authority as a believer and then he started to get more hopeful. Then we

235

asked him to forgive people that had hurt him in the past. Through words of knowledge, the Lord revealed to us the cords and spiritual forces of alcoholism, rejection, fear of rejection, anger, and rebellion, the occult, fear, confusion, etc., that were binding him. When we started to talk about the occult activity in his life, he suddenly started to get rigid, his face grew contorted and he said that he was getting cold inside. Then a demon spoke in a different voice from his and said, "I'm not coming out of him. He's mine." I commanded the demon in the name of Jesus be quiet. Addressing the man, I encouraged him to confess God's words, "Greater is He that is in me than he that is in the world" (I John 4:4). "Satan, I bind you now in the name of Jesus and I refuse your plan for my life which can only destroy. I choose God's plan. I am protected by the blood of Jesus." He no sooner confessed this than his whole countenance changed from one of fear to that of peace.

The demons had to obey his faith-filled confession. When it came time for him to take authority over these demonic things in his life, he became confident in the power of Jesus to set him free. In the name of Jesus, he cut the cords of iniquity that had bound him and his family and renounced these spirits that had used them to oppress him. There were no manifestations, no fight. With him, we had confessed that we were more than conquerors through Jesus who loved us. And because of his feelings of rejection, we had him confess positive statements of Jesus' love for him. Together we asked Jesus that the Holy Spirit would take over every area of his life producing fruit. Together we confessed healing for body, soul, and spirit. We anointed him with oil for the healing of his memories and wounded (human) spirit, and the man lit up like a Christmas tree. The promise of Jesus, "I have come that your joy may be full," became a reality for him. He said, "I feel so clean inside and so light." And then he started laughing and praising the Lord. Faith upon faith came to that man as he exercised his authority as a believer and confessed the truth of God's Word. His confession turned him from a demon-possessed man to a God-possessed man. Truly as scripture says, "God watches over His Word to perform it" (Jeremiah 1:12).

The Bible says that without faith it is impossible to please God (Hebrews 11:6). Therefore, we are encouraged to fight the good fight of faith. But many times, as Charles Capp has observed, the fight is lost about one inch below the nose.[19] Many people wonder why they don't receive healing, provision, peace of mind, or any of the other promises of God. And the answer is in what they say. Most of the things they say are not faith-filled words based on God's Word. They are, rather, words of doubt, unbelief, defeat, fear, etc. In the very deepest sense, we are what we confess to be. And if our words are not faith-filled, they can only lead to defeat.

Many people have experienced the frustration of praying the prayer of faith with someone for healing and seeing him immediately express his doubt and confess his fear about not being healed, thus nullifying the prayers. The doubt and fear, of course, were based on their circumstances; in this case, the symptoms of the disease. The natural tendency would be to say "when the symptoms go away, then I'll believe." But that is not the faith of God. The faith of God believes before it sees. That's what it says in Mark 11:24:

[19]Charles Capp, *The Tongue, A Creative Force*, Harrison House, Tulsa, OK 24135, 1976, p. 58.

237

> Therefore, I say to you, all things for which you ask, believe that you have received, and they shall be granted you.

We are called to fight the good fight of faith. A fight isn't a passive thing. We need to know that for each step of faith we take, we have to fight three things: 1) the world (circumstances), 2) the flesh (feelings), and 3) the devil. If we are passive and put up no fight of faith, our only recourse is to look at the bigness of the problem, instead of the bigness of God. When we keep our eyes on the problem, the devil will use the problems and feelings to defeat us and cast doubt on God's Word. Let me hasten to say here that faith in God's Word does not deny the reality of our problem (as do Christian Science and many eastern religions) but refuses to accept the finality of the problem.

I'm still learning this for myself, but God has shown me that the Word of God may be compared to a sword (Ephesians 6:17). When combined with faith (the shield), it is the only offensive weapon we have. Faith based on God's Word not only fights off Satan, but is able to cut through our feelings (a part of the soul) to the spirit (see Ephesians 6:13f. and Hebrews 4:12). Faith based on the Word of God also raises our eyes from the circumstances and sets our mind on the things (promises) above (Col. 3:2). But faith based on God's Word only becomes activated as we confess the promises of God's Word.

This is precisely what I did when I claimed healing for my bursitus and sinusitis. God's Word says, "By His stripes we were healed" (I Peter 2:24). Therefore, I am healed. I was always fearful of vain repetition until the Lord showed me how to meditate on His promises by personalizing them and thanking Him for them. As I held on to that confession by thanking Him for it (Heb. 4:14), I let the Word of Christ richly dwell in me (see Col. 3:16). As I let the Word of Christ richly dwell in me, I was able to put my

238

thoughts into captivity to Jesus (II Cor. 10:5). The end result was that Jesus, as the Creative Word, healed me. Jesus said, "The words that I speak are spirit and life" (John 6:63).

Because faith and confession are so important in our life, is it any wonder that Jesus made some of the hardest statements on this subject? In addressing the Pharisees, He said:

> You brood of vipers, how can you, being evil, speak what is good. For the mouth speaks out of that which fills the heart.
>
> The good man, out of his good treasures, brings forth what is good; and the evil man out of his evil treasures, brings forth what is evil.
>
> Words that men shall speak, they shall render account for them in the day of judgment.
>
> For by your words, you shall be justified and by your words, you shall be condemned (Matthew 12:34-36).

That is a hard saying. But if we understand that by our words (confession) we can deny Jesus as our high priest and the Creative Word (that brings life), then it becomes a serious matter. There is such a thing as a wrong confession. A wrong confession is not only an expression of lack of faith, defeat and failure, but also an affirmation of Satan's supremacy in our life.

While we were ministering at a full gospel meeting, a man gave his testimony to the above fact. After undergoing much defeat in his Christian walk, God spoke to him and explained his problem in the context of Matt. 18:19, which says:

> Again I say to you, that if two of you agree on earth concerning anything that they may ask, it shall be done for them by My Father, Who is in heaven.

The Lord, speaking to him gently, reproved him for his

239

grumbling and negative confessions. Jesus revealed to him that the failures he had in his finances, personal relationships, and even in health were due to his grumbling and his confession of defeat. It didn't matter how many people he had praying with him, agreeing with him for victory in his life. By his words, he had shortened God's hand and prevented Him from opening up the windows of heaven. He was in perfect harmony with the devil, who is a liar and comes to destroy and render God's Word as false. This so shocked the man that he repented of his unbelief and grumbling. He asked God to help him guard his tongue. This was in keeping with what King David says:

> I said I will guard my way that I may not sin with my tongue.
> I will guard my mouth as with a muzzle (Ps. 39:2).

> Set a guard, O Lord, over my mouth, keep watch over the door of my lips (Ps. 141:3).

This man concluded his testimony by saying that gradually as he started to affirm God's Word for himself, God started blessing his business and healed him of his arthritis. The whole atmosphere in his family life changed. He no longer felt the frustration and tension in his relationship with his family and friends.

King Solomon, with the anointing of God's wisdom, understood the power of words. Consider the following passages:

> He who guards his mouth and tongue, guards his soul from trouble (Proverbs 21:23).

> With the fruit of a man's mouth, his stomach will be satisfied; he will be satisfied with the product of his lips. Death and life are in the power of the tongue, and those who love it will eat its fruit (Proverbs 18:20-21).

> The one who guards his mouth preserves his life. The one who opens wide his lips, comes to ruin (Proverbs 13:3).

240

> Pleasant words are a honeycomb, sweet to the soul and healing to the bones (Proverbs 16:24).

Because of the power of the tongue, the apostle James even goes so far as to define true religion on the basis of what we say:

> If anyone thinks himself to be religious and yet doesn't bridle his tongue, but deceives his own heart, this man's religion is worthless (James 1:26; see also James 3:1-12; I Tim. 6:20; II Tim. 1:13; II Tim. 2:16).

In the book of Numbers 13:1-14:39, there is a good illustration of what happens when we choose to confess and believe God's promises or choose not to. Moses had led his people out of Egypt. They were camped in the wilderness of Paran. The Lord counseled Moses to spy out the land of Canaan with the promise that He would give it to His people. The spies were sent out and they saw the promised land and the enemy they would have to fight. When they returned, they gave two reports. One was a negative or bad report, and the other was a good report. Why was one report bad? Answer: because they didn't take into consideration God's promise of the land. They looked at the enemy instead of God and took the counsel of their fears. They confessed defeat. They said the enemy was too strong for them, the enemy were giants and compared to them they were like grasshoppers. When the rest of the congregation heard this, they wished that they had never left Egypt. They said, "We might as well have died in the wilderness." And that is what happened. The whole generation died in the wilderness and never received the promise.

Let's take a look at your situation. What are the giants in your life? Sickness? Psychological problems? Finances? What is preventing you from getting to the promised land? Maybe your confession needs to line up with God's Word and His promises. That is what made Caleb and Joshua's report a good report.

241

Caleb quieted the people down and tried to allay their fears by giving a good report. He told them, "Let's go and take it. We'll overcome the adversary." But the people, shaking in their boots, wanted a new leader to take them back to the fleshpots of Egypt. Undaunted, Caleb and Joshua stood up to the crowd and made a beautiful confession of faith. They confessed that God was going to bring them into this land. "He'll give it to us. Don't rebel against God. Don't fear the people of the Land."

Both Caleb and Joshua had seen the same giants as the ones who gave the bad report. What was the difference? Did they have rocks in their heads? No, but they were about to have rocks thrown at their heads. When the people heard their confession, they wanted to stone them to death. The big difference between Caleb and Joshua, and those who gave the bad report was that Caleb and Joshua had the Word of God in their hearts. They confessed and believed that God would give the victory over the giants. Because of their good report and confession of faith, Caleb and Joshua were the only ones to make it to the promised land.

God has all kinds of promises for His children. Like Caleb and Joshua, we need to give a good report and line up our confession with the promises of God's Word; and then let Jesus, the Creative Word, make it a reality for us.

Chapter 13

Be in Harmony and in Order
Part I — Under Authority

Most of us have been to a concert. Before the concert
starts, the instrumentalists try to get on key. At first, you
hear a lot of discordant notes as they try to get in the same
key. But then in no time at all the instruments are in
harmony and they are ready to play a beautiful symphony.
God, the Father, is trying to create beautiful harmony
and unity in His family and in His church. We need to be
united in the key of J — JESUS. Harmony within the body
of Christ is the major key to God's creative power working
in our lives. Harmony is the necessary ingredient in exercising our authority as believers.

Jesus, Himself, calls attention to this truth in Matthew 18:19:

> Again I say to you, that if two of you agree on earth about anything that they may ask, it shall be done for them by My Father in heaven.

What does the above passage really mean? Does it mean that if my wife and I agree that John Doe is to be healed, God will heal him? I used to think that until I read this passage in the Greek. In the Greek, the word "agree" is rendered "symphonedzein" from which we get the word symphony or harmony. And so if we were to translate this passage literally, it would read as follows:

> If any two of you would harmonize together or together make a symphony about anything and everything, whatever you shall ask, it will come to pass and be done for you by My Father in heaven.

This means it is not enough for me to simply agree with my wife that John Doe needs healing. What Jesus is saying here is that my wife and I must first of all be in harmony with each other and with God relationally. In other words, my wife and I not only need to agree about healing for John Doe, but we need to be in harmony with each other and God's Word as we agree for His healing. Jesus, in the sermon on the mount, stressed that the vertical relationship that a person has with God is directly related to his horizontal relationship with this fellow man. Before a person lays his gift on the altar, be it a thank offering, a sin offering or even a prayer request, he is supposed to be reconciled, in harmony with his fellow man (Matthew 5:23-24).

Before He went to the cross, Jesus' last prayer request was that His disciples would be one as He was one with the Father (John 17:20-22). Many people want to do the works of God. They want to exercise their authority as believers. But they somehow knowingly or unknowingly shorten the hand of God by the disharmony in their lives.

The truth of these passages came crashing on me when I ministered to a particular woman at a Full Gospel Businessmen's meeting in Iowa City. She came forward after the regular meeting and asked me to pray with her for a friend that needed healing. She wanted to be a proxy for her friend. I replied that I'd be glad to pray with her and lay hands on her. I started praying with her, but I couldn't get anything out of my mouth. I felt like I had cotton in my mouth, or had eaten salted peanuts all day long. Then I heard the still small voice of the Holy Spirit speak to me, "Ask her how she's getting along with her husband." I said, "Before I pray (I couldn't pray anyway), could you tell me how you are getting along with your husband?"

She stared at me and for a moment she looked like she wanted to bash my face in. She was big enough to do it. In a loud angry voice, she shouted, "What's that got to do with praying for my friend?" Hesitatingly, I told her I didn't know, but the Lord seemed to be telling me to ask her that question. I started to sweat and get uncomfortable as I watched people staring at us. But after what seemed to me to be an interminably long time, she started to melt. The Holy Spirit was convicting her. In a sad and halting voice, she blurted out, "Well, we are not getting along at all." Just then, her husband had walked up to her side. As I recall, he was a pretty thin fellow, as thin as she was wide. We went off into another room and I encouraged them both to air their hurts and difference and be reconciled. As they started talking with each other and dealing with their rejection of each other, God began to heal their relationship. The Holy Spirit convicted this man that he should love his wife as his own body. He had neglected her and she compensated for that neglect by over eating. After they forgave each other, they hugged and kissed each other. Then the woman shared with me that they were celebrating their thirty-fourth anniversary. I commented that this was a great way to celebrate their anniversary — reconciled and forgiven. They both nodded and the woman asked if I would now pray for her friend's healing. I laid hands on her and the words inspired by the Holy Spirit just poured out of my mouth, like a gushing artesian stream. I never saw that couple again, but I know God honored that prayer. I also realized from this incident that God could not use her as a vessel for healing until she was in harmony with her husband.

God won't use us until we are reconciled and choose to forgive people that have hurt us. He will not honor the promise of Matthew 18:19 until we are completely reconciled with Him and our fellow men. God's creative power works in harmony. Just as in an orchestra, we may be different instruments, we may have many different talents, but God wants to produce a symphony of renewal and growth and healing to His people. He wants to answer our prayers and meet our needs and use us to meet the needs of the world. But this can only happen when we have peace and harmony in Jesus Christ.

Let's take a look at the results of harmony in the early church. In Acts 1:14, we read that all of the disciples were together in full agreement, devoting themselves to prayer. What was the result of these unified prayers and unified hearts? In the second chapter of Acts, it says suddenly there came a sound from heaven as a rushing mighty wind and they were all filled with the Holy Spirit. What happened? The miracle of Pentecost came to them. It came to them because they were unified in prayer. Further on we read that they continued daily with one accord and what happened? Peter came upon a lame man and scripture says he took him by the right hand and lifted him up and immediately his feet and ankle bones received strength (Acts 3:7). In the unity of God's spirit, a miracle of healing

246

took place. In Acts 2:42-44, it says they were all in one accord and immediately following this it says believers were added to the Lord day by day. In the unity and harmony of God's spirit, revival broke out.

God wants these same things to happen in our church family and in the world. The only condition is that we be in perfect harmony with Him and our fellow Christians.

But along with harmony, there needs to be order. By order, I mean being under authority. In the Gospel of Luke (7:1-10), we see this is an essential ingredient for releasing the faith of God in our lives. Jesus had traveled to Capernaum. A centurion asked the Jewish elders to contact Jesus to see if He would come and save the life of his slave who was sick and at the point of death. The elders vouched for the centurion and shared with Jesus that he was friendly to the Jewish nation and that he was responsible for the building of the synagogue. (Genesis 12:3 promises that those who bless the Jewish nation will be blessed by God. Jesus fulfilled that promise.) So Jesus proceeded towards the centurion's house only to be intercepted by the centurion's friends. They relayed to Jesus the centurion's message. And this is the message that I would like to focus on.

> Lord do not trouble yourself further, for I am not fit for You to come under my roof, for this reason I did not even consider myself worthy to come to You, but just say the word and my servant will be healed. For indeed, I am a man "under authority with soldiers under me; and I say to this one, "Go!" and he goes and to another, "Come!" and he comes and to my slave, "Do this." and he does it.

When Jesus heard this message, scripture tells us that He marvelled at the faith of the centurion. Because of that faith, the servant was healed. The centurion had a faith which Jesus said was without parallel in all of Israel. Why is that? Because faith is rooted in authority. The centurion recognized the authority of Jesus because he himself was a man under authority with authority. He was a delegated authority under Caesar with authority to command officers and slaves under him. By faith he recognized that Jesus in His humanity had the authority of God to exercise His healing power. His faith honored and submitted to that authority. While faith comes by hearing and hearing by the Word of God, it is released with great power when our lives are in order and under authority. Simply put, we only have authority when we are under authority. To put it another way, in order to be submitted to God, we need to be submitted to His delegated authorities.

Many people are trying to exercise the power and authority of Jesus without being fully under Jesus' authority or His delegated authorities. Because of this, their faith is not only hindered, but God's power is diffused and short circuited. The Bible compares our walk with God to a race that God has set before us. What are the variables that enter into a race? Well, there is the condition of the track for one. This variable affects all the runners equally whether the track is good or bad. All things being equal, there remain just three other factors to be considered that determine whether the contestant is to win or lose: 1) the ability of the runner; 2) the physical condition of the runner; and 3) his mental attitude. These three all play a part in winning a race. In the spiritual realm, although we are not in competition with each other, there are similar conditions. Some people have more talent than others and the Bible recognizes that (e.g., the parable of the pounds in Luke 19:13f and the talents in Matthew 25:14f). But talent does not matter as much as our spiritual condition and mental attitude. How many talented people have you known in the area of athletics, or business, or ministry who have wasted their talents because they have refused to get their lives in order and be submitted to the discipline of authority (be it a coach or a boss). Whatever success they had, if at all, was short-lived (or at the expense of their friends or families) because of their refusal to be under God's authority or His earthly representatives.

Now this might sound strange to people, even Christian people, who conceive God's world as being democratic. This is even more foreign and comes as more of a shock to some who are caught up in the liberation theology of today and the "rights movement" (be it children's rights, gay rights, grey rights, women's rights, etc.), but God's order is not democratic, it is theocractic and it is hierarchical.* He is ultimately the head and as the head, He has delegated leadership over His creation. In fact, Paul in Romans 1:18ff tells us that even natural man has no excuse before God, because it is possible to come to know God through His ordered creation.

In Romans 13, Paul explicitly reveals that *all authority is ordained by God.* What delegated authorities do we have over us? Besides our submission to God through Jesus Christ, there are basically four areas where God has delegated His authority in His creation:

1) Governments, both ecclesiastical and political: we are called to submit to them and honor them.
2) Husbands: wives are called to honor and submit to them.
3) Parents: children are called to honor and submit to them.
4) Employers: employees are asked to honor and submit to them.**

*Even in a democracy, we choose leaders and submit to them by trusting them, so that everything can be done in decency and in order.

**The master/slave relationship, which was the management/labor order of Paul's day is a transferable concept.

249

God has ordained these above authorities in His creation. Paul concludes that, because these authorities are ordained by God, we are to honor them, otherwise we will be in rebellion to God.

> Therefore, he who resists authority has opposed the ordinance of God and they who have opposed will receive condemnation upon themselves (Romans 13:2).

It is important to note that these scriptures do not always refer to Christian authorities or institutions. The scriptures are not referring to governments worthy of respect. In many cases, these authorities did not know that they were God's representatives. When Pilate, for instance, confronted Jesus with his authority to free him or crucify him, Jesus responded, "You only have that authority because my heavenly Father has given it to you" (John 19:10-11). Many of these authorities were despotic and outright evil in the apostle's day. The Romans conquered the then-known civilized world and ruled with a harsh and heavy hand. Yet both Peter and Paul emphasized the need to honor the government. They were only echoing what Jesus said, "Render unto Caesar the things of Caesar, and to God the things of God (Matthew 22:21). Jesus, even when He castigated the Pharisees for their hypocrisy, encouraged the people to submit and honor them because they claimed the authority of Moses (Matthew 23:1-3).

Many pastors are finding it difficult to minister to their flock. After worship service, many people not only go home and have roast turkey or roast beef for lunch, but also roast preacher. There is a spirit of rebellion even within the body of Christ. And yet God's Word says:

> Obey your leaders, and submit to them; for they keep watch over your souls, as those who would give account. Let them do this with joy and not with grief, for it would be unprofitable for you (Hebrews 13:17).

250

You will notice it says the pastor will have to give an account for his faithfulness (or unfaithfulness) towards God. You aren't asked to second-guess him, but pray for him. Notice it says "otherwise it will be unprofitable for you." That can mean that we will not receive the blessings of God or be used by Him.

What applies to the congregation also applies to the pastor as well. I recall counseling a pastor and his wife who were newly baptised in the Holy Spirit. They were having difficulty with their church. Many of the people were up in arms with their new-found enthusiasm. As we listened, it was quite obvious the minister wasn't always discreet and understanding in his sharing of the Baptism in the Holy Spirit. But neither were the members of his congregation. Many, as a result, were withholding their pledges to the church, so this pastor had consulted with his supervisor on what to do. In sharing with us, he was rather cynical about his supervisor's advice to leave his church and take an interim pastorate. He had judged his supervisor as not too spiritual; in his own words, "an ecclesiastical functionary." The pastor may have been right, but in the midst of the conversation, the Lord had a prophecy for this pastor. The word was that he was not to disregard that authority over him, because He had spoken His wisdom through that man, and that is what He desired for this pastor and his family. The Lord went on to say that the position that He had for him was not yet open and He wanted him to be in a refuge so that He could minister to him. This situation reminded us of the fact that if God used a pagan authority such as Cyrus to be an instrument in the return of the exiled Israelites to the promised land, He can use anyone as a delegated authority to fulfill His divine purpose.

So we are called to honor and submit to governments, husbands, parents, and employers, not because they are worthy of it, but because they are authorities ordained by

251

God. We need to honor the office. Does this mean that submission is absolute? Yes, because God's authority is absolute. Does it mean that we are to blindly obey all authorities, even when they command someone to do evil and go contrary to God's will? No.[20] While submission is absolute, obedience isn't, because as Peter put it, "We are to submit to every institution for the Lord's sake." The condition is "for the Lord's sake." This same Peter who tells us to submit to all governments for the Lord's sake, when asked to stop preaching the gospel answered the authorities, "We cannot stop speaking what we have seen and heard (Acts 4:20). When the ordained authorities go against the will of God, the Christian has no recourse but to say no. However, this must be done in a spirit of humility, not rebellion. While we will define this more in the next chapter, we need to see that a person can still be submissive and say no to an authority without being rebellious. How can that be? Because submission is an attitude, just as rebellion is an attitude. Too many of God's children, instead of appealing, have justified their rebellion to authorities by questioning the integrity of the authorities and their right to rule. That is playing the part of God. It is not trusting God to deal with the matter. David, for example, honored God by honoring Saul's position as king even when Saul tried to kill him. As a result, God protected him and blessed him.

Many of God's people come to us and say, "I'll submit and honor my husband, parents or pastor if and when they shape up." But is that what God's Word says? No. It has no conditions; we are to honor these ordained authorities, not because they are right, not because they are Christian,

---

[20]Watchmen Nee, *Spiritual Authority*, Christian Fellowship Publishers, Inc., N. Y., 1972, p. 108.

but because God's word tells us to do so. Anything else is simply rebellion. When we refuse to honor them and submit to them, we are going against God's ordinances. We in turn are questioning His sovereignty and authority, and are in direct rebellion against him. This is the ultimate sin of man. The apostle John calls this the sin of lawlessness (I John 3:4).

Everyone who practices sins also practices lawlessness and sin is lawlessness.

When a believer thinks of lawlessness, he usually thinks of some sinister criminal type who robs and steals and commits murder, but according to scripture, lawlessness is rebellion against God's authority. Many Christians would be surprised to learn that they are guilty of lawlessness in some area of their life. The result of that lawlessness is that they have become ineffective Christians. They would be further surprised to learn that Satan is the lawless one. That is what it says in II Thessalonians 2:7-8. And this is fitting because this lawlessness, this rebellion against God's authority began with Satan himself. The prophet Isaiah (14:12f) speaks of Satan trying to usurp God's authority. Jesus, who witnessed the fall of Satan, recounted to His disciples that He saw Satan fall like lightening from heaven (Luke 10:18). If you have seen lightening, you know that Satan didn't wait around for his gold watch. No, God can't stand rebellion and the questioning of His authority. When we question God's authority, we question His being and we are in league with the ruler of this earth who is in direct opposition to God Himself. That is why scripture compares rebellion to the sin of witchcraft and insubordination the sin of idolatry (I Samuel 15:23).

When Satan failed to usurp God's authority in heaven. he decided to usurp God's authority through His creation. In Genesis 2, Adam and Eve were given authority, they were allowed to name the creatures of God's creation. They

253

held that authority in trust as long as they were in fellowship with God and obedient to His Word. But then came the test. God told them they could eat any fruit except the fruit of the tree of knowledge of good and evil on penalty of death.* Satan came on the scene and tempted Eve by questioning God's Word and His authority with these words:

> You surely shall not die. For God knows that in the day you eat from it your eyes will be opened and you will be like God, knowing good and evil (Genesis 3:4-5).

While mankind lost his authority over creation when he rebelled against God's authority, Jesus, the second Adam, regained it for us as we believe and live in Him. In the meantime Satan is still present today. If he can't prevent a person from becoming a Christian, he still continues to blunt the authority of the believer by allowing him or her to stumble and rebel over the authorities and governments which God has delegated in His creation (See II Cor. 11:3).

In ministering to thousands of spirit-filled Christians who desire to do the word of God, I find that Satan has short-circuited their authority because they have somewhere along the line run against a delegated authority that God has put before them. Take, for example, our need to be submitted to the body of Christ and its leadership. God's Word assures us that we need to be submitted to the body of Christ and not neglect the fellowship of believers (Hebrews 10:24f). And yet, we find an alarming number of spirit-filled Christians whom we call "silver bullet" or "Lone Ranger" Christians. They are the spiritual tramps who may

---

*Notice that while Eve ate of the fruit, it was only after Adam, her head, ate of the fruit that they suddenly became aware of their nakedness. Conceivably, Adam, as the head, could have nullified the consequence of Eve's sin by not choosing to eat the fruit.

or may not have their Bible study or prayer groups, but see no need to submit to spiritual leaders and the body of Christ. They never are committed or stay in one place long enough to receive the exhortation, reproof, correction, the pruning that needs to take place in the body of Christ. Many of these same people are what we also call the "Glory Hoppers" who want to be under the spout where the glory comes out. That in itself is not bad, but what they end up doing is following, even idolizing, certain gifted teachers instead of Jesus Himself. Rock stars have their groupies, but certain Christians are their counterparts. They are the spiritual groupies who say, "I follow such and such a teacher." Paul had to contend with this problem even in his own day (I Corinthians 3:1, 4-8):

And I, brethren, would not speak to you as to spiritual men, but as to men of the flesh, as babes in Christ. (v. 1)

For when one says, "I am of Paul, and another, "I am of Apollos," are you not mere men? (v. 4)

What then is Apollos? And what is Paul? Servants through whom you believed, even as the Lord gave opportunity to each one. (v. 5)

I planted, Apollos watered, but God was causing the growth. (v. 6)

So then, neither the one who plants nor the one who waters is anything, but God who causes the growth. (v. 7)

Now he who plants and he who waters are one; but each will receive his own reward according to his own labor. (v. 8)

God's people need to be planted and rooted in His body and submitted to it. Submitting to the body of Christ and its leaders involves adjusting and accommodating oneself to God's people just as newlyweds need to adjust and accommodate each other. Can you imagine a husband saying to his wife, "If you don't get supper on time at 6 o'clock, I'm going to call it quits. The marriage is off." Many of us might not be able to conceive that. Nevertheless this is precisely what some Christians do in the area of the church. A good pastor friend of mine was threatened by a parishioner of some 30 years membership that if he changed the 9 o'clock service to 9:30, he would quit the church. Paul tells us to "walk in a manner worthy of the calling with which you have been called, with all humility, gentleness, with patience, showing forbearance to one another in love, being diligent to preserve the unity of the spirit in the bond of peace (Ephesians 4:1-3). The apostle Peter gives us another image and insight in the fellowship we are to have with a submitted body.

> You also as living stones are being built up as a spiritual house for a holy priesthood to offer up spiritual sacrifices acceptable to God through Jesus. (I Peter 2:5)

What kind of sacrifice is Peter talking about? How about the sacrifice of ourself, our pride, our ambition, our natural desire to be committed to no one but ourselves? Like it or not, we are being placed together by God and cemented together by the Holy Spirit to be a holy priesthood. In submitting to one authority and its leadership, we automatically become priests to one another and minister life and health by the power and authority of Jesus. Submission and having our life in order opens the door to our finding out our spiritual gifts that make the body of Christ complete and whole.

This is precisely what happened to a distraught woman who called me from one of our neighboring towns. From the tone of her voice, I could discern that she was at a point of despair as she shared her spiritual odyssey. She confessed, for example, that she had several nervous breakdowns and received every kind of counseling, both Christian and non-Christian, without any results. Divorced, in her mid 40's with three teenage children, she emphasized that she had received Christ as Savior and Lord, and was baptized in the Holy Spirit, but with no freedom. She still felt harassed and nervous, frustrated, powerless to cope with herself and her family. She ended with the statement that she had no joy in her life. We made an appointment. When she came for ministry, the Lord immediately, through a word of knowledge, told me that she had a wounded spirit and several cords of iniquity that had to be cut, one of which was rebellion. We prayed together and I asked her to forgive her former husband and some other people in her life that had hurt her. As we took authority over these cords and renounced the spiritual forces that used the cords to harass and oppress her, the Lord prompted me to ask her about fellowship and submission. I shared with her as I'm sharing with you that God only uses us and empowers us as we are fitted into His body. Did she have a church? Her response was no. She wasn't a member of any church. But she was attending one more regularly than others. I asked her if she was submitted to the leadership of any church. She no longer had a spiritual head in her husband so she needed to submit to a pastor, elder, or deacon of the church, so that Satan could no longer harass her. After we anointed her with oil for the healing of memories and a wounded spirit, the Lord had a prophetic word for her, assuring her of His love for her and again exhorting her to be a part of His body. A week later, she called up and said while she felt better, she still had this nervousness problem and her joy wasn't full. While I was still on the phone, I asked the Lord what was the matter, and the Lord told me that she had not submitted to His body. I shared this revelation with her and surprisingly I found myself promising her that when she did submit and become a part of God's body, she would see the inner healing complete.

God would also use her to minister to other people. At first I thought I was putting my foot in my mouth but as I was later to learn, God was putting His thoughts into my mouth.

Two weeks went by. The oldest daughter came for ministry and I asked her about her mother submitting to God's body and a spiritual leader. She said she hadn't gotten around to it yet, but she was planning to do it that week.

Another week went by followed by another phone call from the woman. She asked if she could bring her youngest daughter for ministry. When I greeted her and her youngest daughter, I immediately recognized a change in her countenance. Her face was radiant with joy. The peace of God was in her. Even the worried lines on her face had disappeared. Without asking her, I knew that she had finally submitted herself to the body of Christ and its leadership. She nevertheless volunteered what had happened. Within a week of her submission to the church, her nervousness went away. She experienced a peace and joy in her life that she had never experienced before. The inner healing was complete, but that wasn't all. God independently gave both her and her oldest daughter a word of knowledge about her youngest daughter. He told them that she was being approached by a homosexual classmate and she needed to be protected from her advances. Her youngest daughter, who seemed pretty naive about this whole incident, received ministry for some of her problems. And then without prompting on my part, the mother started to pray and deal in spiritual warfare for this homosexual classmate so that she might receive ministry. She prayed an anointed prayer for that girl and literally stormed the gates of heaven. A week later, both her daughters came back with this girl. They had already led her to Christ and prepared her heart to receive ministry and the baptism of the Holy Spirit. I share this incident with you because this story is typical of what happens when people get under authority. Like Jesus, who was under the authority of the Father, we need to be under authority so that we might wield His authority and do the same works of Jesus.

Chapter 14

Be in Harmony and in Order
Part II — God's Order for Families

While many Christians claim the ultimate authority and Lordship of Jesus in their lives, they need to realize His Lordship is not something abstract. His Lordship is directly related to the authorities that God has placed over us. This is particularly true in the area of families. God is a God of order and we need to have order within our families. Families are the basic unit of the body of Christ. They are the two or three gathered in His Name. In I Corinthians 11:3, Paul explains the order of families and ties it directly into the order of the Godhead.

> I want you to understand that Christ is the Head of every man, and the man is the head of a woman and God is the Head of Christ.

First, there is God the Father, and then Jesus Christ and the husband and wife. While both husband and wife and family are under the authority of Jesus, the husband is the delegated authority over his wife.

In ministering, and counseling thousands of Christian families, I find that Satan has played havoc with so many marriages. He has created disorder within the family structure and with that disorder much of the authority and power of God is diffused. There are many Christian families that are out of order. Either the husband by default refuses to take a responsible leadership role over his family or the wife is unwilling to be submissive to her husband or both. I dare-say 80 to 90 percent of all marital problems involve this area. The reason is that many Christian couples have bought the lie of the devil and have based their marriage on a 50-50 proposition. But God doesn't want us to have a marriage on a 50-50 basis. Rather He wants us to be 100 percent husband and 100 percent wife.

In Ephesians 5:21, Paul encourages both husband and wife to be subject to one another in the fear of Christ. When both are submissive to each other, there is mutual esteem for one another and the ideas of authority and order, submission and leadership become a way of life. Paul prescribes the right ingredients for this mutual submission and mutual esteem to flourish:

> If therefore there is any encouragement in Christ, if there is any consolation of love, if there is any fellowship of the Spirit, if any affection and compassion,

> Make my joy complete by being of the same mind, maintaining the same love, united in spirit, intent on one purpose.

> Do nothing from selfishness or empty conceit, but with humility of mind let each of you regard one another as more important than himself;

> Do not merely look out for your own personal interests, but also for the interests of others. (Phil. 2:1-4)

This mutual esteem is important for the body life of the church as well as families which are the basic unit for that body life.

Once we have this mutual esteem for one another, what is the role of the wife? In verses 22 through 24 of Ephesians 5, Paul lays out the role and order of the wife and encourages her to be submissive to her husband. He goes on to make an analogy of the church, the body of Christ, being submissive to Jesus as its head.

Now, many women have understood submission as sell-out, that this means the woman is inferior or a slave to her husband. One angry woman in fact, when confronted with this passage, proceeded to explain and define the word submit in her own terms. She said, "Sub means 'under' and mit means 'hand' and together it means being underhanded." But nothing can be further from the truth. This is not God's or Paul's conspiracy against women. Paul says in Galatians 3:28 that all are one, all are equal, both female and male, in terms of status in Jesus Christ. Peter encourages husbands to be understanding of their wives and give honor to them as fellow heirs of the grace of life, otherwise God will not listen to their prayers (I Peter 3:7). In terms of salvation and status, God considers us equal, but in terms of function, He asks the woman to voluntarily submit to her husband as a delegated authority. This is no different than Jesus' role in the Trinity. Jesus is equal to God the Father and God the Holy Spirit, but in Philippians 2:6-8, Paul tells us that Jesus didn't regard His equality with God a thing to be grasped. On the contrary, He voluntarily emptied Himself of all His glory and became a bondservant and obedient to the point of death on the cross. Because of that, God highly exalted Him and gave Him authority over all things. Jesus throughout His ministry said, "I only do what I see my heavenly Father do" (John 5:19, 30). In the garden of Gethsemene He said, "Nevertheless, not my will, but Thy will be done" (Matthew 26:39). In His relationship to the Father, He set the pattern for us all as He chose to voluntarily submit Himself to the Father. Submission then is a voluntary act. It has nothing to do with a person being inferior — no more than Jesus is inferior to the Father.

If submission is a voluntary act of an equal partner, it is also an attitude, as we have mentioned in the preceding chapter. Paul says in the same chapter of Philippians that we (this includes all Christians, regardless of sex) are to "Have this attitude that was in Christ Jesus" (Phil. 2:5). Many people that we have counseled have accepted this as God's Word, but they have never been able to implement this in their lives in very practical ways. I often hear the words, "I try but . . . I haven't succeeded." Submission isn't a matter of trying, it's effortless; as effortless as receiving Jesus as Lord and Savior and Baptizer in the Holy Spirit. We cannot be submissive in and of ourselves. Only Jesus in us can make us submissive. All we have to do in faith is ask Jesus to do it in us, then act in a submissive way and believe He has given us a submissive heart. This is part of the righteousness of Jesus that Paul asks us to put on in Colossians 3:12-14. Putting on the righteousness of Jesus is acting in a submissive way; that is, providing the outward form. Just as a contractor or mason constructs the framework for curbing with the understanding that it is going to be filled up with concrete, so we act in a submissive way and by that put legs on our faith with the assurance that God is going to put the real thing, the concrete attitude of submission in our lives.

Besides being an attitude and a voluntary act, submission involves the element of trust — not so much with respect to the delegated authority — in this case, the husband — but trust in the Lord to work through the husband. The wife is called to honor the husband's office, but trust the Lord. This is what Sarah did with respect to her husband. She honored her husband and trusted the Lord. On two occasions, her husband foolishly decided to pass her

263

off as his sister since he feared being killed because his wife was so beautiful. (See Gen. 12:11ff; Gen. 20:2-18) Sarah, despite this foolishness, trusted the Lord to intervene on her behalf. In both instances, God intervened, with a plague in Egypt and a message to King Abimelech in a dream, threatening to kill him if he did not release Sarah. In the process, Abraham was reproved by both King Abimelech and Pharaoh for lying about Sarah.

From a very practical standpoint, one friend demonstrated the power of God to work on her behalf when she became submissive and trusted the Lord. She came to me one day and shared a problem. The problem was that her dentist husband — a beautiful, spirit-filled Christian — wasn't always wise in his business investments. Because of his past ventures, he was heavily in debt and his wife suddenly felt that she needed to take this burden on herself. The end result, however, was that she found herself nagging her husband. Although she prayed about this, she became frightened and anxiety ridden, even depressed, because her husband wouldn't listen to her.

I shared the above passages about Sarah honoring her husband and trusting the Lord. I told her that she wasn't trusting the Lord nor honoring her husband by nagging him. I told her that she was taking on the responsibility and burden as provider and protector that was her husband's. She needed to voluntarily submit herself to her husband and trust that the Lord would work through him. In discussing further with her, I discovered that she really had a lot more wisdom in the area of finances than her husband. I pointed out to her that being submissive does not mean that you don't share your God-given wisdom. Otherwise, she would not be fulfilling her role as a helpmate. In order for her to fulfill her role of submission, she was simply to give her husband her wisdom and release this burden to him and trust the Lord to deal with him just as

Sarah did with Abraham. Submission is an act of will. It means that you are willing to even suffer the consequences (in this case, another bad investment) so that the Lord would deal with the husband. (A husband learns a more powerful lesson when God Himself says, "I told you so," than when a wife says, "I told you so.")

My friend prayed a brief prayer, something like the following:

> Father, you know the turmoil I've been in, I know that part of that has been my unwillingness to trust you to work through my husband. Lord, I ask your forgiveness for my resentments toward my husband and my unbelief. I ask for your attitude of submissiveness. And with that I release this burden to my husband and I trust You to work it out. Amen.

A week went by and suddenly she called me, ecstatic about what God had done. She said, "Denis, this really works! I gave my husband my wisdom about a certain financial matter and dropped it. I must say I was tempted to nag him and pick up the burden again. But when I was tempted, I simply prayed, 'Lord, I trust You to do it!' and all of a sudden, a delicious peace would come over me. But that wasn't all, my husband later came to me and said, 'You know honey, I feel you really are right about the investment. In fact, I feel convicted about it.' " This really blew her mind. Because, you see, by trusting God, she allowed God to lend weight to her word of wisdom. By honoring her husband, the weight of the burden came off her and onto him. She opened the door for God to intervene. Her wisdom became identified with His wisdom. Rather than be threatened by his wife's wisdom, he began to see that her wisdom was God-ordained. This was an asset to him because she was his helpmate; and she completed what was lacking in him.

My friend demonstrated another aspect of submission which is important to recognize. You'll notice, she said "as soon as she honored her husband and trusted the Lord, she felt a delicious peace that came over her." She was attesting to the fact that headship is a protective covering against Satan's darts. While she thought the anxiety and frustration was a direct result of her husband not listening to her, she actually was being harassed by Satan. Satan has unlimited access to people that are not under authority. He had tied up my friend emotionally. He was playing on her emotional strings, just like a pianist plays on a piano; only his kind of music is constant discord.

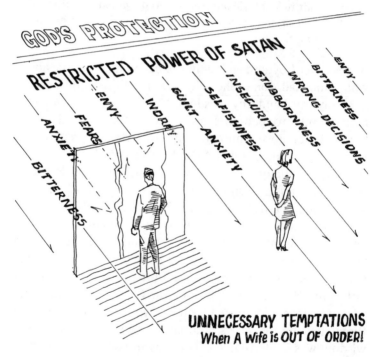

UNNECESSARY TEMPTATIONS
When A Wife is OUT OF ORDER!

We have counseled many women who have blamed their circumstances or their husbands for their emotional

266

problems. But they failed to see that they were responsible for their own reactions to their husbands or circumstances. Their emotions were fed by their lack of trust in the Lord and their subsequent lack of submission to their husbands. When we are not submitted to God's delegated authorities, we are submitted to the Lawless One, Satan himself. Paul warns that in the last days there will be men who will enter households and captivate weak women weighed down with sins and various impulses (II Timothy 3:6). These men are undoubtedly in league with the devil and tempt unsubmitted women who are unprotected by their husbands.

As soon as my friend chose to voluntarily submit to her husband and thus honor him and trust the Lord to work things out, she immediately found herself behind her husband's shield of protection where there was peace.

At this point, many of our readers will say "Well, this is all right if your husband is tuned into God, but what if your husband is an unbeliever?" I have personally witnessed countless women who have honored their husbands, even their unsaved husbands and trusted the Lord and have seen God mightily use them and have a tremendous effect in shaping their husband's attitudes. Many wives who have been dying for their husbands to come to know the Lord have, through the simple act of submission, opened the doorway for God to work in their husbands. This, after all, is the promise of I Peter 3:1.

> In the same way, you wives, be submissive to your husbands
> so that even if any of them are disobedient to the Word, they
> may be won without a word by the behavior of their wives.

The attitudes that we need to take both as husband and as wife is not one which says, "I'll be submissive (to a spiritual leader) only when and if he shapes up." Rather our attitude should be "I want to fulfill my role as a wife (or

267

husband) regardless of the circumstances, because this is the will of God."

But what about men who need to be under authority? It goes without saying that men need to be in order, too. They need to have an attitude of submission toward Jesus and fellow Christians — employers, pastors, etc. The more submissive a man becomes, the more transparent he becomes to the authority of Jesus working through him. The man can be compared to a greenhouse, and his family the plants in the greenhouse. And as the light of Jesus shines through him (with this attitude of submissiveness), the more authority and protection he will offer for his family to flourish and grow.

Since authority is established by God, there is no need for a husband as delegated authority to try to secure his authority. It isn't his to claim. Being an authority does not mean lording it over the wife and the rest of the family. It isn't being "boss." On the contrary, it is being a servant head. When the sons of Zebedee, James and John, were arguing who was to be greater in the kingdom of God, Jesus said, "I don't want you to be like the Gentiles, lording it over the people." (Mark 10:42-43). In the gospel of John, Jesus demonstrated God's authority by washing the feet of His disciples (John 13:5-15). By this act, He was demonstrating how to be a leader. And yet He never did deny that He had received authority from the Father. As husbands and fathers, we have been given this kind of authority over our families.

The motivation for this authority is to express God's love. In Ephesians 5:25, Paul, having pointed out the woman's role to submit, goes on to show the husband how to lead. He encourages the husband to love his wife just as Christ loves the church and gave Himself up for her. Ideally, the wife should be submitted to her husband who is loving her as his own body. If we are to compare the kind of love that Jesus had for the church, we can see that this love was not a natural love, but the supernatural self-giving (agape) love described in I Corinthians 13. Just as the Lord woos people with love, so a husband should continually woo his wife with his love. The more a husband loves his wife, the easier it is for the wife to trust the Lord to work through him and even trust him. On the other hand, rejection, abuse, and neglect are three enemies of submission.

A man at a Full Gospel conference shared with me that when he was first baptized in the Holy Spirit, he prayed, "Lord, I want to serve you. I want to minister by your power and in your name." The Lord spoke to him and said, "I desire that you do that, my son; begin by ministering my love to your wife and ten children."

Just as the church is the message of Jesus' ministry, so the husband's wife is the message of his ministry. Many times in our marriage seminars, I tell husbands if they don't like the way their wives turned out, chances are it is their fault. They are responsible for building a message of love and Christ-likeness in their wives and families. They are to sanctify their wives just as Christ sanctified the church without spot or wrinkle. As priests of their family, husbands are to give up their rights and initiate forgiveness and reconciliation. It doesn't matter who is right or wrong. They are to initiate love and forgiveness just as Jesus did for the world and the church.

One young Pentecostal pastor came with his wife for ministry. His wife had problems adjusting to the role of a pastor's wife. She grew jealous of his time at the church and blew up in frustration at various ladies' groups. The Lord revealed to us that she had a problem of rejection and fear of rejection. As a believer, she dealt with it, but the Lord wasn't entirely satisfied. Through a prophetic word, He emphasized the need for this young man to love his wife and cherish her. Previously, when she asked for affection and

time with him, he would say, "Jesus comes first in my life."
The Lord said, "My son, it is because I come first in your
life that I command you to love your wife as I love the
church. My love isn't abstract, my love is expressed in relationships." The Lord then directed our attention to
Ephesians 5:28 and showed us that the husband is supposed
to love his wife as his own body. This means that in a very
practical way he can no longer look at his wife and say to
her, "That's your problem." Her problem automatically
becomes his problem. Paul, with respect to the church,
shares a spiritual truth that if one person in the body of
Christ is hurting, all of them are hurting. And so if I
neglect to take care of part of my body in the family, I
am going to be affected by it. This is especially true in the
spiritual realm. Scripture warns husbands to honor and be
understanding of their wives lest their prayers be hindered
(I Peter 3:7). In other words, God won't listen to their
prayers if they are harsh with their wives.

In the course of conversation with another young
couple, I had learned that the husband had been a Christian
for only two months. His wife, who was sitting next to
him, spoke in a quiet and loving voice and shared that though
she had prayed for a number of years that her husband
would receive Christ, her prayers were only recently
answered as she asked Jesus for a submissive heart and
claimed the promise of I Peter 3:1. She went on to say
that although they were still struggling to get order in their
family, she was thankful for God's answer to her prayers.
While we were on the subject of answered prayers, the husband started sharing his financial woes. He had learned
through his church the blessings that come through tithing
to the Lord, and so he was faithful in his tithing, but he
was receiving none of these blessings. On the contrary, it
was precisely here in the area of finances where he was
having the most trouble. In utter frustration he shared,

270

"I've prayed and prayed until I'm blue in the face and it doesn't seem that my prayers are getting beyond the ceiling. My creditors are hounding me for $500 that I owe. I know in the past I haven't been wise in buying things on credit. We have tried to get out of this burden by cutting our expenses to the bare bone. But somehow, this isn't enough. I need $500 badly, otherwise they are going to garnishee my wages."

I started to share with him how sometimes God delays an answer to test us and purify our motives and allow us to build up our spiritual muscles. But as soon as I mentioned this, I felt the Holy Spirit saying that this was not the case. I then asked him about how he was getting along with his wife. The two of them looked at each other and the look in his eyes indicated that things weren't quite right. Then the scripture passage of I Peter 3:7 leaped into my mind.

> You husbands, likewise, live with your wives in an under-standing way as with a weaker vessel, since she is a woman; and grant her honor as fellow heir of the grace of life, so that your prayers may not be hindered.

I asked him, "Could it be that your prayers, particularly your prayers for God to meet your financial needs, are blocked or hindered by the way you've treated your wife? Have you expressed love towards her and honored her?"

I then started to explain how God commands the husband to love his wife as his own body and minister to his wife as Jesus ministered to the church. I asked him if he were building Christ's message in his wife and the rest of his family. He admitted that he wasn't leading and being responsible for family devotions. He was letting his wife do it. He also confessed that lately he wasn't faithful in attending church. He added that the church he was going to was pretty dead. I suggested that if he wasn't satisfied with the church he was in, that he was responsible for finding a

271

church home where the full message of Jesus Christ was preached. I asked him if he wanted to recommit his life to Christ and also get reconciled with his wife and ask her forgiveness for his unloving attitude. He nodded and I lead him in a prayer of recommitment. With a little prompting, he asked his wife's forgiveness and tears came to her eyes as they hugged and kissed each other. I felt the Holy Spirit prompting me to introduce them to the Baptism of the Holy Spirit. As I proceeded to explain this to them, the wife started glowing and mentioned that their best friends were trying to tell them about this new dimension in their lives. She said that she was holding back because she wanted to receive this with her husband. As we looked at him, he said, "I need all the help I can get." I laid hands on them to receive the Baptism of the Holy Spirit and the husband promptly fell under conviction. He asked the Lord's forgiveness for the way he treated his family and he asked God to help him to be a better father and husband. With that we all said, "Amen."

"Before we go," I said, "let's pray about that need that you have for $500." We made our request known and left. Less than a week later, I received a call from his wife. Excitedly she cried out, "Praise the Lord. It's a miracle! We just received a check for $500 in the mail. It was some paid-up insurance policy that my husband's folks made out for him. They were suddenly impressed to give it to him." I rejoiced with her, thanking the Lord for demonstrating His power and the truth of His word to this young backsliding husband. But that wasn't all . . . two days later, I received another call and another witness to the miraculous power of God which is released when a family is in order. The wife shared with me a miracle that had the doctors dumbfounded. It seems they had car problems and the husband got out of the car to look under the hood. In the process he forgot to shut the door and his five-year-old

272

daughter wriggled off the front seat and was run over by an oncoming car. The left front and rear tires of the car ran completely over her legs. They rushed her to the hospital praying as they went. The doctors examined her and observed the tire marks on her legs, but except for a few scratches and bruises, they could find nothing wrong. There was no internal injury, no crushed legs. This was another example of what God will do when we choose to be in order, when men dare to be heads of their own families.

But what about the authority of parents? If Satan can't get us out of order in our husband/wife relationship, he tries to work against parent/child relationships. I find in ministering to numerous families that parents do not understand their authority over their children. Many times the children are frustrated because they do not know where they stand with their parents. They want limits. They want authority over them even though they may continuously test that authority. Many parents are giving in to the standards of the next door neighbors. Parents who abdicate their God given authority over their children usually have a tendency to vacillate in two directions; between permissiveness and an authoritarian approach.

The authoritarian approach is one where the key phrase is "children should be seen and not heard." They are not encouraged to make responsible decisions. Children are treated as subhuman, without much respect. We have observed the product of this kind of upbringing. When these children come of age, they are unable to make responsible decisions in their adult life. Some on the other hand, have reacted to the parental heavy-handedness and become wild as soon as they are out of their parents' presence. Other parents, in reaction to the authoritarian approach, take the permissive approach and let their children grow up like weeds without rules or any parental discipline, reaping the fruits of rebellion and anarchy.

Many parents do not know that they have the authority of God to rule and protect their children from temptations and Satanic attacks. One father, for example, shared with me that many times while his older children were off to college exposed to all kinds of temptations, he would find himself exposed to these same temptations and be in a position to take authority over them and intercede on their behalf.

This authority that parents have was never more dramatized than when we engaged in spiritual warfare for one particular family's daughter. Typical of many today, this family was hamstrung by divisions in their home. The father and mother were spirit-filled and longed to be used by God. They had attended all kinds of full gospel conferences and seminars and were eager to learn everything they could to be effective witnesses for Jesus Christ. But Satan had them tied up with their own personal problems. While attending one of our marriage enrichment seminars, they exercised their authority as believers and broke some of the spiritual inheritances — cords that were preventing them from fulfilling their roles as husband and wife. In the course of our conversation, the wife brought up the question, "What can we do with our twenty-year-old daughter?" She shared that their daughter had a child out of wedlock.

This incident became a point of contention between the husband and wife. The husband wanted her to keep the baby and the daughter wanted to put it up for adoption. The mother sided with the daughter and from that point on a deep wedge was made with the wife continually siding with her daughter in all disputes. Now the wife who had, among other things, a spiritual inheritance of rebellion, broke the cord of rebellion and renounced the spirit of rebellion that had attached itself to the cord. Together with her husband, we broke cords down through their daughter and by the power of Jesus stood against Satan's hold on her. In this whole process, the husband reaffirmed his headship over his family and was reconciled with his wife. Except for their daughter, their house was in order.

A few months later, the husband and wife shared what God can do when a family is in order. Besides restoring the wife's loyalty to her husband and the husband becoming more loving toward her, God immediately began to work on the rebellious daughter. The change was so dramatic that the father had to learn to tone down his voice when he reproved her. Instead of growing angry and reacting to what he had said, which was the usual response before, she would break into tears. Her strong will was being broken. This is the authority that God gives parents who are in order. Once that family came in God's order, the husband and wife soon began to move and minister in the power of the Holy Spirit to many people in their church and community.

Another couple that came for ministry brought their eight-year-old son, along with a friend of the same age. They wanted ministry primarily for their son, but the Holy Spirit prompted us to send the young son out to play in the back yard. He wanted to get the husband and wife in order before He dealt with their son. The husband and wife shared that they had recently come to know the reality of Christ. This joyous experience, however, was being overshadowed by their son, whom they said was uncontrollable. They revealed that their son would prowl around in the night, without provocation, destroying things in his wake. The situation was so bad that they felt that they had to lock him up in his room. Sometimes, they would observe him, in a trance-like state, cursing them and God. They tried to present Christ to him, but he would back off, start cursing and run away from them. As they shared more of their frustrations and their unsuccessful attempts at having the child undergo psychiatric treatments, the Lord began to show us that a cord of the occult was involved in the wife's background. As we taught them how to take authority over these cords of iniquity and dealt with some of the problems that were affecting them as well as their son, the Holy Spirit told us that we were ready to deal with the child.

As soon as we called in the child and his friend, we could see the softening of his countenance. We presented the Gospel of Jesus Christ to him and in a simple way asked him if he wanted Jesus to come into his life. Without hesitation he said yes, and prayed the sinner's prayer with us as his parents looked on increduously. Together with the parents, we refused Satan's plan for this child and told him to get out of that child's life. The boy's friend, who was viewing this whole thing, had such a longing-to-belong look on his face that we asked him if he wanted to have Christ in his life, too. He nodded and together we led him in a prayer to receive Christ. Part of the blessing of an ordered family spilled over to their son's friend. Again this was a typical example of what God can do when families dare to be in order.

But what about young people being under the authority of their parents? This is part of God's order for His family. As an assistant pastor of a large Presbyterian church in the early 1970's, I found myself in charge of young people who were suddenly turned on to Jesus as Savior, Lord and

Baptizer in the Holy Spirit. This dynamic element of Pentecost proved to be threatening to many parents, who may or may not have known the reality of Christ. A young person confided with me that her mother had confessed that she could handle her former drug and illicit sex habits better than her new experience with Christ. By that statement, the mother more or less intimated that if she had a choice, she would have preferred her daughter's former lifestyle to this present one. To further complicate matters, some of the young people with their new-found spirituality began to see some of the shallowness of their parents' faith and they did not know how to relate to them. Some found themselves preaching to their parents, judging and alienating them. While the Lord was blessing the young people's fellowship with many healings and people coming to know the Lord, many were finding themselves at the same time under spiritual harassment. Why? Because they had consciously or unconsciously taken themselves out of their parents' protective care.

This is about the time when I came into the picture. The Lord gave me one basic message for these young people and that was the fifth commandment; namely, "honor your father and mother that your days may be prolonged in the land which the Lord your God gives you" (Ex. 20:12). Paul in explaining the order and authority of families, starting with husbands and wives, goes on to quote this commandment:

> Children, obey your parents in the Lord, for this is right. Honor your father and mother (which is the first commandment with a promise), that it may be well with you, and that you may live long on the earth (Ephesians 6:1-3).

I reminded the young people that obedience to the word was more important than personal sacrifice or their ministry for Him. The injunction was for them to obey their parents, not because their parents were always right or even Christian, but simply because God wants them to do it. With this honoring and obedience, there come two promises: The first one is that they would be blessed by God and that it would be well with them. At this point, things weren't well with them, because they did not have an attitude of submission towards their parents. The second promise was that they would live a long life. There was a possibility that their life may be shortened by their disobedience to their parents.

One director of a Full Gospel Businessmen's Fellowship International shared with me that his son learned that it was in his own self-interest to obey his parents even before becoming a Christian. After fourteen car crackups, he decided to quit rebelling and submit to his parents. He had no furhter accidents.

Many of the young people at the church that I served also discovered some more fringe benefits from obedience. As soon as their lives were in order, many of the parents received Christ as Savior and Lord and experienced their own Pentecost. This parallels the promise of I Peter 3:1. Just as husbands can be won by the submissive attitude of their wives, so parents can be won by the submissive attitude of their children. Many of these young people began to see the truth of this commandment for their own lives and their families. The few that didn't see it quickly lost their zeal for the Lord, and some even got caught up in the Children of God or similar cults. Those who honored their parents made a tremendous impact on that Presbyterian church and in their school. Some moved on to full-time ministries with long lasting effects.

The power of God is always activated when people are in order and under authority. He is the ultimate authority and we honor Him by honoring His delegated authorities.

278

Chapter 15

Following the Highway of Holiness

When we take a vacation, especially to a place where we have never been before, we usually consult a map. If we have an automobile club membership, the maps may even supply information on what to expect while we are on the trip, such as road conditions, detours, tourist attractions and accommodations, as well as what we will encounter at our destination. The Bible offers this same kind of direction and guidance in our spiritual walk. This is important because there are many of God's people who have grown weary and fainthearted in the walk of faith. While we know that our final destination is to be with Jesus in heaven, many of us have not understood the goal that God has in mind for us while we are sojourning here on earth. God has a divine purpose and destiny for each one of us as we travel through this life. But unless we discover this for ourselves, we are apt to grow discouraged and even give up, never exercising our authority as believers.

On this divine sojourn, we can be assured we are not alone. Jesus, as the author and finisher of our faith, promises that He will be with us always. He sends His Holy Spirit to dwell in us and reveal His truth. He also assured His disciples that He and the Father were One. So we have the whole Trinity with us. If this isn't enough, Scripture assures us that we have ministering angels to meet our needs. We also have the fellowship of believers encouraging each other. We have a full carload of interesting company along the way.

But what kind of way is it? For the Christians, there is only one road to take. In the thirty-fifth chapter of Isaiah, we find precisely what kind of road it is.

> Encourage the exhausted, strengthen the feeble. (v. 3)

> Say to these with palpitating heart, "take courage, fear not. Behold, your God will come with vengeance; the recompense of God will come, but He will save you. (v. 4)

> Then the eyes of the blind will be opened and the ears of the deaf will be unstopped. (v. 5)

> Then the lame will leap like a deer and the tongue of the dumb will shout for joy. For waters will break forth in the wilderness and streams in the Arabah. (v. 6)

> And the scorched land will become a pool, and the thirsty ground springs of water; in the haunt of the jackals, its resting place, grass becomes reeds and rushes. (v. 7)

> And a highway will be there, a roadway . . . (v. 8)

This is the highway we are all to take.

> . . . and it will be called a highway of holiness. The unclean will not travel on it. But it will be for him who walks that way, and fools will not wander on it.

> No lion will be there. Nor will any vicious beast go upon it; these will not be found there, but the redeemed will walk there. (v. 9)

280

And the ransomed of the Lord will return, and come with joyful shouting to Zion, with everlasting joy upon their heads. They will find gladness and joy, and sorrow and sighing will flee away. (v. 10)

The highway of holiness is the road that all God's children will take. Notice the blessings and promises of healings and miracles that will be a part of our walk with God. The eyes of the blind will be opened. The deaf will hear. The dumb will shout for joy. The lame will leap like a deer. We will be refreshed by spring waters. Jesus in John 4:14 promised the living waters of the Holy Spirit so that we would never thirst. In spite of all turmoil about us, He will save us. No lion will be there. That includes Satan who is like a roaring lion intending to devour all those who come his way (especially those who do not know their authority and his ways). In Proverbs 16:17, there is also a promise and a condition.

For the highway of the upright is to depart from evil and he who watches his way preserves his life.

Now that we know the name of this highway, like any map we need to check with God's word to see what kind of road this highway of holiness is. Is it a two-lane or a four-lane highway or what? In Matthew 7:13-14 we have a clear understanding of what type of road way this is.

Enter by the narrow gate; for the gate is wide and the way is broad that leads to destruction, and many are those who enter by it.

For the gate is small and the way is narrow that leads to life, and few are those who find it.

So the road is narrow. It isn't a four-lane highway. It starts at a small gate. This gate opens up to us when we are born again. As we enter this gate and walk this highway of holiness, it gets narrower and narrower. Narrower that is, as far as the world is concerned:

THE NARROW ROAD

The things I could get away with years ago, God won't let me get away with anymore. Take, for instance, my driving habits. I've always had a bit of a lead foot, but as I have walked down this highway of holiness, God will not let me get away with passing over the speed limit. "Why?" you might ask. It isn't only because it is against the law, but as I have walked down this highway of holiness, I have given over more and more of my life to Jesus' Lordship. He wants to be Lord of every detail of my life and He wants my will to be His will. Jesus wants me to be pure in heart as He is pure in heart. When we start this highway of holiness, God is always gracious towards the young Christians. He lets them go their way and blesses them and overlooks many things. But there comes a day when He lightly pulls in the reins and reminds them that they have taken off the yoke of slavery and replaced it with the yoke of His Son, Jesus.

282

Even though His yoke is easy, it is nonetheless a yoke. We need to get under it and submit to Jesus' Lordship and the promptings of His Holy Spirit.

I used to think God was pretty petty with respect to His servant Moses. Do you remember how the people of Israel tested the Lord by grumbling at Rephidim? (See Exodus 17:1-7). They wanted water and God, who was angry, accommodated them by having Moses strike a rock with his rod and letting water spring forth. The place was called Massah and Meribah − a place of testing and quarrels. Thirty-five years later Moses comes to Kadesh-Barnea with the second generation of Israelites (Numbers 20:1-2). The first generation of sojourning Israelites died in the wilderness because of their unbelief and grumbling against God. But the same identical scene takes place with the new generation of Israelites. They, too, are quarreling and bickering about God leaving them to die in the wilderness. Once more God accommodates them and instructs Moses to speak to the rock so that water would pour out from it. But instead of speaking to the rock, the exasperated Moses raps the rock twice and the water pours out. Because of his disobedience, God reproves Moses and tells him that he would not be allowed to enter the promised land. Now doesn't that sound petty and insignificant? In the natural it does. But we need to recognize that as Moses walked with God, he was given a full revelation of God. He spoke to Him face to face. He experienced the Lordship of God and with that, the responsibility. The Bible says of him, to whom much is given much more will be demanded. (Luke 12:48).

So the way is narrow and gets narrower as we walk closer with God and experience His Lordship. But as we walk this highway of holiness, we begin to see the wider dimension of God's ways and His Rulership in direct opposition to the world's ways and the rulership of Satan. The

283

narrower it gets, the more we see and understand with God's
eyes the working of His kingdom and His will

GOD'S LORDSHIP

THE NARROW ROAD

INSIGHT INTO KINGDOM LIVING

This is in keeping with the Lord's prayer when Jesus taught
His disciples to pray into reality "Thy kingdom come, Thy
will be done." Paul, in his walk with the Lord, was able to
put his faith in the unseen world of God and set his mind
on things above (Col. 2:3; II Cor. 4:18).

Like every road, there is a destination. There is a pur-
pose for our trip. We don't travel aimlessly. God has a final
divine purpose for us as we travel the highway of holiness.
That divine purpose is Christlikeness. We are to put on His
righteousness (Eph. 4:24) and be His ambassadors
(II Cor. 5:20). We are the letter of Christ read by all men
(II Cor. 3:3), the fragrance of Christ to God among those
saved and those who are perishing (II Cor. 2:15; see also
I John 3:1-3). It is Christ in us the hope of glory (Col. 1:27).
The Christlikeness that God wants to build into us is His
character. And the character of Christ is the fruit of the
Holy Spirit: love, joy, peace, patience, kindness, goodness,
faithfulness, gentleness, and self-control (Gal. 5:22). Jesus
said, "You will know them by their fruits." (Matt. 7:16).

284

But along with the character of Christ (the fruit of the Holy Spirit) we need to reproduce the good works of Christ, because faith without works is dead. When Jesus was walking on this earth, He expressed the compassionate heart of God. It is out of the loving, compassionate heart that God saves, heals, and delivers us in body, soul and spirit. Out of this same character, He desires us to do these same deeds. Paul reminds us, "we are His workmanship, created in Christ Jesus for good works." (Eph. 2:10). Within the realm of God's character, He has placed His mantle of authority and power on His people. By faith, we need to receive that authority and power. Jesus also said, "If I cast out Satan by the finger of God, then you know that the kingdom of God is in your midst." (Luke 11:20). We are called to live in God's kingdom and Jesus is on the highway training us to live and express the Father's heart in His kingdom. Two thousand years ago some Greeks approached Jesus' disciples and they said, "Sir, we wish to see Jesus." (John 12:21). The world in our day is still saying the same things, "Sir, we wish to see Jesus." They will only see Jesus as we walk the highway of holiness and put on His character and express His love through His good works.

Many times our traditional churches have emphasized the authority of Christ, but lacked the power or the character of Christ. Many of the Pentacostal churches have emphasized the power, but lacked the authority or the character. And finally, there are many holiness churches that have emphasized the necessity for the character of Christ, but lacked the power and authority to express it. But the world wants to see all of Christ, His power, His authority, expressed through His character. That is what God is completing in this day and age through His church as we walk the highway of holiness. (See illustration.)

CHRISTLIKENESS

HIS CHARACTER
HIS POWER
HIS AUTHORITY

The highway of holiness is also a training ground for that day when we shall rule with Him in heaven and in the Millenial Kingdom. We are being changed from glory to glory and what isn't revealed now will become evident when we become fully joint heirs with Christ and win the crown of righteousness.* (See Romans 8:16-30; Revelation 4:10; II Timothy 4:8).

Many times when the going would be tough, and we'd be discouraged, God in a prophetic word would tell us, "You don't quite understand it all yet, but I'm preparing you to reign with Me in all My Glory." On another occasion, He shared the following words:

And it shall be that as we sit upon the shores of the new millenium I plan to create with you in the days ahead, we shall sit and remember these days, and you shall say, "Why was it so hard for me to understand? And we shall laugh

*Scripture speaks of other crowns. The incorruptible crown (the victor's crown, I Cor. 9:25). The crown of life (martyr's crown, Rev. 2:10, James 1:12). The crown of rejoicing (soul winner's crown, I Thess. 2:19). The crown of glory (the elder's crown, I Pet. 5:4).

286

together. For then you shall know all things and it will all be clear to you, and we shall enjoy remembering these moments — glad that they are past, glad that they were part of My process in bringing you into the full sonship and daughter-ship in My kingdom, so that we could think together the thoughts that come. We shall remember them with joy when this is no more, and we shall chuckle together and say, "Wow, why was that so difficult?" And we shall rejoice, because it all is true, and I am faithful to fulfill all that I have promised. So rejoice with me, my loved ones. It's a beautiful land that I have planned, and you shall help me create it, and our joy shall be sweet.

So God is not only preparing and teaching us to rule and live in His kingdom while we are here on earth, but He is also preparing us to reign with Him in all His Glory. All these things are what God is doing and building in us on the highway of holiness. These represent His ultimate intention and, therefore, our final destination in our walk with God.

But just how does that process take place in our life? How does He work His righteous character in our lives and make us responsible heirs and rulers in His Kingdom now and to come? C. S. Lovett, founder of Personal Christianity, recounts an American reporter's interview with Prince Charles.[21] The question was asked of him, "What's it like to know that you will one day wear the crown of England?" Without hesitation, he said, "Rough." He began to explain the disciplined training he needed before he would rule the British throne. For instance, he had to be fluent in a number of languages, master history, mathematics and sciences; and become an expert in heraldry, diplomacy and protocol, as well as serve in the military. The interview ended with

[21] C. S. Lovett, "Welcome to the School of Kings", *Personal Christianity,* Vol. 19, No. 7, 14932 East Pacific Avenue, Baldwin Park, CA 91706.

the potential monarch reiterating, "It's still rough. I don't have a life of my own."

Now Prince Charles' experience parallels our experience in our walk with God. We don't have a life of our own, because our life is bought with a price — the price of God's Son, Jesus. The highway of holiness is a disciplined life of obedience even to the point of death. It is not only the way of blessings, but also the way of the cross that leads to death of the self.

THE WAY
OF THE CROSS

·TRIALS
·PRUNING
·REFINING

Paul came to that point in his own life when he confessed that death of his old nature.

> I have been crucified with Christ; and it is no longer I who live, but Christ lives in me; and the life which I now live in the flesh, I live by faith in the Son of God, who loved me, and delivered Himself up for me (Gal. 2:20).

He reminded the Ephesians to lay aside the old self and put on the new man which in the likeness of God has been re-created in righteousness and holiness of the truth (Eph. 4:22-24). In addressing the Colossians, he stressed that they have died and their life was hidden with Christ in God (Col. 3:3). By the power of the Holy Spirit, they were to put to death whatever was earthly in them. To the Roman church, Paul admonished:

> So then my brothers, you can see that we have no particular reason to feel grateful to our sensual nature or to live a life on the level of the instincts. Indeed, that way of living leads to certain death. But if on the other hand you cut the nerve of your instinctive actions by obeying the Spirit, you are on the way to real living (Romans 8:12-13 Phillips)

In our obedience to the Word of God and the promptings of the Holy Spirit, we are to die to self. Have you died yet? From God's side, it is an accomplished fact. It becomes a reality when you believe it and walk in it and allow the Holy Spirit to translate this fact into our everyday lives. You already agreed to it when you were baptized, whether you were sprinkled as a little baby and later confirmed it for yourself, or were immersed in a believer's baptism. In either case, the water symbolized the dying to self and the rising up unto Jesus Christ. Jesus said the following to His disciples:

> Truly, truly I say to you, unless a grain of wheat falls into the earth and dies, it remains by itself alone. But if it dies, it bears much fruit (John 12:24).

Jesus was comparing Himself to the kernel of wheat that needs to die to bear fruit — the fruit of salvation and re-demption, healing, and deliverance. We ourselves need to

289

die to self so that we bear the fruit and character of Christ Jesus — living vessels for that salvation, redemption, healing, and deliverance. Jesus further instructed His disciples:

> He who loves his (soul) life, loses it and he who hates his (soul) life in this world shall keep it to life eternal (John 12:25).

> He who does not take up his cross and follow after me is not worthy of me. He who has found his life shall lose it and he who has lost his life for my sake shall find it (Matthew 10:38-39).

God's word attests to the fact we don't have a life of our own. God wants us to be ruled by His Holy Spirit and not by our human psyche or physical drives. He's not in the business of building an addition to our spiritual house. Rather, He's in the business of substituting His son Jesus' life for our life. This is the way of the cross that leads to the death of self and brokenness of the old man. A person isn't broken and dead to the self until all resentment and rebellion against God and man is removed. A person who resents, takes offense, retaliates, or needs to justify himself is not broken or dead. In fact, all discontent and irritation with circumstances and situations betrays the old man in us that needs to die. God doesn't want us to react to people and things, but rather to respond with the mind of Christ. Dying to the self through the way of the cross is the way of coming to the end of our resources and the total reliance on God's resources. As Paul Billheimer so aptly put it, "God's great purpose in His dealing with us is to reduce us. This is because any confidence in one's flesh is fatal to confidence and faith in God. Until one is broken, he is full of

290

himself, his plans, his ambitions, and his value judgements."[22] In this respect, even man's best intentions can get in the way of God's divine intention. Like John the Baptist, we need to decrease so that Christ increases in our life.

Charles Price in his book *Spiritual and Physical Health* has this striking comment on this need for us to be nothing so that God can be everything.

> The day was when I used to pray for power to become something and do something. That day has gone. Today I pray for power to become nothing. I realize that self is the brake that holds the power back. I know that if I surrender my life, He will give me His. Then this life, touched with depravity, robed in impatience, with a heart that is deceitful above all things, is swallowed up in the glorious majesty and power of the resurrected life.[23]

Abraham was given the promised child Isaac. There was a delay of twelve years between promise and fulfillment, but finally the miracle happened. Isaac was born. God brought life from dead bodies. Abraham's body was too old to be father of many nations, and Sarah was also beyond child-bearing years. Abraham's faith produced new life. God wants us to have the same faith of Abraham to let Him produce the life of Jesus in us. Our life is already reckoned as dead. But there came a day when God invited Abraham and his son to a mountain. He asked Abraham to sacrifice his own son. That may sound strange to us, just as strange as God reckoning us as dead. God wanted to make

[22]Paul E. Billheimer, *Don't Waste Your Sorrows,* Christian Literature Crusade, Fort Washington, Penn. 19034, 1977, p. 75.

[23]Charles Price, *Spiritual and Physical Health,* Logos International, Plainfield, N.J. 07060, p. 53.

sure the promise didn't get in the way of Abraham's allegiance to Him. God doesn't want even our blessings to get in the way of trusting Him. Only when we have trusted Him with our life will He trust us with His blessings and His kingdom.

If the highway of holiness is the way of the cross and death of the self, how does God implement this death of self? Does it come about through study and obedience to His word? Does it happen when we fellowship with other believers and exercise our faith based on the promises of God's word? Does it occur when we exercise our authority to receive healing in body, soul, and spirit? Yes, in all accounts, but there is another way which the Holy Spirit uses that we have not touched on in this book and that is through trials and tribulations. While we have the blessings on the highway of holiness, we need to recognize the trials and tribulations that God allows to test our faith and make us complete.* Just as an athlete needs to test his strength and stamina in an athletic event, so the Christian needs to have trials to test his faith and the death of self. This is precisely what it says in God's word:

> Consider it all joy my brethren, when you encounter various trials, knowing that the testing of your faith produces endurance. And let endurance have its perfect result that you may be perfect and complete, lacking in nothing (James 1:2-4).

That perfection and completeness which the apostle is talking about is the perfection and completeness of Jesus

---

*Trials and tribulations do not in themselves bring maturity. We grow into maturity when we stand firm in our faith, believing in God and His word in and through the trials and tribulations.

in us. The apostle James goes on to promise a blessing and a crown of life for those who persevere under trial (James 1:12). Paul essentially says the same thing in Romans 5:1-5:

> Therefore, having been justified by faith, we have peace with God, through our Lord Jesus Christ.

> Through whom also we have obtained our introduction by faith into this grace in which we stand; and we exult in hope of the glory of God.

> And not only this, but we also exult in our tribulations, knowing that tribulation brings about perseverance,

> and perseverance, proven character; and proven character, hope;

> and hope does not disappoint, because the love of God has been poured out within our hearts through the Holy Spirit who was given to us.

I must say I wish someone would have informed me about this a long time ago. Instead of reacting and questioning God about what and why a certain problem came into my life, I could have simply relied on His love to see me through it and use it to complete me. That was essentially the problem with Job, wasn't it? In the prologue of the book of Job, you have a brief scene where Satan tells God that the only reason why His servant is faithful to Him is because he is being blessed. Take away Job's blessings and see if he remains faithful to God. God agrees to it, but He says, "You can't take my servant's life." As the blessings are taken away from him, Job ignores his wife's suggestion to curse God and die. He even makes a valiant affirmation that he knows that his redeemer lives, but nevertheless, fear comes on him and his faith wanes. Against his better judgment to be silent and teachable, he complains of his

293

lot and grows bitter (Job 7:11). The main body of the book of Job, some 714 verses, asks the question "why?" His friends offer reasons for his suffering and end up accusing Job of some sin he did against God. Job, in reacting to these accusations, tries to justify himself. Near the end, a fourth character comes on the scene by the name of Elihu. His name means, "He is God," and that is significant because God always leaves a witness to His people. Elihu rebukes Job's friends for condemning Job and Job for justifying himself (Chapters 32-37). Then God himself appears in a whirlwind and confronts Job who, in justifying himself, really questions God's sovereignty and providence (Chapters 38-41). In the final chapter, Job repents of his self-justification and God heals him and blesses him with twice as much. The accusers of Job were to make a sacrifice and ask for Job's prayers. In this book, we see that Job was a righteous man, dead to sin, but in his great sufferings, he dies to his theology and all his simplistic views of God's providence. He dies to a great many things which in themselves were not sin, but which hindered his greatest union with God.[24]

If we understand what God is doing in these trials, we can shorten, if not eliminate, the questioning, the reacting, the need to justify ourselves. With Paul, we can be content in all things and even get to the point where we praise Him in all things. Why? Simply because it brings us more closely to the point of stretching our faith and allowing the Holy Spirit to further destroy the old nature and build the righteousness of Jesus in us.

I personally know of many people (including myself) and I'm sure you do, too, who have run away from trials in their life. Instead of growing through them, they run away

[24] Billheimer, *Op. cit.*, p. 25. ᛵ

from the tests. I'm thinking, for example, of a pastor friend who quit the ministry when the going got rough. God, through many people, had spoken prophetically that He was going to use this man not only for a mighty revival in his own church, but also in his city. But the man walked away from it. He refused to stand with God and "faith it" in the trials that were coming his way.

Let me assure you that if we walk away from one trial, God will provide another one for us to walk through with Him. Bob Mumford, a teacher with Christian Growth Ministries, puts it in his own inimitable way:

God fixes a fix to fix you. If you fix the fix before it fixes you, God has to fix another to fix you.

Now while I have no quarrel with those that say most trials are obviously from Satan, I believe the whole context of Scripture speaks of God in His sovereignty using people and circumstances (yes, even Satan) for His divine purpose. God allowed Peter, for example, with all his brashness and bravado to be sifted by Satan and face up to the shallowness of his commitment.* In the same manner God allowed Paul's thorn in the flesh to keep him humble and make him totally dependent upon Him.

Jesus illustrated the way of the cross another way when He compared Himself to the vine and His Father to the vinedresser (John 15).

I am the true vine and My Father is the vinedresser. (v. 1)

Every branch in me that does not bear fruit, He takes away; and every branch that bears fruit, He prunes it that it may bear more fruit. (v. 2)

---

*Jesus, addressing Peter said, "Satan has asked permission to sift you , , , " (Luke 22:31). Whose permission did he have to ask? God's, of course.

You are already clean because of the word which I have spoken to you. (v. 3)

Abide in me, and I in you. As the branch cannot bear fruit of itself, unless it abides in the vine, so neither can you unless you abide in Me. (v. 4)

I am the vine, you are the branches; he who abides in Me and I in him, he bears much fruit, for apart from me you can do nothing. (v. 5)

Here, Jesus indicates the intimacy that we need to have with Him — that has already been established on the cross. Just as the branches cannot sustain themselves apart from the vine, so we cannot sustain ourselves, let alone bear fruit. But notice. Here Jesus tells His disciples even though they were clean by the Word, they need to be pruned so that they may bear more fruit. This also includes the fruitful works and character of Christ. I saw the reality of this spiritual truth one day when I was asked to prune a pear tree. The tree belonged to my wife's Aunt Opal. She said, "Denis, I love this beautiful pear tree, but it's not producing very much." I looked at the tree which was just to the right of her picture window. I could see how it was solid leaves with suckers growing all over. I asked her, "Will you trust me to prune as much as is needed?" I could see that she was a bit hesitant, but she nodded. As I proceeded to lop off all the unnecessary branches, every once in a while, through the corner of my eye, I could see her peek nervously out of her picture window to see if I killed the tree. After I was done, I could see by the look on her face that she wasn't quite sure whether I pruned it or butchered it. But the following year she gave us a glowing report of the results. The pears were so big and so many that the branches had to be propped up with stakes.

296

Now God asks us to do the same thing with our lives. He says, "Will you trust me to prune the things that may seem important to your life, that limit my working in your life?" This could mean our possessions, our job, our security, our friends, even our television habits. It could mean everything and anything. Every time, for example, we abuse our privilege of TV watching, it seems that, almost as if by divine fiat, the TV doesn't work. We discover that God is pruning us from the TV because He wants to redeem our time with Him. The Word of God says even Jesus, the Son of God, learned obedience through suffering (Hebrews 5:8). If Jesus, who was perfect, learned obedience through suffering, can we not do the same as we follow the way of the cross?*

We have established that the highway of holiness is a narrow road where we enjoy blessings as well as the way of the cross, with its trials, tribulations, pruning and refining. The final destination is Christlikeness. Like many travelers, we often get side-tracked. We go off on the wrong road. Sometimes we sin by thinking we know better than God's road manual (the Bible). By sinning and trying to do our own thing, we try to make a narrow road into a four-lane highway and that, of course, is impossible. We simply end up on a dead-end street and as a result, we must be chastised by God.

At this point, we need to see the difference between a trial or pruning as a way of the cross, and chastisement and suffering as a result of sin and disobedience. Many people complain about the trials and sufferings that they have undergone. They tell me with a sigh and stiff upper lip,

*The Bible uses other terminology, such as the baptism of fire and God refining His people. In all these cases, it leads to the way of the cross and death of ourselves.

that it is their cross to bear. This is a trial that God has placed on them, but the truth of the matter is, they are not suffering for righteousness sake. They are simply suffering because of their sinful attitudes and out-and-out disobedience to God's Word. The apostle Peter points out the difference between suffering for righteousness' sake and suffering due to sin.

> For what credit is there if, when you sin and are harshly treated, you endure it with patience? But if when you do what is right and suffer for it, you patiently endure it, this finds favor with God (I Peter 2:20).

Suffering then, as the consequence of our own sin, is not the way of the cross. It is the way of chastisement, and we need to see the difference. Many times we reap what we sow

298

and God has to simply chastise us either by His word or by a brother or sister in Christ or allow us to suffer the natural consequences of our sin. In the latter case, for example, if I have a heavy foot and disobey the speed laws by going through town at 80 miles an hour, chances are I'd be caught for speeding, fined and possibly imprisoned. But whatever the case, out of His love for us God spanks us and reproves us just as an earthly father spanks his child. What we need to do is repent and get back on the narrow road of the highway of holiness. Consider Hebrews 12:4-11, for example:

You have not yet resisted to the point of shedding blood in your striving against sin. (v. 4)

And you have forgotten (many of us have) the exhortation which is addressed to you as sons, 'My son do not regard lightly the discipline of the Lord, nor faint when you are reproved by Him. (v. 5)

For those whom the Lord loves, He disciplines and He scourges every son whom He receives.' (v. 6)

It is for discipline that you endure; God deals with you as with sons; for what son is there whom his father does not discipline? (v. 7)

But if you are without discipline, of which you all have become partakers, then you are illegitimate children and not sons. (v. 8)

Furthermore, we had earthly fathers to discipline us and we respected them: shall we not much rather be subject to the Father of spirits and live? (v. 9)

For they disciplined us for a short time as seemed best to them, but He disciplines us for our good that we may share His Holiness. (v. 10)

All discipline for the moment seems not to be enjoyed, but sorrowful, yet to those who have been trained by it, afterwards it yields the peaceful fruit of righteousness. (v. 11)

In verses 10 and 11, we see again the ultimate purpose in chastising us is for holiness which yields the fruit of righteousness. There is only one righteousness and that is the righteous character of Jesus and there is only one righteous work and that is the righteous work of Jesus.

After God chastises us, what then? We need to repent and get back on the narrow road of holiness. Paul, who was used by God to chastise the Corinthian Christians, shows what must be done (II Corinthians 7:1, 8, 9, 10).

> Therefore, having these promises, beloved, let us cleanse ourselves from all defilement of flesh and spirit, perfecting holiness in the fear of the Lord . . . (v. 1

> For though I caused you sorrow by my letter, I do not regret it; though I did regret it — for I see that the letter caused you sorrow, though only for a while — (v. 8)

> I now rejoice, not that you were made sorrowful, but you were made sorrowful to the point of repentance: for you were made sorrowful according to the will of God, in order that you might not suffer loss in anything through us. (v. 9)

> For sorrow that is according to the will of God produces a repentance without regret, leading to salvation, but the sorrow of the world produces death. (v. 10)

Paul in these verses makes the distinction between worldly sorrow that produces death and godly sorrow that leads to salvation and, I would add, the highway of holiness. There are many people in the world that are sorrowful for the situation in which they find themselves. They are suffering because of their sin, but they are not sorrowful for their sinful nature. For instance, a thief that gets caught in a robbery is sorrowful mainly because he got caught and has to go to prison. But if he were sorrowful to the point of repentance, he would be sorrowful because of his sinful nature that expresses itself in his thievery. I never completely understood this until I counseled a sixteen-year-old girl. She was sorrowful for the situation she was in. She reaped what she sowed, in this case, an illegitimate baby. Taking the world's way, she killed the child by having an abortion. As a result, she was feeling guilty. As I talked and prayed with her, it suddenly dawned on me that she was not sorrowful to the point of repentance. She intended to go on living with the man who was the father of their baby and she refused the message of salvation. Once we have been convicted of our sin, we need to repent and agree with God that it was a sin against Him. We need to have the godly sorrow to the extent that we would rather die than to do it again. Then asking for and receiving God's forgiveness, we need to claim His grace to redeem us from this sin (and the old sinful nature for those who are not Christians already). We need to see the importance of repentance because once God chastises us through His instruments, we either respond by repenting and being reconciled, or react and grow bitter towards Him and our circumstances. This can lead us down another dead-end road, the road of bitterness (with the insidious emotional twins of self-pity and resentment) which ultimately leads to depression. The letter to the Hebrews, Chapter 12, verses 14 and 15, gives us fair warning about this:

> Pursue peace with all men and the sanctification (holiness) without which no one will see the Lord.
>
> See to it that no one comes short of the grace of God; that no root of bitterness springing up causes trouble, and by it many be defiled.

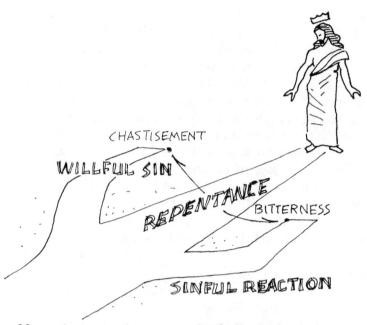

CHASTISEMENT

WILLFUL SIN

REPENTANCE

BITTERNESS

SINFUL REACTION

Many times people react to God's chastisement or even a trial (or pruning) that comes their way and they grow bitter instead of better. Larry Christenson points out that there is only one letter difference between the words "better" and "bitter" — the letter "I" and God wants to remove it from our life.[25] Repentance helps us remove that "I", the ego, and replaces it with an "E" for Emmanuel, God with us.

Finally, there is another thing that we need to consider when we travel the highway of holiness. Like any trip we may run into a roadblock or barrier. A roadblock in general prevents or hinders us from getting to our destination. In this respect, we need to see the difference between a chastisement, the way of the cross, and a barrier that we need to take authority over so as to fulfill our divine destiny.

[25] Larry Christenson, *The Renewed Mind,* Bethany Fellowship, pp. 99-100.

302

SATAN'S BARRIER

In the sixteenth chapter of Matthew, we can see the barrier that can hinder and prevent us from walking with God along the highway of holiness. In this chapter, Jesus asks the disciples who people think He is. And they offer that some thought He was John the Baptizer, some said He was Elijah, others, Jeremiah or some of the other prophets come back alive. Then He addresses the disciples and asks, "Who do you say I am?" Peter confesses that He is the Christ, the Son of the Living God, whereupon Jesus blesses him and tells him that this revelation and confession were not inspired by his own understanding, but revealed by His Father in heaven. Immediately after this confession, Jesus explains to His disciples God's plan for His life — that He was to suffer by way of the cross, and die and be raised from the dead. Peter, who had previously spoken by the inspiration of the Father, rebukes Jesus and says, "God forbid it."

303

Jesus immediately discerns that Peter was inspired by Satan to hinder Him from His divine destiny. That barrier was Satan. Satan did not want Him to go the way of the cross and save mankind. By the same token, Satan does not want us to go the way of the cross, either. He does not want us to participate in God's kingdom and put on the likeness of Christ. Jesus had an answer for that barrier. He said, "Get thee behind me, Satan. You are a stumbling block to me for you are not setting your mind on God's interests, but man's." There are times as we travel the highway of holiness when we need to exercise our authority as a believer and say, "Get thee behind me Satan. You are a stumbling block to the way of the cross." Satan is a stumbling block, a barrier, when he lies to us and tries to prevent us from walking with God. He is a barrier to our walk with God when he tries to bind us and curse us with sickness in body, soul, and spirit. He is a barrier when he lies and deceives us and breaks our spirit. He is a barrier when he brings fear into our hearts. When we recognize him for what he is, all we need to do is exercise our authority as a believer in Christ and rebuke him and claim the promises of God.

To sum up, the highway of holiness is a narrow road. It gets narrower as we become mature and responsible Christians. But with the narrowness (according to the world) there comes the broad freedom in the spirit to rule and live in God's spiritual kingdom. Our experience on this road is a preparation for the time when we will rule with Jesus in the millenial kingdom. Our ultimate destination, however, is to gain Christlikeness — the righteous character of Jesus — and express His compassionate heart to the world with His power and authority. This Christlikeness comes through a disciplined obedience to His Word. It also comes by way of the cross where we die to ourselves through the pruning and the trials that God allows to come into our life. When we choose to sin and be disobedient, God also

304

chastises us and calls us to repentance which leads us back to the highway of holiness. Finally, when Satan tries to hinder our walk and keep us from fulfilling our divine destiny, we have been given Jesus' authority to deal with him.

In the next chapter, I want to show you just how that has worked in my own life.

Chapter 16

The Highway of Holiness
A Personal Testimony

As a child I was always shy and withdrawn. I was pretty much a loner and had difficulty making friends. My parents were separated during most of my early life. When my sister contracted rheumatic fever, my mother had to make the decision of keeping her in a cold-water flat in Montreal, Quebec, and risking her health or sending her to live with my uncle and aunt in a warmer climate in the United States. She chose to do the latter and I felt even more lonely. And yet it was through her nurture that I can't remember not knowing about Jesus and God. In my loneliness, I would always talk to Him and I knew His hand was upon me. There was the time, for example, when I fell through a porch railing on our second story apartment and somersaulted, landing on my feet with no broken bones or even a scratch. The Bible says that God is a Father to those who have no father and that was true in my case.

I can remember when I was particularly lonely and cried out to Him and I heard an audible voice call my name. I looked around but I couldn't see anyone. It completely jolted me out of my despondency.

When I was eleven years old, my mother and I immigrated to the United States and were reunited with my sister in Milwaukee, Wisconsin. We grew up in a German-Polish neighborhood. My sister and I faithfully went to church and Sunday school — our lives centered around that church. But it wasn't until I was 17 years old that I really discovered the reality of Jesus as my Lord and Savior. I was going out with a date and the girl suggested we stop by a Youth for Christ meeting. Although I had led a pretty moral life, I discovered that my righteousness was as filthy rags. God doesn't have a sin meter where one person is more of a sinner than another. We all stand in need of salvation. When the invitation was given and I raised my hand, I felt, as John Wesley put it, "my heart strangely warmed." My spirit had become regenerated, my name had been written in the Lamb's Book of Life. In humility I had stooped down to get into the narrow gate and chosen the narrow road. But there was no follow-up or anyone to teach and disciple me. I had no idea what was expected of me. And so I stayed at the small gate and had for-better and for-worse commitments with Jesus along the way. And yet somehow, God always gave me a friend who had some spiritual dimension to him and we would be able to stand against the prevailing sins of our youth.

My parents were reunited about the time I graduated from high school. This presented a time of mixed blessings. It was a time of adjustment where I found myself no longer the head man in the house. It was a particularly painful point in my life; I remember vividly having to die to my status as head of the family and submit to my father. Although, I did not appreciate it then, God used my father to

307

reprove me and chastise me and make up for the lost time that I had experienced when I was growing up pretty much by myself.

When I went to college I had no idea that I should have asked for the Lord's guidance on what I should do. Since I had an interest in the natural sciences, I decided that I would become a wildlife biologist. Besides, I ventured, shy people like myself can always get along with animals; they are easier to relate to. When I graduated from the University of Michigan, I found out that there were not too many positions available. After sending out 150 applications and writing civil service exams, all I could find was seasonal work in the summer time. It was quite a blow to my ego. It seemed all doors were closed to me in this area. As I struggled working in factories and odd jobs, a friend directed me to a Christian Fellowship where they were turned on to Jesus. There was a very dedicated and committed corps of young people. We held Christ-centered meetings, retreats and participated in crusades. Whether I was aware of it or not, I was involved in the rudiments of discipleship.

About this time, the Lord was laying on my heart that He wanted me to go into the ministry. I struggled against this because it didn't fit in with my plans and ambitions. There was a great fear also, because I had such a difficult time getting up and sharing with a crowd of people. I felt about as qualified for the ministry as a blacksmith for neurosurgery.

One day, as I was wallowing in self-pity (offering every excuse that I could think of not to go to seminary), my eyes fell on a scripture passage where Moses received a call to go and set the Israelites free (Exodus 4:10). Moses offers a similar excuse for not going. He claimed he was slow of speech (tongue-tied). God answered, "Never mind, I will be your mouth." The Lord was chastising me through that scripture and saying, "enough of your excuses, just let Me be your mouth." God wouldn't give me any peace. Finally, like a reluctant Jonah, I said, "Okay, but I'm sure not going to like it." Satan was setting up a barrier of lies, too. He was telling me, "If you go to seminary, you'll never laugh and enjoy yourself again (I wasn't happy now). This religious stuff is pretty serious business." By that he meant it would be pretty boring. In spite of his lies, I went off to seminary. I resolved to try it for a year and if it didn't work out I'd go home. When I agreed to go, God's peace finally came to me. But Satan had to get his last dig in. When I was on the campus, I asked a college student for directions to the seminary. His response was, "Oh, you mean the angel factory?" He proceeded to give me directions as I groaned inside.

But God proved Satan a liar! Because, as I chose to obey Him, I never enjoyed myself more or laughed as much in my whole life. While we had our serious moments, it was exciting and sometimes downright hilarious. Certainly, it was far from boring. The fear of rejection and feelings of rejection were pretty well kept in abeyance. It would only crop up when it came to practice preaching. But even here on certain occasions when I would go out in fear and trembling and read a manuscript in a little pastorless country church, the Lord would bless that. On one occasion as I started preaching, a strange thing happened, I forgot my fears, I felt confident. As I looked out in the faces of the people, I saw people gasping, and even weeping. I thought to myself "O God, am I that bad?" I didn't realize until years later that what happened was a special anointing of God and these people weeping were under the conviction of the Holy Spirit. The Lord was proving that He could use anyone, including me.

The time came to graduate. I was graduating magna cum laude. I had won a Hebrew Scholarship and spent one year in Paris, France, on a denominational work-study scholarship. I had accomplished a lot while I was there. Seminary and the academic life was like a refuge to me. Now I was to graduate and the fears of inadequacy came upon me again. And so I decided rather than go out and preach, I would go to a School of Religion at the state university and maybe get a Ph.D. and teach. Notice, I said "I decided." I didn't consult the Lord about this either. At this point, I was beginning to feel pretty confident in myself, at least in the academic field. Later, the Lord revealed that it wasn't confidence so much as it was arrogance and pride. Learning and study apart from the Spirit makes a person arrogant. In spite of fear and feelings of inadequacy, I thought I was pretty hot stuff. When I left seminary I began to question the authority of God's Word. While many of my professors were godly men, some felt that modern scholarship and hermenautics was the only way to interpret the Bible. Little did I know then that much of modern scholarship is a throwback to 18th and 19th century Rationalism. This, of course, did a lot to cast doubt on the inspiration of the Bible. We were told to demythologize the Bible and recognize that many of the healings and supernatural events in the Bible were the mentality of that age. A reader must wade through the tradition of the church and the theology of Matthew, Mark, Luke, John, and the other writers who were not contemporary with Jesus to get a kernel of what Jesus said and who He was. And so I bought that — not all of it, but some of it. Enough to eventually dry me up spiritually. Since my major was New Testament Studies at the University, I got more of this kind of scholarship and with that, more doubt about my faith. Some of our seminary professors were spiritual fathers to us; there was no such thing at the School of Religion.

Along with this spiritual dryness, I was beginning to feel more lonely than ever. It was about this time that I said, "Lord, if You want me to remain single, give me the

310

grace to be single, but if you have someone for me, send her soon. I trust you with that part of my life." God honored that prayer in less than a year. He didn't give me the grace to remain single, He simply gave me Grace — that was her name. Although she was just an undergraduate, she was a Christian woman mature beyond her years. When I met her it was as if I had known her all my life. There was no need for coyness or social one-up-manship. On our first date, the Lord wanted me to read scripture to her. I protested and said, "But God, she'll think I'm a religious stuffed shirt or something." But when I obeyed Him, I saw her light up like a Christmas tree. I simply knew from that day on that we were destined by God to be life partners in Christ's service. As unromantic as it might sound, before I could afford to buy her an engagement ring, I bought her a yoke brooch as a symbol of our life of service together.

We were married in her little home (country) church in southern Iowa. While life as a married student added a plus in my life, graduate school left me cold. I was beginning to lose my motivation. Life as a half-time instructor was not as challenging as I thought it would be. I found it difficult, if not impossible to teach world religions without beinging in my own convictions of Jesus Christ. I found people coming up after class, not so much concerned with understanding world religions or getting a better grade, but seeking truth and meaning for their lives. I felt torn up inside trying to play the role of straight academician, which was demanded of me, and a longing to share my faith, which was prohibited. After struggling through comprehensive exams and writing a dissertation, I knew I had to leave. God was closing the door on my academic life.

Grace and I took a two-point charge in northern Wisconsin vacationland. One church was strictly a resort church. The other was an Indian mission church. Most of those who attended the mission church were white resort owners.

311

While I was pastoring these two churches, I read an auto-biography of a priest who came to northern Wisconsin 100 years ago to minister to the Indians. In his diary, he commented that this particular band of Indians where we were living were hardened to the Gospel. He said he could have spent the rest of his life ministering here and not get as far as he would somewhere else. And so he turned his attention to other Indians who were more receptive to the Gospel. After a couple of months living on the reservation, I was convinced he was right. The Indians had abandoned the best of their culture and accepted the worst of the white man's culture. Alcoholism was rampant among them, along with that came the sins of the flesh described in Galatians 5:17-21. The real eye opener was waking up in the morning and finding twelve-to fourteen-year-old children dead drunk on our lawn. Church activity for most of the Indians was confined to funerals, marriages, and baptisms. Among the resort owners and white residents who attended church, there was a religious apathy towards the church. Many of them were refugees from the cities escaping from its race problems and problems of urbanization. In the mission church, I was confronted by two social strata — abject poverty on the part of the Indians and considerable wealth on the part of the white community. The only thing that could bridge that gap was Jesus and so I preached the most Christ-centered messages that I knew. I had Bible studies and I could see a gradual awakening to spiritual things but somehow it wasn't enough. By and large, my words seemed to fall to the ground. When I talked about the love of God, I could not convey the reality of it because of my own hurts that needed to be mended and healed. With the reluctant approval of the elders in the church, I made changes in the liturgy and on occasion held more up-to-date guitar services. But there was still no response. I had Wednesday night prayer services and only a few would come. I got involved with Project Headstart and did other social services in the community and still felt empty and unfulfilled. I could see no significant change in the lives of the people. I started an AA group with the help of some dedicated members. A lot of people outside the community came, but none from the church or the immediate community. One of my summer assistants approached me about having a boys' club for the kids in the community. Something happened, but not what I had expected. A window in the church was broken and someone wrote some graffiti on some bulletin boards. This caused a furor and the end of the boys' club. I later found out that the town gossip had turned the graffiti into pornography. There finally came a day when I told God, "I'm tired; that's it, I'm quitting. You know, I didn't want to be in the ministry in the first place."

After I handed in my resignation, I said to the Lord that unless something happened, I was not only quitting these churches, I was quitting the ministry. There had to be something more. In desperation I started to look to scripture for answers for my life. Before that I used to look to scripture mainly for next week's sermon. My eyes fell on the Book of Acts and I saw the authority and power working in the apostles. I wondered if this were for today. If it were, I had nothing to lose and everything to gain. In my case, I was willing to die to my theology; it hadn't gotten anywhere so far. And so I knelt down in front of the altar and asked God's forgiveness for my sins, my pride, my stubbornness, and asked Him to baptize me with His Holy Spirit. At that time I didn't know about claiming it by faith; I thought that somehow I would feel different. After an hour on my knees, I went about my business making pastoral calls. That same week at our AA meeting, I found myself gravitating to one of the leaders in the group. In our previous encounter, I discovered that this cherubic

50-year-old man was a grocer in Eagle River, Wisconsin. He had been an alcoholic for fifteen years. I noticed the enthusiasm he had for the Lord. I was astonished by the authority that he had, especially when he spoke about Jesus. In fact, everything was Jesus-this and Jesus-that. This unlearned man had a tremendous knowledge of the Bible. I knew he came from a Pentecostal church. Later I found out he was a Full Gospel Businessmen International Director. After the meeting I invited him to come to the manse (parsonage) and I explained to him that we felt the need to have the Baptism of the Holy Spirit. So, my wife and I knelt before him and had him lay hands on us. He later invited us to attend a Full Gospel meeting at Green Lake, Wisconsin, and it was there that I was released in the Spirit to speak in tongues.

After that, the Word of God came alive to me. One of the more perceptive saints in the church said, "Denis, what happened to you? You preach differently." God's love poured out from the pulpit in spite of myself. I would pray for a parishioner and he would be healed. The town gossip, who was a member, came to my study after a service and with tears in her eyes asked forgiveness for all the nasty things she had said about me.

After leaving this parish, I eventually accepted a call to central Minnesota as an assistant pastor to an 800-member church. While the baptism in the Holy Spirit gave me a better balance in my spiritual life, I still felt insecure about myself, especially working with young people. And yet God richly blessed us and we were accepted by many of the parishioners, as well as the senior pastor. He was just looking into the Baptism of the Holy Spirit which he and many of the parishioners received while I was there. Like myself, he was insecure about himself and was fearful about what this would do to the church, which was basically liberal. Not all the members were open to a born-again experience,

let alone the Baptism of the Holy Spirit. Some were involved in Spiritual Frontiers — a mixed bag of spiritualism
and psychic phenomena — and Edgar Cayce studies. This
brought a point of conflict, but God eventually dealt with
these people as He showed them the difference between
soul power and the power of the Holy Spirit. While I was
there I received the encouragement I needed for spiritual
growth — sometimes through the pastor, but more often
through some of the elders. God was slowly breaking me of
my intellectual pride and showing me how much I needed
to convey His compassionate heart. In spite of this, I still
felt lonely and inadequate in my role as assistant pastor. I
did not know what was expected of me. Part of that frustration would sometimes be expressed in my frustration
with unbelief or noncommitment of so many parishioners.
I still did not feel free in the few occasions that I did preach
or teach. Eventually I was told that the church could no
longer support an assistant pastor. I knew that it wasn't
the only reason; it was because I wasn't carrying my own
weight and because of my offending some members of the
congregation who deemed me too evangelical. Once again,
I felt like I was a big failure.

   With the next call, the Lord gave me two choices. The
first choice was to stay in the same town and pastor a
broken-down church which couldn't afford a full-time
pastor. The second choice was as an associate pastor in a
rather affluent church further north where the senior pastor
was spirit-filled. That sounded like an easy choice, but then
God told me His first choice was my staying in town and
pastoring the broken-down church. The other choice was
only within His permissive will and I would miss His divine
will for me. With fear and trembling I decided to choose
His way. A lot of people, when they heard of my choice,
thought that I must be desperate or out of my mind. But I
consoled myself because a few years back I had read

Father Dennis Bennett's book, "Nine O'Clock in the Morning," and learned that he, as a spirit-filled Episcopalian priest, was assigned to a little mission church in Seattle. [26] The church had no way to go but up. God resurrected that church. I felt and hoped that this might be God's plan for this church, too. Undoubtedly, He was sending me here to help do a resurrection job on this little church.

I was wrong. Before a resurrection takes place, you need to have a death. The one that died was me. It did not take me too long to find out the reason why this little church was in such sad straits. Years ago, the church was a congregational church and as membership dwindled, it was handed over to the Presbyterian church. After supplying and yoking it with two other churches, they were able to hang on. When, however, the other two churches grew in numbers and were able to support a full-time pastor, they were left alone to forge for themselves. Although it was in the middle of a residential area, it never grew. After the Presbytery supplied it with part time student preachers, and short term supply preachers without much success, they provisionally handed it over to the Christian Reformed Church. Part of the congregation did not want to be under the discipline of the Reformed Church which had a ruling against Masonry. As a result, the church split. Part of it, the more evangelical wing, went off to be with the Reformed Church and the rest remained. This is the part that I had to work with, plus a few families that had come in who were refugees from a past split in the Mission Covenant Church. The situation was so chancy that the Presbytery officials refused to install me. Here was a bunch of people feeling rejected, hurting and angry about their lot, led by a not-fully-recognized pastor who had this same problem.

[26] Dennis Bennett, *Nine O'Clock In the Morning,* Logos International, Plainfield, N.J., 1970.

Any thought that I may have had about them being grateful in having a full-time pastor at half-time pay flew out of the window. One very frustrated man, who refused God's call into the ministry earlier in his life, managed nearly every Sunday to corner me and correct me on every sermon. He just had to tell me how I should have preached my sermon; and the Lord told me to say nothing, simply to thank him and love him. That was the death of me. While I was dying to myself, the Lord little by little added to our numbers. Some would come to the Lord and still others came into the Baptism of the Holy Spirit. But more than anything, the Lord was opening the doors for me to minister to people in the larger community, people who were hungry to know about the Baptism and their walk in the Spirit. I found myself ministering to hundreds, yes, thousands of people outside that little church: to Catholics, Lutherans, Baptists in the community. Many of these people were disenfranchised in their own churches. Little by little, God was showing me my authority as a believer and where He intended me to be. Slowly He was weaning me from a life of guaranteed wages and preparing me for a life totally reliant on him.

A few years later, this was to become a reality as I joined with two other pastors and their families who started an interdenominational faith ministry. As we ministered together, the Holy Spirit began showing us the ministry of Jesus and our authority as believers. We were called to teach His people how to minister by His power and in His Spirit, but before we received that call, we needed to exercise that power for ourselves and receive healing and deliverance. As freely as we had received from God, we were to freely give.

One day as we were ministering to a person who had the problem of rejection and fear of rejection, the Lord said to me, "Denis, that is your problem. This has been a barrier to my ministering through you and I want you to deal with that as well as other things." As we prayed in the Spirit, the Lord revealed that these cords had come down through my father's side. I needed to break them by the power of Jesus and renounce the spirit of rejection, which had used that cord to oppress and harass me. As soon as I did that, I found that perfect liberty that Jesus has for all His children. Before I exercised my authority, the Holy Spirit allowed me to put a lid on that problem, but now God was saying, "I want you to be totally free of it and to fulfill your divine destiny." A few days later after I had dealt with the barriers in my life, I was meditating on a passage in Revelations where the elders in heaven were worshipping Jesus, casting their crowns before Him. In my prayer I said, "Lord, I would like to gain a crown of life to cast before your feet." Unknown to me, one of the saints was praying for our ministry at that same time. The Lord spoke to her and said, "Share this with Denis." And I share this with you now, not to bring any glory or attention to myself, but to simply show what your divine destiny is. In fact, place your name in place of mine:

> My servant, Denis, is glorious in My eyes. I have brought him through fiery furnaces. I have tested him and have given him an enduring heart. Denis is clothed in royal robes, upon his feet are velvet slippers which quietly lead him to the heart of my people.

> The hands that reach out to the fallen have been bathed in the blood of the cross; the eyes which gaze from his face are pools of living waters where My people come to be refreshed. The words which issue forth from his lips are as thunder from My mountaintops. Hearts will rejoice for my rain will soon follow.

God is not only preparing me, but you and all of us to reign with Him. As we travel this highway of holiness, we

318

need to endure the testing, the refining, the pruning which is the way of the cross that leads to the righteousness of Jesus. Along the way, we also need to exercise our authority as believers and draw on our inheritance. When Satan challenges us or binds us, like Jesus we need to rebuke him and take authority over him. When we rebel against God and try to make that narrow road a four-lane highway, we need to accept the chastisement of God, repent and get back on the highway of holiness. Whatever the cost and whatever the situation we find ourselves in, we need to look to Jesus, the author and perfector of our faith.

A CALL TO LIVE ETERNALLY NOW

Several years ago, as we were beginning to understand our authority as believers, the Lord spoke these words of encouragement. It is a timely message for today for those who have ears to hear and a desire to please Him.

Move quickly, my children. Move quickly. You know I am moving quickly. You must move right along with me bringing in the harvest; shouting from the rooftops what is about to take place; touching the hearts of people who are afraid to believe. My excitement I give to you, and my peace. Trust Me. Cling close to Me. Be with Me always. I want to hold you and bless you and be with you for all eternity. I want you to know that I love you. Rejoice with Me, My children, for it is a time for great rejoicing. Not for mourning any more, the mourning is gone — rejoicing is come. Celebrate Me. and My Life; the Resurrected Life that I have given you. Be resurrected in your minds and your spirits and your bodies. Don't be limited anymore by the limitations of the world. Those limitations are broken — the bonds are gone. I CALL YOU TO LIVE ETERNALLY NOW, RIGHT NOW!!! You stepped into Eternity already — now begin living it! Because you really have. The enemy has tried to tell you that you haven't, but he's the Liar of all the liars. I told you that. Stop listening to his lies and start listening to My Love and the certainty of My Eternity and the reality of My Life in you. My power is so much greater than anything you could imagine or dream and I am pouring it out into you and through you. That power must be disseminated into all the world so that they may have light...may see the Light...may become the light...so that darkness cannot be anymore.

The river of living water must be poured out and cleanse the world; refresh the world that is so dead...cleanse, refresh, renew, rebuild. And out of you shall come that living water. It is coming as a trickle right now and it is going to come forth as a mighty river...a tidal wave of MY Love that is not limited or stopped by anything. Be unlimited people. Be My unlimited Body. Know that I am God; that I am in the midst of thee, and that I am mighty to fulfill all that I have purposed and planned to fulfill from the very beginning of the foundation of the earth. I love you, I love you, I love you. I bless you, I bless you, I bless you. I need you. Come let us walk together. Let me show you the Glory you have inherited, that is upon your heads and your dwelling places and being poured out into all the world.

320

BIBLIOGRAPHY

Bennett, Dennis, *Nine O'Clock In The Morning,* Logos International, Plainfield, N.J. 1970.

Billheimer, Paul E., *Don't Waste Your Sorrows,* Christian Literature Crusade, Fort Washington, Penn., 19034, 1977.

Bittlinger, Arnold, *Gifts and Graces,* William B. Eerdman's Pub. Co., Grand Rapids, Michigan, 1967.

Capps, Charles, *The Tongue, A Creative Force,* Harrison House, Box 35055, Tulsa, OK, 74135, 1976.

Christenson, Larry, *The Renewed Mind,* Bethany Fellowship, Inc. 6820 Auto Club Road, Minneapolis, MN 55438, 1974.

Frodsham, Stanley Howard, *Smith Wigglesworth, Apostle of Faith,* Gospel Pub. House, Springfield, Missouri, 65082, 1972.

Grossmann, Siegfried, *Charisma, The Gifts of the Spirit,* Translated by Susan Wiesmann, Key Publishers, Inc., Wheaton, Ill., 1971.

Lovett, Dr. C. S., "Welcome to the School of Kings", *Personal Christianity,* Box 549, Baldwin Park, CA 91706, Vol. 19, No. 7.

Malz, Betty, *My Glimpse of Eternity,* Spire Books, Fleming H. Revell Co., Old Tappan, N. J., 1977.

McGraw, Francis A., *Praying Hyde,* Bethany Fellowship, Dimension Books, Bethany Fellowship, Inc., 6820 Auto Club Rd., Minneapolis, MN, 1970.

Menninger, Karl, *Whatever Became of Sin?,* Hawthorne Books, Inc., Publishers, New York, N.Y., 1975.

Miller, Basil, *Charles Finney,* Dimension Books, Bethany Fellowship, Inc., 6820 Auto Club Rd., Minneapolis, MN.

Mowrer, O. Hobart, *The Crisis in Psychiatry and Religion,* D. Van Nortrand Co., Inc., Princeton, N.J., 1961.

Watchman Nee, *Spiritual Authority,* Christian Fellowship Pub. Inc., New York, N.Y., 1972.

Price, Alfred, *Healing, The Gift of God,* St. Stephens Episcopal Church, Tenth Street, Philadelphia, Penn., 19107.

Price, Charles S., *Spiritual and Physical Health,* Logos International, Plainfield, N.J., 07060, 1972.

Tari, Mel, *Like A Mighty Wind,* Creation House, Inc., Carol Stream, Ill., 60187, 1971.

"Evangelism", *New Wine,* Don Basham, Editor, Christian Growth Ministries, Ft. Lauderdale, Fla., Vol. 8, No. 7, July/Aug., 1976.

Bible Translations

Phillips, J. B., *The New Testament in Modern English,* Geoffrey Bles, 52 Doughty Street, London, WCL, 1960.

Eight Translation New Testament, Tyndale House Pub., Wheaton, Ill. 60187, 1974.

The New American Standard Bible, A. J. Holman Co., Division of J. B. Lippincott Co., Philadelphia, 1973.